(continued from front flap)

mour and slave girl who became the first

Fifty-five centuries old, Cairo is today the largest city of the Arab world. Its development from the time of the ancient pharaohs to the present Nasser government is traced in this vivid history.

Desmond Stewart compares Cairo to Troy in the building of successive cities on or near the same site. This occurred, he explains, because the founders of Muslim dynasties disdained occupying the capitals of their predecessors. Thus the first Muslim conqueror built Fustat, the "City of the Tent," where his armies had camped outside the walls of Christian Babylon-in-Egypt. The sultan Ibn Tulun, builder of the city's largest mosque, chose higher land to the north of Fustat. Saladin, defeater of the Crusaders and pioneer town planner, encompassed and greatly enlarged the previous capital in his walled fortress-city guarded by a citadel on the Mokattam Hills.

Situated strategically on the Nile, Cairo's predecessor, Memphis, had controlled both the fertile valley and the caravan routes between East and West. A series of foreign conquerors occupied this important site—the Persians in the sixth century B.C., the Greeks under Alexander the Great, the Romans, Byzantines, Arabs, Ottoman Turks, and finally the French under Napoleon.

The author portrays the rulers whose personalities affected the history of the capital. Among them are Al-Hakim, the Arab Nero, who ordered the city burned and watched from a nearby hill; "Tree of Pearls," a para-

(continued on back flap)

---

state expenses Victoria. He ed mercenary ho fought and the late Mid-

unequaled by uling Fatimid ounded a uni- with the West. n-story dwell- irkets teeming

Stewart evokes iose exotic life *lights*. He de- it patrols on a e tells of weird ines, amorous gery.

he afterlife has Egyptian his- with eternity s and mosques, nd an enthusi- ian and Islamic

ith fifty-eight ues, minarets, s from Cairo's

MOND STEWART years in Bagh- of his Middle ovels set in Iraq and his recent trilogy, *The Sequence of Roles*.

He has taught at the University of Baghdad, and contributed articles to *Holiday*, *Encounter*, and *The Spectator*. His eight books include *New Babylon: A Portrait of Iraq* (with John Haylock) and *Young Egypt*.

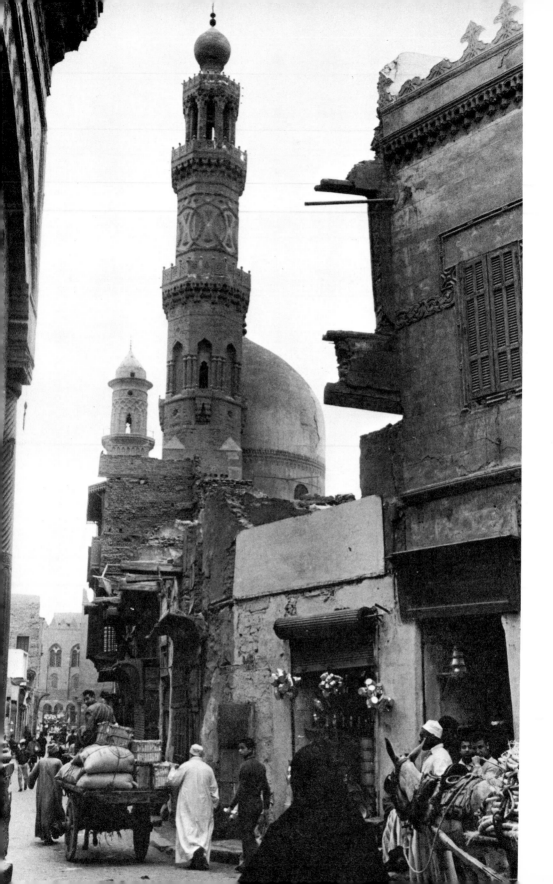

DESMOND STEWART

Cairo

 5500 Years

THOMAS Y. CROWELL COMPANY   NEW YORK   ESTABLISHED 1834

ACKNOWLEDGMENT is made to George Allen & Unwin Ltd. for permission to adapt material from *The Eastern Key,* Ivy E. Videan and Sayid Zand's translation of Abdul Latif al-Baghdadi's *Kitab al-Ifadah,* and to Jonathan Cape Ltd. for permission to quote from *The Travels of Ibn Jubayr,* translated and edited by R. J. C. Broadhurst. Acknowledgment is also made to Ibn Iyas's *Journal d'un Bourgeois du Caire,* translated and edited by Gaston Wiet (Paris, Librairie Armand Colin and S.E.V.P.E.N.).

To A. M. Stewart

FOREWORD

In extricating the constants and variants in this history of the largest
African and Arab city I have been prompted by a purpose which explains the formula of my book. I have wished to make my favorite
city known as I myself should like to know, for example, Peking.
Knowing little of Chinese history, I should want to be told the most
basic information about the strands of information and belief which
have woven China. In this spirit I make no apology if I bore, or madden, the expert, if I repeat what is known to him already or explain
what he understands. I am writing for potential converts to an interest in Cairo, who may know as little of Egyptian history as I know
of Chinese. I am writing for the reader in the armchair as much as
for the traveler in the airplane. I hope that the traveler will com-
prehend better the significance of the city he visits; I hope the reader
in the armchair will understand better what he hears of modern
Cairo as a result of what he reads.

To make reading easy I have spelled Arabic and Turkish names
as simply as possible. My system of transliteration is bound to annoy
somebody. Detesting the armory of diacritical signs, I have omitted
indications of several Arabic letters which do not exist in English,
and which English speakers would mispronounce anyway (for example, the initial *ain* in words like *Ali* and *Aziz*); sometimes I have
made indications which are approximate only (as for the terminal
ain in the Arabic word for *street,* which I have written *sharia,* not
shar', as is sometimes done). I have used the form *al* for the definite
article, although the Egyptians (under a French cultural influence)
have usually spelled it *el.* Where Egyptian names are concerned I
have written the Arabic *j* as *g,* since this is how Egyptians pronounce
it.

I have made a simple rule about notes. I have used them from
time to time to point a connection between the present and something or somewhere referred to in the past. Where I name a source
in the text, I leave the interested reader to consult the bibliography;
where I do not, I have inserted a note.

My sources are in large part the illustrious dead. I have quoted
from them gratefully in little and in large. I owe debts to those who
have preserved and edited their works. This debt will be apparent
throughout the book, but I acknowledge it here.

Abdul Latif of Baghdad, whom I quote often, visited Cairo at the time of Saladin. Ivy E. Videan believes that the spirit of the long-dead pnysician prompted her and her husband to produce an edition of his book about Egypt. "Our first meeting with Abd el-Latif was in August, 1957, when he spoke to my husband and to me during a conversation with a sensitive, Mrs. Ray Welch, in London. Since then we have had very many long talks with him, through Mrs. Welch and also through Mr. Jim Hutchings. It was not unexpected, therefore, that he should tell us in 1960 that he wished my husband to make a photographic copy of the Bodleian manuscript of the *Kitab al-Ifadah.* . . ." Though my own conversations with the dead have been less dramatic, I have found myself haunted in the streets of Cairo by those who walked them in the past and bequeathed their impressions or explanations: Nasir Khosrau, the Persian; Ibn Maimun, as the Arabs know Moses Maimonides; Volney, the Frenchman; Edward Lane, the Englishman; and a host of others.

From the present I draw on experience over almost twenty years, of which the second decade has been more concentrated than the first. My connection with Cairo has been of a different order from the intimate bond that linked me with Baghdad, where a dozen households made me welcome at all times. During the years 1957 to 1967 Cairo was traversing a period of revolutionary change; the Egyptians, besides, have never displayed the spectacular hospitality characteristic of the more purely Arab states. But although I visited fewer houses I received as many impressions and innumerable acts of kindness. I must thank in particular the staff of the Egyptian Geographical Society for their cooperation. Mr. Mahmoud Ali uncovered some little-known Arabic texts and Mr. Muhy Digwy gave me interesting sidelights on the modern Cairo character. In Tangier, Mr. Donald Angus allowed me free run of his considerable library.

CONTENTS

ILLUSTRATIONS

Illustrations

Cairo
5500 Years

CHAPTER 1

Mother of the World

Cairo: the world's oldest monuments in stone mark its site; the world's longest river pours through its heart. A sphinx couching among palms, a prostrate Pharaoh, recall "the middle of the universe," Memphis, first capital of the Egyptian empire. The oldest surviving obelisk stands as the sole survival of Heliopolis, twenty miles to the north. Memphis and Heliopolis had been flourishing for thousands of years when Alexander visited them; their awe was so potent that the conqueror preferred to build his Egyptian capital not where the Pharaohs had reigned but on an island joined to Greece by the sea and divided from Egypt by a lake. Alexandria remained the capital when Augustus made Egypt an imperial province on the death of Cleopatra, its last Greek sovereign. But under Roman rule, when Egypt was the granary of the empire, the urban nexus of Memphis and Heliopolis remained important. The man whom Christians call the Word of God (the term *Logos* had been coined by philosophers living in Egypt) first spoke words within its purlieus; his mother washed his linen in a trough inscribed with hieroglyphs. After being Christian for many centuries, Egypt became a bulwark of Islam in the seventh century. In the Middle Ages this African city was the largest metropolis in the three continents of the Old World.

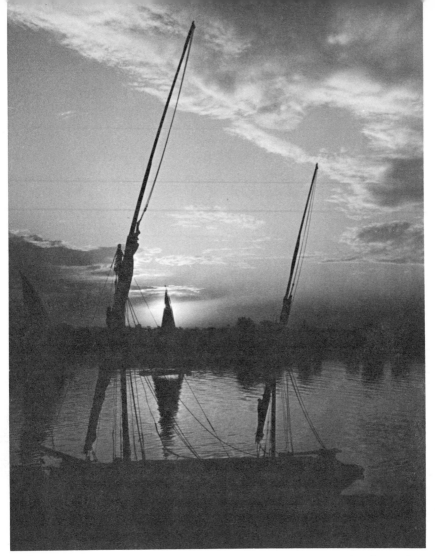

Sunset over the Nile. In the foreground, the Arab felucca resembles the ancient Egyptian boats in shape and sail. (Sayid Hassan)

Its luxurious way of life, its order and scholarship, impressed visitors from Europe and Asia whose trade passed through its bazaars. As the link between a spiceless West and a remote but luxuriant East, Cairo was rich enough to afford public buildings uniquely splendid.

Its triumph was, however, incomplete and discontinuous. For twenty-five centuries it suffered the indignity of foreign rule: Macedonian kings and Roman prefects, Arabian governors and Turkish sultans, French conquerors and British proconsuls concerned themselves with interests other than those of the people they ruled. The city's prosperity, dependent on a river and a geographical position,

2

could turn to sudden dearth. When the Nile ran low, men died of famine; when in 1498 Vasco da Gama sailed round Africa, Westerners found it possible to reach the Far East without paying Egypt its long-accustomed fee. Under the rule of the Ottoman Turks Cairo had shrunk to a huddle of splendid mosques girt with rubbish hills and evil lakes when Napoleon brought the West to detonate the East. But even then its pyramids inspired his oratory. In a century and a half of consequent effervescence its unique prestige gave it a leading position in the struggle of the Arab and Muslim peoples to throw off Western rule. The opening of the Suez Canal in 1869, the cultivation of cotton, restored it to a position of strategic and commercial power. In the mid-twentieth century, under its first Egyptian ruler since the seventh century B.C., it has come to be the voice of those who at once resent and admire the West, the capital not just of Egypt and the Arabs, but the entire Third World.

The fluctuating names of Egypt's capital long puzzled Europeans. John Ogilby, the seventeenth-century English geographer, listed more than a dozen names by which the city had been known to such people as the Chaldeans, Armenians, Hebrews, and Turks. The modern Egyptians use two names when referring to their capital. Each has a meaning and a nuance of its own; both names are used loosely. The first is ancient and popular, the second official and Islamic. Either can refer to the amalgam of towns and cities that have blurred within municipal boundaries which today bind more than four million souls. For no one city (unless it be the peripheral village of present-day Memphis) has survived intact or separable from the rest. Each has devoured the past and each has been devoured by its successor. "For this is the practice of kings," wrote a tenth-century Arab, Maqdisi. "They always efface the traces of their predecessors. This is the prime reason why they destroy cities and fortresses. They did this before Islam, and after it."

The first and most important name is Misr, pronounced more like Musr. This name, far older than the Muslim Arabs, is vague and haunting. Like the Hebrew Mizraim, it refers to the whole country as well as to its capital. Someone who announces: "Tomorrow I travel to Misr," may mean, if he speaks in Paris, that he is going to Egypt; if he speaks in Alexandria, that he is going to Cairo. The sharing of one word for country and capital makes things easier for a writer who would in any case have to interweave the two. It also underlines the extent to which Egypt, since its unification under a first-dynasty

3

Pharaoh, has been a centralized state. In no other country in the world, not even France, are the provinces felt to be so provincial; the desert is not felt as being part of Egypt at all. "Misr" carries with it the attachments of the past, the half-forgotten links with the Memphis and Heliopolis of the Pharaohs, with Babylon-in-Egypt, with the earliest cities of Islam. Egyptian peasants are not content with speaking of Misr alone. They expand it to Misr, *um al-dunya*, Cairo, mother of the world.

While Misr is timeless, the second name for the city is linked to a date: August 5, A.D. 969. On that day, in one bold move, a new east-bank capital, an approximate square of about 1200 yards each way, was pegged out by a conquering general. The astrologers in whom the general reposed his trust "consulted together to determine the auspicious moment for the opening ceremony. Bells were hung on ropes from pole to pole, and at the signal of the sages their ringing was to announce the precise moment when the labourers were to turn the first sod. The calculations of the astrologers were, however, anticipated by a raven, who perched on one of the ropes and set the bells jingling, upon which every mattock was struck into the earth, and the trenches were opened. It was an unlucky hour: the planet Mars (in Arabic, al-Qahir) was in the ascendant; but it could not be undone, and the place was accordingly named after the hostile planet, al-Qahira,[1] the 'martial' or 'triumphant,' in the hope that the sinister omen might be turned to a triumphant issue." [2]

The general's city, the first true Cairo, had its epithet also: "the Guarded." This originally derived from the high walls that hedged it in. On Egyptian lips it came to include an implicit prayer against the baleful planet that had presided at the city's birth.

Mother of the world, the Guarded: such Arabic hyperbole has echoed from Morocco to Kuwait. It has annoyed non-Arabs. Writing when Constantinople ruled the Ottoman empire (and in theory Egypt), the Turkish poet Fazil Bey retorted: "Misr, mother of the world? She is only a whore who has given herself up to the world each century."

The Arabic phrase "mother of the world," *um al-dunya,* has the same force as those German compounds that begin with *ur.* Cairo (used loosely to include all the cities on this site) is the *Urstadt,* the primordial city. In the same way Muslim theologians speak of a "mother of the Book," a primordial scripture laid up in Heaven from which both Bible and Koran derive. Cairo's stresses and pains, its

4

triumphs and problems, cut a stencil which fits the experience of later cities. Most cities are, indeed, later. When Constantinople was being founded the southern tip of the Egyptian delta had already witnessed a formidable history of urban living. The earliest city on this site, the Memphis of the Pharaohs, antedates almost every other human conglomerate larger than a village; as an imperial capital it antedates them all.

Cities were themselves the spoor of a new kind of man. For un-numbered millennia human beings had wandered in search of their food; in tribal migrations they followed the animal tribes they hunted or the berries and fruits that flourished in different places in different seasons. Such nomadic peoples would sometimes build forts or permanent structures to which they would periodically return. But the settled village became a necessity when cereals began to be culti-vated; the village houses, huddled together, guarded the fields and the corn which the fields produced. As such villages multiplied—

The fertile, adhesive Nile silt is the basis of Egyptian agriculture. It is brought down the Nile with the summer floods from central Africa and Ethiopia. (Costa Alifrangis)

their traces have been found, among other places, in Anatolia, Kurdistan, the Indus valley—villages joined together in common defense against the remaining nomads or alien groups. Primitive Egypt, a land of marshy thickets thronged with wild fowl, was divided into two such states: in the north, the delta; in the south, the valley stretching from the delta's apex to the first cataract at Aswan. Each of these states had its own capital and its local gods. Around 3000 B.C. the two states, Lower and Upper Egypt, were linked into one great kingdom. Its capital was founded about fifteen miles from the heart of modern Cairo.

In building where they did, the builders of Memphis showed strategic sense. They built on the west bank of the Nile. At that time the delta—whose southern apex is pushed approximately one mile north every five hundred years—started to fan out where Memphis now is. (The point of the delta is now more than ten miles north of Cairo.)

The strategic motives that inspired the choice of site are as evident today (taking into account the changes of the river and the retreat of the delta) as when those first engineers set their men to work.

There are geographical constants which time has hardly touched. These constants accompany the Nile on its northward journey from the granite islands that form the first cataract at Aswan. There are variants which, like the thematic variations in an Arab musical theme, surround a monotonous core. This central monotone, these slight variations, can be seen from an airplane flying from the south. For five hundred miles the Nile follows a natural rift through limestone hills. Some seasons the color of the water is reddish brown; at other times it takes the greenish hue after which dressmakers have named their *eau-de-Nil.* The cliffs, now approaching, now drawing back, maintain an average of ten miles' fertile soil; this is *kemi,* the "black land" of the early Egyptians. The "red land," *toshri,* or desert, seen from above, shows the brainlike whorls of convoluted bluffs, savage and bare. Sometime, long ago, the wild mountains were worn away by tributaries whose ghosts are flattened wadis where freak storms even now may cause tidal floods. This flatter earth resembles a photograph of a beach enlarged by an instrument as tall as the Eiffel Tower.

And then after this momentous passage—flights of geese or stands of palm make the monotony a delight to the traveler on the river or on the ground—there begins to be a change. The enclosing hills [3] move farther apart; and then, as a twenty-mile stretch of pyramids appears to the west, the hills abruptly change direction as though they were teams of horses obeying a circus master's whip. Instead of running parallel with the northward-pushing Nile they pivot west-northwest and east-northeast, allowing the river to flow broad and free. To the east, a broken line of beige and khaki cliffs are the Mokattam heights; they rise 550 feet above the Nile; their storm-worn, eroded cliffs once overlooked the Mediterranean, before the delta had begun to form, when the Nile poured its Congo water and its Ethiopian silt deep into the sea. The western hills, the Libyan plateau, are the start of the Sahara. As the two groups of hills swerve from the river, the Nile is constrained no more. The artery of Egypt has changed into an intricate web of capillaries and veins. The slim growth which ran beside the artery's banks turns into a vast open fan. In color the fields are emerald green; yet they shimmer with the evaporation from the little canals which make the green possible, which permit the heavy-sailed feluccas to navigate from one up-piled village to another in a landscape that seems limitlessly rich until, if the plane persists on its northern flight, the green merges with the sea.

The Greeks compared the rich part of Egypt not to an opened fan, but to the fourth letter of their alphabet written in capital form with its base facing north toward them: ∇. The delta might also be compared to an open hand, to one of those signs for good luck which the Muslims were to inherit from the past. Where Cairo stands is the pulse, the wrist. Whosoever controls this pulse can control both the valley and the delta: the men from the south, who make trouble or, when properly trained, control it; and the men of the north, whose agricultural wealth makes the country worth controlling. The Nile is not the only route controlled by this point. Northeast from Cairo, skirting the Mokattam hills, a broad waterless valley, the Wadi Tumilat, leads to the Isthmus of Suez. Caravans following this natural road could thus link Egypt with the Red Sea and the land route to Palestine.

Other ancient cities were built with a similar regard to controlling agriculture and territory. Ur and Babylon guarded the river system of Iraq. But the Tigris and Euphrates were less cooperative rivers than the Nile.

"The Nile increases," a twelfth-century Arab was to write,[4] "when all other rivers diminish and their waters are lowest, because

7

it begins to rise at the moment when the days are longest in summer and finishes its rise at the autumn equinox." This convenient flood was linked with the Nile's direction of flow from the tropical south to the moderate north, from the uplands of Ethiopia and the jungles of the Congo where rain falls in summer. The Tigris and Euphrates flowed south from the uplands of Asia Minor and Iran. The melting snows of the northern spring would pound south at a time when Mesopotamia had no particular need of water; they could cause floods of the enormity described in Genesis. When summer began to parch the land both rivers were tame and low; there was no easy way of storing water.

Cairo's position on the Nile was no less strategic than that of Troy, built on narrows through which ships from the Black Sea brought corn to the Greek archipelago. Troy persisted through sixteen lives; but wars, earthquakes, and political change achieved its final and post-Homeric death. From Roman times until the nineteenth century Troy was a silent hillock where goats clambered through the winds.

Cairo guards more than a breadbasket and a strategic pulse-point. It dominates a waterway far easier to navigate than the Euphrates or the Dardanelles.

To this day uneducated Egyptians refer to their river as *al-bahr*, or "the sea"; and this was the first sea on which men learned to sail. Apart from being sheltered, the Nile, as a sea, had two advantages. Its constant tide was from the south to the north. Its dominant wind was in the opposite direction. The man who wished to travel north from the first cataract had merely to launch a raft upon the Nile and the impetus of the river would carry him and his goods as far as he wished to go. And the man who wished to journey to the south did not need to fight the current with oars. A strong and persistent wind blew steadily south. It made the up-river journey, against the stream, easy for any craft with sails. (The same wind alleviated the Egyptian summers. From earliest times until today the people of the country have sought to place their houses so that the windows catch a breeze as pleasing to the settled as it is useful to the sailor.)

When the capital at the tip of the delta grew, when its resources and its need expanded, its central position could be exploited further. Caravan routes to the east would be followed by man-made waterways making it possible to ship goods from the Nile to the Red Sea.

A city lulled in too much convenience would die of a yawn if its citizens, unused to challenge, were not first clubbed to death like drunken seals.

Part of the stencil which this primordial city cuts is one of dialogue with nature, sometimes of violent dispute. Such disputes stimulate like good arguments—unless one of the parties loses his temper, takes to arms, and kills. When a city's dispute with nature is unfairly balanced, the city may be destroyed. An earthquake or a flood may destroy it forever.

Cairo's dispute has been with water, the humblest and strongest of elements. It has been a dispute in which need has been balanced by dread and in which the Nile has often repaired the catastrophes it has itself caused.

All those who have built on this site—Pharaohs, kings, governors, caliphs, sultans, slaves, and beys—have had a double preoccupation: their city must be near enough the Nile for its water to be freely available; at the same time houses must be high enough above the river bank to escape the engulfing floods which are the occasional counterpart to drought.

The Nile has not only pushed its delta forward in the last millennia, it has also constantly changed its course. While in Pharaonic times it had had a pronounced westward bend, in later centuries it deposited more and more of its agglutinative silt toward the east, so that in historical times the channel has moved constantly farther from the Mokattam hills, enlarging the area of cultivable or habitable land. The Nile's silt was so cohesive that it would cohere round any stable object, such as a wrecked ship, and begin, quite quickly, to compose an island. There are at the moment two considerable inhabited islands: Gezira to the north, and Roda to the south. Gezira is comparatively new. Roda has moved steadily north over the centuries; its southern tip was once its northern limit. At the same time the channel between Roda and the eastern bank of the Nile has tended to grow narrower, making the provision of water for the thousands living on the east bank constantly more difficult. A canal which the Pharaohs had designed to link the Nile with the Red Sea would become in medieval times an instrument for bringing water into the heart of Cairo, from whose walls the river had progressively withdrawn. Throughout the centuries this canal (in Arabic, *al-Khalig al-Misri,* the canal of Misr) was kept dammed until the height of summer, when its breaching was the secular feast of the year. The dry canal would then flow with water which for three

9

pleasant months would be clear and sweet; after November it would be stagnant and smelly; it would then become a dry ditch of rats and refuse until in August it would be filled again.

Only in the early twentieth century were the upper reaches of the Nile itself to be dammed, for flood control and storage. Until then the annual supply of water was entirely dependent on the rains in Ethiopia and the Congo basin, or what the Egyptians fancied were springs in the Mountains of the Moon. No measures to bring the Nile water nearer the capital, no system of canals, was any use if there was not enough water to bring. There was no way of storing water in a sodden year for use in a year of drought. The wells which filled after the annual flood lasted some months but were brackish and drinkable only in an emergency. The fields which were watered by one annual inundation depended on a flood large enough to overflow the banks.

If the ruler could not control the amount of water, he could, by the use of measuring instruments, estimate from the level of the annual flood the agricultural prospects for the coming year. Since at least 3600 B.C. the height of the Nile flood was recorded annually as the major statistic of the year. The Pharaonic priests had devised the first Nilometers; the Copts had maintained their secrets; and the Arabs learned from them. The southern tip of Roda island was the site of the city's chief Nilometer, an instrument marked out in cubits, a measure based on the distance from the elbow to the tip of the middle finger. "Upon another side of the island standeth a house alone by itself, in the midst whereof there is a foursquare cistern or channel of eighteen cubits deep, whereinto the water of Nilus is conveyed by a certain sluice under the ground. And in the midst of the cistern there is erected a certain pillar, which is marked and divided into so many cubits as the cistern itself containeth in depth. And upon the 17th June when Nilus beginneth to overflow, the water thereof conveyed by the said sluice into the channel, increaseth daily, sometimes two and sometimes three fingers, and sometimes half a cubit in height. Unto this place there daily resort certain officers appointed by the senate, who viewing and observing the increase of Nilus, declare unto certain children how much it hath increased, which children wearing yellow scarfs upon their heads, do publish the said increase of Nilus in every street of the city and the suburbs, and receive gifts every day of the merchants, artificers and women, so long as Nilus increaseth." This account of the Nilometer and the public interest in the Nile was written in the sixteenth

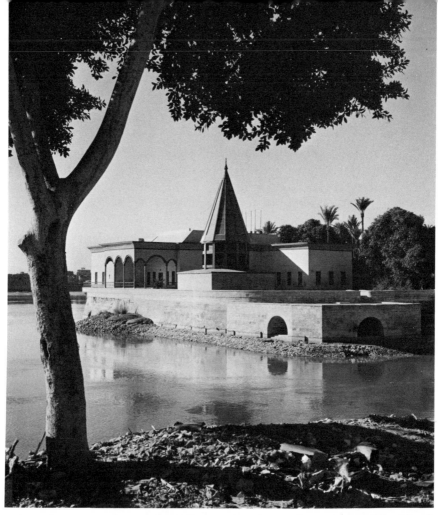

A modern restoration of the Nilometer on the southern tip of Roda Island. The conical structure covers the Fatimid well, into which the rising Nile flowed to be measured against a central pillar. In ancient times the prosperity of Egypt depended on the river level. Now the rise and fall are controlled by modern dams, in particular the High Dam at Aswan. (Costa Alifrangis)

century by Leo Africanus, a Moor converted to the Christian faith; it would have been equally true at any time until the twentieth century.

The Nile rose between its banks, then overflowed them, during the astrological signs of Cancer, Leo, and Virgo. Its waters spilled out over all the cultivated land in the valley and the delta. Receding, they left behind a glutinous deposit of silt which was then ploughed and sown.

For Egypt to avoid the twin perils of flood and drought the Nile had to rise between limits known to all. If it rose more than twenty cubits, higher ground was invaded, houses overwhelmed, and stagnant lakes were formed; the water did not recede from the lower ground in time and was thus without use for crops. Such high floods were rare. For an excellent harvest an ideal level was eighteen cubits. Anything between twenty cubits and sixteen would provide enough food to last two years. It was therefore important for the country's rulers to estimate the future. If there were signs of coming dearth, precautions could be taken in advance. If there were signs of coming bounty, plans for storage could be made.

The rulers were particularly preoccupied with the vegetation on which they and their subjects lived; they were less concerned with the water their subjects drank. The aqueducts built by various rulers were to carry water for palace or citadel. Not until the early nineteenth century was an aqueduct used to bring water for general use. The city's needs for clean water were always great. They were keenest in summer, when May to July was torrid and July to October humid from the flood. These needs were met by an army of water carriers as highly organized as London taxi drivers but enjoying higher popular esteem.

"From water all that lives . . ." The Koranic phrase with which the water seller (or *saqi*) would salute his client expressed the pride of a respected if ill-rewarded caste. (As late as 1830 the *saqi* earned a penny for carrying one of his huge skins full of water a mile and a half.) Since all life not only came from water but depended on it, the *saqi* was a benefactor of the city. He had many colleagues. A traveler of the fourteenth century (not, admittedly, a century of precise statistics) estimated that 12,000 employed camels and another 30,000 employed mules.

The water sellers were governed by an intricate accumulation of laws and customs. They must not draw water from places contaminated by sewage or the outflow of slaughterhouses; they must avoid stagnant pools. In order to qualify for this profession, a British traveler wrote in the 1690's, an apprentice must carry a skin weighing sixty-seven pounds for three days and nights without a pause. Once enrolled, the *saqi* had to be ready to play the role of municipal fireman; to assist him in this work, a law required householders to keep Ali Baba-sized jars filled to the top with water in case of fire.

Every prosperous household had its cistern, which was constantly refilled. Like a modern tradesman, the *saqi* kept careful note of his account: he either scratched figures on his clients' doors, or used a string of blue beads, ticking one off for each skin of water.

The poor could not afford cisterns of their own. It was therefore considered a pious act to endow a public cistern, or sebeel. The public cistern would often occupy the ground floor of a two-story building. Here behind intricately fretted grilles the poor women of the quarter would fetch water free; here they would gossip with the *saqis,* who besides being benefactors of the city were famous go-betweens, having a right of entry to houses denied to other males. Above the cistern, on the second floor, would be a school. Here boys would rock back and forth on their heels as they memorized the scriptures of Islam. As water for the body, so religion for the soul.

Animals were not neglected. One hot day the Prophet Muhammad had seen a harlot using her slipper to scoop up water for a dog. "For this action," he had proclaimed, "you will enter paradise." Troughs for animals (including the camels and mules of the water sellers) stood outside mosques.

The *saqi* had an honored place in the major religious occasion of the year: the pilgrimage to Mecca. Without him and his supplies the journey could not take place. He was also a target of war. Anyone who wished to invest the city on the high ground to the east of the Nile would try to cut it off from its water supply. In 1711, for example, a body of Turkish soldiers combined with Bedouin Arabs against the citizens of the town. Their tactics were not to assault Saladin's walls (which were never carried by storm) but to occupy the places opposite Roda Island where the water sellers filled their skins. Cut off from the Nile, Cairo could not long survive.

Primordial in its strategic site, primordial in its dialogue with nature, Cairo has epitomized urban life in showing how a mature city produces citizens of a recognizable mold. This mold is shaped by the city's hinterland and its people's experience.

Cairo's hinterland is complex. It combines the narrow Nile valley, the rich Nile delta, and the vast expanse of encompassing desert. A city where farmers sell their crops, a city where bureaucrats tax and judge the farmers, a city where travelers meet, it has been a cosmopolis with a history sometimes jubilant and often harrowing.

Though their shrouds preserve less than their buildings, though their words and deeds are forgotten by their heirs, men and women are the most interesting results of the civilizations they build. Observers have been summing up the Cairenes for centuries. Ibn Redwan, physician to an eleventh-century caliph, found them "greedy, avaricious, idle, timid, lying, given over to intrigues." Another added to these adjectives "mercurial, indecisive and given to swift change of mind." Yet in one of their worst periods, the sixteenth century, Leo Africanus saw them in a more kindly light: "They are of good company, leading amusing lives, fast to promise yet slow to effect; few of them study; their women disdain to spin, sew or cook; their husbands have to buy the meat ready cooked; their households are disunited."

The product of this city, the Cairene, is in a sense the hero, sometimes antihero, of this book: what he did, what he made, and what others did to him. But one primordial problem of all cities can, without fear of putting the last first, be abstracted here.

Since man is often violent when strong and malicious when weak, the first problem of a city where thousands rub shoulders is the problem of violence. Unless the fact of living together in the human equivalent of an ant hill modifies human nature, the city falls into anarchy and chaos. Young cities can sometimes afford violence; they have the energy to rebuild. They often cannot avoid it: their citizens have not learned to cohere. But violence is something that cities must tame if they are to survive.

The solution of the problem of violence in Cairo has been difficult. The Egyptian stock is sturdy, in particular when it derives from the south. Sudden rages can be fired by a hot, dry climate. As long ago as the age of Constantine an observer complained that "the Egyptians showed an appetite for quarrel and strife and unparalleled deceit and litigiousness, not only to their superiors, but also among themselves. These otherwise gloomy people would then be seen aflame with fiery anger and wild insults, perhaps only because a greeting had not been returned, or place had not been yielded in the baths, or because their insane vanity had otherwise been injured." [5] The novelist Towfik al-Hakim, who spent many years as a country prosecutor, marveled at the capacity of the Egyptian peasant to lose his head over women and over land. Rancor could express itself in killing neighbors or burning their crops.

The interaction of this basic violence with the congestion of Cairo has produced a remarkable solution: a folk ballet of violence, the *dowshah*.

Almost any visitor to Cairo may expect to witness a *dowshah*. It may erupt beneath his hotel window; it may be in progress as he visits a bazaar; or at any street corner, by any stall for nuts or cigarettes, its peculiar staccato sound may suddenly be heard. There is no

View from the southeast of the Great Pyramid on the Giza Plateau. (Sayid Hassan)

need to write a modern description. This ritual of defused violence has been noticed through the centuries. Leonardo Frescobaldi, a prosperous fourteenth-century Florentine, arrived in Egypt from an Italy where all men carried swords. He first marveled that "the Egyptians are scarcely the warrior type and do not carry weapons." He then went on to give a classic account of what happens in a *dowshah:*

When they begin to quarrel the onlooker expects them to tear each other to pieces. But the moment one of them cries *Istafurla,* which in their language means "Peace for God's sake!" they at once calm down.

Leo Africanus, whose description of the Nilometer has already been given, describes, two centuries after Frescobaldi, the *dowshah* in similar terms:

And if any of them chance to fall out in the streets, they presently go to buffets, and then a great number of people come flocking about them

15

to see the conflict, and will not depart thence, till they have reconciled them.

In other, newer cities trivial incidents—the arrest of a dangerous driver, interference with children splashing in a hydrant—have set off destructive riots. Cairo is too old, too fragile, too combustible, for such riots to be tolerable. The Cairene's experience has been of violence from others; against it he tends to shut his doors and pull his quilt over his eyes.

Modern annals offer one exception. On January 26, 1952, an organized mob destroyed cinemas, cabarets, and hotels associated with the power then occupying Egypt. But the cause was not trivial. The previous day, in the Canal Zone, a large number of Egyptian policemen, ordered by their government to resist the British, were shot dead on their own land by foreigners. The Cairo police refused to support a system which had permitted this to happen. They did nothing to stop a riot which expressed the despair of a city without hope.

The *dowshah* deserves applause. It is an institution for the relief of tension which could arise only in a city with a millennial past. Cairo has ruled an empire comprising most of the known world; it has been a provincial city in a Greco-Roman province, the awesome powerhouse of a caliphate, the leave center of European armies. Its people, having seen and remembered a great deal, have learned the lesson that serious violence brings a bitter harvest. Violence of emotion cannot be abolished by law. It can be sublimated in a ritual pantomime. The vile words fly, the fierce fists are raised. But when "a great number of people come flocking about them," the contestants will, with a great show of reluctance, with fists held back as though against bands of steel, allow themselves to be parted, so that, till the next disturbance, the street is calm—or calm but for its daily sound: the cries of vendors, the hurly-burly of traffic, and the oaths of men exaggerating in the name of God.

CHAPTER 2

Memphis and Heliopolis

The cardinal event in Egyptian history—the event as a result of which Egypt was to influence the world—was the act whereby the southern valley and the northern delta were linked in one state. This act has been traditionally ascribed to Menes, an Upper Egyptian who lived approximately 3500 years before Christ. The new unity was symbolized by the god-king, or Pharaoh, who wore the high conical crown of the south and the complex, high-backed crown of the north, and who reigned from his new capital at Memphis, a city built precisely where delta and valley met.

The Greek historian Herodotus visited Egypt in the fifth century B.C., when the unification was as distant in time from him as he is from us. He obtained his story from the living repositories of Egyptian tradition:

The priests informed me that Menes, who first ruled over Egypt, started by protecting Memphis with a mound; for the whole river formerly ran close to the sandy mountains on the side of Libya; but Menes, beginning about a hundred stades above Memphis, filled in the elbow towards the south, dried up the old channel, and conducted the river into a canal, so as to make it flow between the two mountain

17

ridges: this bed of the Nile, which flows excluded from its original course, is still carefully upheld by the Persians, being made secure every year; for if the river should break through and overflow in this part, there would be danger lest all Memphis should be flooded.

The purpose of Menes was twofold. The original river bed now provided flattened and fertile ground for a city of small mud-brick houses with gardens; at the same time the new city was protected from the east (the source of most attacks in Egyptian history) by the whole stream of the Nile. Before he diverted the river in this huge operation

This street, known as Sharia Port-Said, was formed at the beginning of the twentieth century when the Cairo canal was filled in. In Roman times this canal connected the Nile to the Red Sea. (Sayid Hassan)

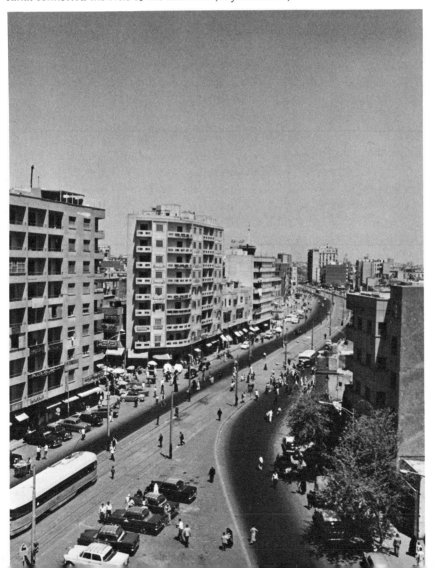

there had been insufficiency of ground on the west bank for a capital of the grandeur he envisaged.

A further reason has been advanced by an English hydrologist.[1] The western bend would have encouraged silting. Since the Egyptians depended on the Nile for transport and drinking water, it was important that "towns should be established on an outward bend where no silting—such as would be probable on an inner bend— would be likely to take place."

The achievement of Menes was to be a great deal more lasting than the work of most town planners. For many thousand years Memphis was to be either the capital of Egypt or its second city. Its tutelary deity, described as "the creator of the gods and of the world," was Ptah, whose temple was the most imposing building in a city commonly known as Hat-ka-Ptah, Place of the Soul of Ptah. This creative god was portrayed as a bearded man clad in close-fitting white garments, his feet joined together as though he were mummified. His head was usually bare, though in later times he was shown in a variety of royal crowns. His complexion was shown as pale yellow, a color often reserved for foreigners in ancient Egyptian art; but it is likely that in the case of Ptah a lack of sunburn is intended to show his reflective, intellectual nature, fitting a god who stayed diligently in his workshop. The Greeks easily identified Ptah with their own Hephaestus, the artificer of Olympus. But there was more to Ptah than creativity. He was shown standing on a pedestal which was later interpreted as the hieroglyph of justice. One text survives in which a man smitten by blindness sees in his fate the punishment for perjury and implores the god's forgiveness:

I am one who swore falsely by Ptah, the Lord of Justice;
He made me see darkness in daytime.
I shall tell his power to the one who knoweth him not, as well as to the
    one who knoweth,
To the small and to the great.
Beware of Ptah, the Lord of Justice!

Memphis was the capital of an empire whose power was to affect its neighbors and whose lure as a commercial center was to draw merchandise from Crete and Lebanon to the great stone wharfs that lined the Nile. But except for the temples, a citadel known as the White Wall, and the city and harbor walls, Memphis was put together from the same sun-dried bricks as form the houses of the fellahin in the villages of Sakkara, Mit-rahina, and Abusir which today mark the site of the ancient capital. The mud houses of Pharaonic times have long since returned to the Nile silt from which they came, while the public and royal buildings have been digested in cannibalistic greed by the capitals which have arisen across the river on the eastern bank.

The process has been continuously destructive.

As late as A.D. 1200 an Arab traveler [2] could muse on the untold wonders of this ruined city. One wonder which was not destroyed until 1449 was "the building called the Green Building. It is made from one vast block of stone nine cubits high and eight long and seven wide. In the midst of this stone a room has been hollowed out; it is formed by leaving two cubits thickness to the side walls as well as the floor and roof. Inside and out it is completely covered with reliefs and paintings and hieroglyphic inscriptions. Outside there are designs of the morning sun as well as stars, spheres, men and beasts. The men are shown in various postures. Some standing, some walking, some with a leg stretched forward, some at rest. Some of them have hitched up their clothes for working; some are carrying things; some are giving orders concerned with the work . . ." This remarkable shrine stood in a magnificent temple made of cyclopean stones, fitted neatly together.

Even then vandals were at work. The Green Building had been undermined by seekers for buried treasure; the single block from which it was made was already cracked. The astonished visitor noted "one statue of very large dimensions from the scalp of which a millstone had been cut, two cubits in diameter, without being greatly deformed by the excision, or even showing much evident change." Where temples were bound together by metal links, "vile and wretched individuals have sought after these bands of copper and torn away a considerable quantity. In order to get them they have smashed a number of stones."

Nor were the vandals always petty thieves. The Green Building was to be destroyed by an important prince.[3] The vandals often had exalted motives. They took columns by the thousand for their own newer shrines on the other bank.

Time and its agents were to be even more destructive of Heliopolis, the City of the Sun, which was the second Pharaonic foundation near the apex of the Delta, the site of modern Cairo. All that remains of Heliopolis today is an obelisk of the twelfth dynasty (around 1900 B.C.), a symbol of solar worship.

Heliopolis was the religious center of ancient Egypt. Standing on slightly raised ground to the east of the delta, in dry air where the power of the sun was visibly potent, this city contained the elements of a cult behind the cults, a system of ideas underlying the worship of birds, beasts, insects, and intellectual abstractions. Its center was a spring of fresh water known to this day as the Spring of the Sun.[4] In this sacred well "the sun was believed either to bathe himself morning and night or to have been born at the beginning of the world, when he arose from the abyss." [5] Another object of reverence was the holy Persea, a large lauraceous tree considered the foremost earthly proxy of the Tree of Heaven.

The Tree of Heaven illustrates, as a concept, the beauties and the confusions of the Pharaonic faith. The notion itself shines with poetic power. The chief of the gods was supposed to inscribe the names of the living on its leaves. The Persea had many different types of tree proxies, growing in different shrines; this various abundance shows the pleasant confusion of Egyptian beliefs, each merging in the next. Sometimes the proxy would be a sycamore, the Egyptian tree with the widest-spreading branches; sometimes a lofty date palm; sometimes the cedar growing in the mountains of Lebanon, a Pharaonic dependency; sometimes the vine, identified with Osiris, the god of death and rebirth. Or because the willow grew near water—the spring at Heliopolis was an earthly prototype of the Osirian abyss from which life began—the willow too could be an earthly type of the transcendental tree.

The priests of Heliopolis made an early attempt to systematize beliefs which in their nature were unsystematic, to reconcile gods who were originally the competing deities of villages and towns. Their greatest achievement, dating to roughly the same period as the founding of Memphis, was the isolation of an "ennead," or genealogy of nine gods. The primal god was the sun (known sometimes as Atum, the primitive deity of Heliopolis, more often as Re) from whom descended in the third generation two couples, Osiris and his sister-wife Isis, and the baleful Seth and his sister Nephthys. Despite this gallant attempt, Pharaonic theologians never produced a coherent or consistent creed.

The greatest religious reformer of the Pharaonic religion was Akhnaton, the fourteenth century B.C. Pharaoh whose short-lived

21

capital was halfway between Memphis and the southern capital of Thebes. For reasons which have been variously interpreted, Akhnaton advocated the cult of one god only, the sun-disc Aton. But even the priests of Heliopolis, within a conservative tradition, reached through sun worship something akin to the conception of one force animating all. Because of the fluidity of Egyptian thought—so alien to the fixed categories of Europe—it was possible for a priest in an eighth century B.C. papyrus to argue that Ptah was himself the antecedent of all the gods, the begetter, through a form of himself, of the sun itself. Ptah is "he who standeth on the earth and toucheth the sky with his head, he whose upper half is the sky and whose lower half is the underworld." This god can change his name to Amen-Re (a synthesis of the local god of Thebes with the solar god of Heliopolis) and at the same time represent the cosmos manifesting itself in plural forms and names:

Thy forms are Nile and Earth,
Thou art the eldest, greater than the gods.
Thou art the abyss when it stretched itself over the ground;
Thou didst return in thy ripples.
Thou art the sky, thou art the earth, thou art the underworld,
Thou art the water, thou art the air between them.

The metaphysics of the Egyptian priests, to whom cult was more important than belief, moved by intuitive analogies rather than by logic; these analogies could be profound when the intuiting minds were still poetic. With the passage of time they turned to meaningless spells. As religion they were to yield before the incisive monotheism of the Semitic peoples to the east, as philosophy they were to yield before the organized thinking of the Greeks from the north. But in one important aspect they were to remain visible to the eye and influential to the heart.

More than any other people in history the ancient Egyptians were obsessed with death. Delighting in the pleasures of this world, they sought through the mechanism of their liturgy and magic to ensure their continuation in the next. They believed this could be done through mummifying the body and preserving it in a lasting house. The people of Memphis and Heliopolis built houses for eternity which have remained to this day.

22   Behind Memphis on the Sakkara ridge, to the west of Cairo and

Muslim tombs near the Pyramids. The Libyan desert rises in the background. (Sayid Hassan)

Heliopolis on the Giza plateau, are the great burial grounds of the Pharaohs and their subjects. Tombs have been preserved by sheer size or concealing sand.

Overlooking the mud-brick houses and dusty date palms of modern Memphis stands the first great architectural monument in stone[6] to be built on the planet Earth: an oblong step pyramid within whose entrails lies a mastaba, a square building 250 feet on each side and 25 feet high. Such mastabas (so named by Arab excavators in the nineteenth century because they resembled the mastabas—or benches—on which they sat outside their homes) covered deep shafts in which the coffins of the dead were laid. (The Sakkara shaft is 104 feet deep and leads to a subterranean gallery 97 feet long.) Imhotep, a scientist of such genius that he was later deified as the god of healing and identified by the Greeks with Aesculapius, worked for Zoser, a third-dynasty Pharaoh of the twenty-eighth century B.C.

23

Imhotep recognized that his master's mastaba, set in a huge courtyard with high walls, would be invisible from Memphis on the plain below. He therefore erected above it, first a four- then a six-tier structure, 195 feet high, the first pyramid in Egypt or the world. It has been well described as "a gigantic flight of steps reaching up towards the sky, which would enable the soul of the dead king to ascend towards the sun, his father Re." [7] This building, at once gigantic and simple, still dominates both the western skyline and the ruins of its own walled courtyard. In one part of this courtyard Zoser would run a ceremonial race in honor of Apis, the divine bull. This

An obelisk of the twelfth dynasty is the only vestige of Heliopolis, "City of the Sun," the religious center of ancient Egypt. (Sayid Hassan)

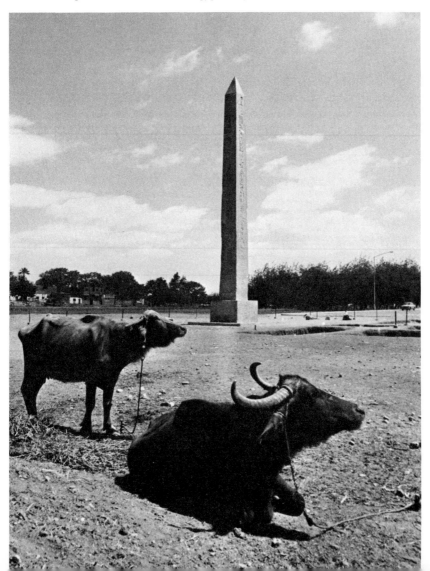

cult of Apis once again displayed the liquidity of Egyptian beliefs, as well as their evident origins in an agricultural society. A particular bull—black with certain white marks resembling an eagle's wings on his forehead and back—was "discovered" by the priests in a manner that recalls the selection of a Tibetan Dalai Lama. Each new sacred bull was supposed to have been conceived by a ray of sunlight on a cow. In his lifetime he was honored as "Ptah renewing himself"; the way he ate his food, the paths he chose, were taken as oracles. When he died he was mourned for seventy days, embalmed and buried in a giant sarcophagus, its granite brought by raft from Aswan.

As well as Pharaohs and bulls, lesser mortals were buried by the thousand round the step pyramid of Sakkara and the yet larger fourth-dynasty pyramids of Giza to the north. Bas-reliefs on the walls of such tombs embodied the delights and comforts which the dead hoped to enjoy in the hereafter; magic formulae empowered the dead to pass into immortal bliss.

The Egyptian attitude to death has sent tentacles of influence through time and space, influencing Christianity through Plato, himself a visitor to Heliopolis. The influence persists in modern Cairo, whose burial customs are unique in the Islamic world. To the east of the clangorous city is a vast duplicate: little houses with doors and windows line roads which differ from ordinary streets only in their silence and lack of traffic. These are the houses for eternity of today's Egyptians. Each well-to-do Cairo family has such a house. Inside are what look like rooms. Under the floors in crypts are laid out the family dead, the men in one crypt, the women in another. Here as in ancient times relatives come to visit the dead on the great religious occasions of the year. There is one difference, however. In ancient times it was important for the *ka,* the dead person's soul, to be offered flowers to smell and food to eat. At the same time it was vital for the dead body to be far below ground to avoid robbers. The art of sculpture arose as a response to the need for surrogate figures for the safely buried. In a ground-level funerary chapel a lifelike statue would stand waiting to receive visits and gifts. The living could in this way make contact with the inviolate dead. Muslims, praying only to God and giving only to the poor, and in a Semitic tradition hostile to representational art, have produced no sculpture worthy of the name.

There was a poetic balance in the two important cities on the   **25**

The ruined al-Gyushi mosque on the Mokattam hills stands in stark contrast to modern Cairo. In prehistoric times, before the delta spread to the north, these hills comprised a cliff overlooking the sea. The mosque was built in the twelfth century. (Sayid Hassan)

opposite banks of the Nile but within easy reach of each other near this strategic site: Memphis, on the west bank to the south, was dedicated to Ptah and the practical tasks of power; Heliopolis, or On, on the east bank to the north, was dedicated to the sun god, Amen-Re, and the metaphysics of Egyptian life. The tension between the two kept Egyptian society alive through the long ages when few challengers from outside threatened the authority of Pharaoh. Even when the challenges began to multiply, the balanced harmony of Memphis and Heliopolis were to impress and change the bringers of challenge.

26

CHAPTER 3

Babylon-in-Egypt

After producing more than thirty dynasties whose average span was at least as long as the United States' existence as a nation, after responding to countless challenges, Pharaonic civilization was to respond no more. Its central spirit, that nexus of interwoven forces which gives a society its distinctive traits, had grown tired; its creative impetus had cooled. Designs which had been fresh and individual at Sakkara degenerated into the stereotyped motifs of the decorator. They had been repeated so often that they turned into the trumpery postcards of religious art, stylized conventions produced by the square yard and without power to move. The gods of the Pharaohs were no longer prayed to with belief; the analogies no longer made sense; the priests were trusted no more. Foreigners created the later dynasties. Libyans from the west, Nubians from the south, then Persians from the east invaded the rich valley, interested in wealth and indifferent to the lot of those who produced it. Yet to the end those who conquered Egypt put on its impressive clothes, adopted its ancient rituals, and bowed to its mysterious gods; they took their place in a hierarchic system whose immense age gave it still a sort of power.

When the Persians occupied Memphis in the late sixth century

B.C., they brought with them, according to one tradition, a host of workmen from Babylon on the Euphrates. These Persian Pharaohs were to complete the canal which the fifteenth-dynasty Pharaoh Necho had begun in 609 B.C. Necho's waterway followed much the same route east through the Wadi Tumilat as a canal which had existed seven centuries earlier in the reign of Seti I. Near where the canal branched northeast from the Nile the Persians built a fortress on the heights of al-Rasad, a spur of the Mokattam. Near this east-bank fortress (commanding a westward view of Memphis and the pyramids which lined the Libyan escarpment) a new city was to grow up. Different traditions account for its name, Babylon-in-Egypt. According to one, the Chaldean workmen, exhausted by harsh treatment, rose in revolt and, crossing from Memphis, seized the fortress and its surrounding site. Granted an amnesty, they were allowed to settle where they were and build a town. By the waters of Memphis the Chaldeans remembered their Euphrates home. They called their settlement "Babylon-in-Egypt."

Another theory derives the name from an entirely different root. Babylon, in this theory, is a corruption of Bab-li-On, meaning the Gate to On. On was the biblical name for Heliopolis; the new city was certainly placed at the southern extremity of the straggling religious ancient one.

Whatever the origins of its name, the city occupied a newly strategic site. After Menes had diverted the Nile to build his west-bank capital, the apex of the delta had moved steadily north. Other changes in the river and the world gave new importance to the east bank. One was the emergence of the considerable island of Roda, lying like a flounder immediately to the west of the heights of al-Rasad. Roda was separated from the east bank (as it is today) by a narrow channel; this channel could be bridged by linked boats and from the west bank of Roda the task of traversing the other half of the Nile was considerably less. Babylon's proximity to Roda gave it an easy link to Memphis and the west; its proximity to the canal (an intermittently functioning thoroughfare from the time of Darius until the early Middle Ages) linked Babylon with an east grown richer and more developed since the time when Memphis had been planned.

Babylon's Persian nucleus was to develop into the chief Egyptian (as opposed to foreign) city during the thousand years in which Greek influence dominated Egypt.

The Greeks had always been aware of the wealth of Egypt. Cretan sailors had docked at the Memphis wharfs; Helen, according to one tale, had landed in Egypt after the fall of Troy. Herodotus had recorded the peculiarities of the Egyptians for his Hellenic readers: it was the only country where women urinated standing up, he claimed, and where men performed the same office sitting down. On a more serious level, he had gossiped with the priests of On. From the same priests Plato had learned the story of Atlantis. According to a modern theory, he got the Pharaonic numerals wrong, thus siting Atlantis too far to the west and too far in the past. Far from being a myth the story was a precise account of the volcanic disintegration of an island in the Minoan empire.

The man who delivered Egypt from Persian rule and implanted Greek culture was a pupil of Aristotle, who in turn had studied with Plato. A Macedonian from the Greek fringe, Alexander came to Egypt with an open-hearted readiness to endorse its values. His attitude to foreign cultures was uncharacteristic of most Greeks, who used the term "barbarian" to signify what was not their own. Nothing in his career pleased Alexander more than the recognition by the oracle in the Siwa oasis that he, the reputed son of Philip, was in fact the son of Ammon.

For the first time in Egypt's long history a foreign force was to affect Egypt deeply and for a very long time. Having visited Memphis, Alexander decided to found a new capital on a fishermen's island off the delta, separated from Egypt by Lake Mariut. From this city of Alexandria a Hellenizing influence was to permeate the adjacent delta, the Nile valley, and the attached oasis of Fayum. One of Alexander's generals, Ptolemaus, inherited Egypt when Alexander died near the original Babylon in Mesopotamia; Ptolemaus bequeathed it as a kingdom to more than a dozen generations of descendants. Ptolemaic Alexandria was a city where Europe, Africa, and Asia met. The Ptolemaic legacy—in particular to the West—was opulent; to the Egyptians it was gained at the price of colonial rule. It was a form of colonial rule whose tolerance made it the more difficult to resist. No instance of modern colonialism affords a parallel. Post-Renaissance empires, varied as they have been, have manifested, each in its own form, the Hebraic principle: Thou shalt have no other gods but Me (the "Me" being an astonishing spectrum of intolerances). The Greeks, imitating Alexander, were to intermarry with the subject races. They had no attachment to one faith. On the contrary they sought for correlations between the occupants of their own Olympus and the gods of foreigners.

To picture an equivalent of the Greek symbiosis with Egypt one would have to imagine an Anglo-Saxon occupation of India lasting not two centuries but ten and marked, from the beginning, by a passionate and continuous absorption of Hindu rituals. Lords Curzon and Reading and ten generations of successors would have dressed themselves in the panoply of rajahs, while English sovereigns would have reigned as avatars of Indian gods from Balmorals rebuilt to resemble the temples of Madura. Their pallid corpses would have

The ruins of a fortress from Roman Babylon-in-Egypt. The Nile, adjacent in the time of Christ, is now some distance to the west. (Sayid Hassan)

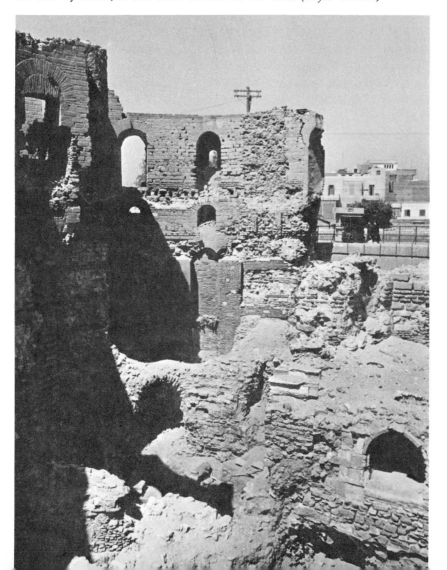

been burned on Ganges pyres or digested by vultures in the towers of silence.

The dynasty of Ptolemaus, and after its extinction, its Roman inheritors, played this role in Egypt. The Ptolemies shook off the taboos of their native land, starting with incest, the most horrendous sin of classical Hellas. Osiris had married his sister Isis; many Pharaohs, inheriting through the female line, had done the same thing. The Ptolemies piously begot children by their sisters; the last effective monarch of the race, Cleopatra, was the comely result of this procedure. They patronized the gods of their adopted land. Sculpted as Pharaohs, they rebuilt derelict temples and scrupulously maintained the timeworn rites. To bind the Greek colonists with the Egyptian majority, a new god, Serapis, was consciously created. (He had a considerable success outside as well as inside Egypt.) Serapis was a fusion of two Pharaonic gods: Osiris, the lord of the afterworld, and Apis, the divine bull; these two deities had more popular resonance than the intellectual of Memphis, Ptah, or Ammon, originally an Ethiopic god. In appearance Serapis was a riverine ancient in the Greek manner: bearded, he supported on his tangled locks a basket of mysteries.

The Greek appetite for mysteries was insatiable. Perhaps because they were so rational themselves, the Greeks eagerly sought what refuted logic. They had practiced mysteries at home in a dull Athenian suburb. In Egypt with its weird animal gods, its nocturnal rites, its cryptic tongue, its ambiguous texts, they had stumbled on a fascinating vein. They would mine its most jaded seams. In a second-century necropolis at Alexandria—an underground Forest Lawn of the pagan world—they stacked their loved ones amidst a fusion of Greek and Egyptian modes: Anubis, the jackal-faced undertaker god, is dressed in Greek costume complete with military boots, while a European dignitary with the curly hair of a Praxiteles stands in the rigid Pharaonic pose.

In return for these mystic borrowings the Greeks brought gifts of their own: a language more supple than any other and a naturalistic style of art which would leave its impress in Egypt, as it would farther east, in Buddhist lands.

Yet linguistic subtleties and the philosophical ideas they made possible did little for the native Egyptians, for the people we may imagine living in Babylon-in-Egypt as well as the now declining cities of Memphis and Heliopolis. Greek naturalism was not only to overthrow the priestly art of Egypt (from which the art of archaic

Greece had distantly derived) but to destroy the credibility of the symbols which this art purveyed. Despite their eager patronage of the mysterious, the Greeks themselves could not quite believe, however hard they tried. They loved philosophic argument more than magic. In the tenebrous vaults of Thebes someone who signs himself "Nicagoras of Athens" has scrawled the following prayer:

> Be gracious to me here also, Plato.

Against their will, the Greeks had killed the mysteries they wished to serve. Plato was more potent as a god than Horus (both hawk-shaped solar god and son of Isis), in whose honor the Ptolemies had rebuilt the Edfu temple. For the Egyptians Plato was no substitute for the gods in whom they increasingly disbelieved.

There was no real fusion between the mind of Alexandria and the mind of Babylon-in-Egypt. The Greeks were inquisitive, experimental, articulate; the Egyptians were patient, conservative, secretive. The Greeks believed in speculation and reason, the Egyptians in magic which could raise them children or crops, or bring curses on a neighbor.

Babylon-in-Egypt was a town where Egyptians lived in surly amity beside their masters. These masters were preponderantly Greek even when, from the death of Cleopatra to the founding of Constantinople, Egypt was a part of an empire ruled from Rome. Latin never became the lingua franca of the eastern portions of the empire, whose culture was consistently Hellenistic. The Roman contribution to Egyptian history was almost nil, though Roman methods of building, transmitted to the Byzantines, strengthened the walls and buttresses of Babylon. Those emperors who took an interest in Egyptian culture—such as Hadrian, who founded the city of Antinoöpolis on the Nileside site of his favorite's suicide—were themselves completely Hellenized. Others merely regarded the delta as a cornucopia for the imperial populace.

Alexandria was the city where the Hellenic mind fused not with the Egyptian, but with the Hebrew. The relation between the Greeks and the Jews was ultimately one of violent antagonism. The majority of pious Jews would always see in the Hellenic tradition a compound of idolatry and human self-worship repellent to Israel. But under the Ptolemies these very opposed ways of looking at the world interacted creatively, if briefly.[1] Thanks to Ptolemaic encouragement the Hebrew scriptures were translated into Greek; a Jewish temple at Leontopolis in the delta was founded under the same kindly rule. A double process was at work. The Jews of Alexandria (more broad-minded than those in Palestine) began to recognize that the terms of Greek philosophy could deepen their understanding of their ancestral faith. The Greeks, always thirsty for a new idea, toyed with identifying the Almighty of scripture with the Platonic absolute from whom lower forms had all evolved. The medium between the transcendent and the near was the Logos, or creative Word.

The incarnate Logos came first not to coastal Alexandria with its sumptuous palaces, its spectacular Serapeum and munificent library, but to the huddled inland town of Babylon-in-Egypt. The Logos, in appearance an infant refugee, passed the customs post at the village of Qantara to enter an Egypt which had become the private estate of Augustus Caesar, Cleopatra's vanquisher. The prefect of the province was Gaius Turranius. With the child traveled his mother, his putative father, and the midwife Salome. They went first to Bilbeis, a delta town not far from the place where the ancient Hebrews had toiled in bondage. On their way to Babylon they passed the colonnades and porticoes of Ptolemaic Heliopolis. As the donkeys of the Holy Family trotted into the decaying city the statues of the pagan gods (recognizing that truth had come) fell crashing to the ground. The Fountain of the Sun, which gave the city its name, delighted the Virgin, many of whose later apparitions, as at Walsingham and Lourdes, were to be concerned with wells and springs. Her sojourn in Heliopolis (on the site of the modern suburb of Mattariya) has made the spring of fresh water and its surrounding trees a place of pilgrimage throughout the centuries. Piloti, a medieval traveler, describes what has hardly changed today:

Near Cairo, going three miles towards Jerusalem, is a garden which is called Mattaria, where is a well worked in white marble which seems as though it had been made today. It is full of sweet water in which Our Lady washed the clothes of Our Lord Jesus Christ.

The Egyptian exile of the Holy Family has been denied by critics. Some argue that the story is a pious fiction designed to fulfill the scriptural prophecy "Out of Egypt have I called my son." [2] Similar criticisms were long leveled at Homer's description of windy Troy

33

or Herodotus' account of a canal across the isthmus of Corinth. Archaeology confirms more often than it refutes such persistent traditions. There can, however, be no archaeological evidence for this journey by humble people. Yet we know enough of the classical world to recognize that the ancients traveled widely. Egypt, with its numerous Jewish colonies, was a most convenient place of refuge. The unanimous tradition of centuries associates Jesus and his mother with numerous places in Egypt, though never with Alexandria. In old Cairo a church contains a crypt that has long been revered as the home of the refugees.

"The fourth church we entered," wrote a traveler in the fourteenth century, as we might write today, "is called St. Mary of the Cave. It is where Our Lady lived with her son when she fled from Syria with Joseph and when they took refuge in Egypt out of obedience to the warning Joseph received in Bethlehem that Herod was looking for Jesus to kill him. They stayed there seven years. It is an underground place. You go down by a staircase of nine steps."

There is no reason to suppose that the Holy Family had a penchant for crypts. The deposit of centuries has laid layer upon layer. What was ground level in the first century is many steps below ground level now. If any place is awe-filled this place is.

From their base in Babylon—only a short walk from an ancient synagogue—the Holy Family are reputed to have traveled upriver as far as the site of Deir al-Muharraq, a later monastery. As traveler's checks Saint Joseph used the gold, myrrh, and frankincense brought by the Wise Men. Then Herod died and the Holy Family returned to Palestine—Christ to study the scriptures which he would fulfill in Jerusalem in Easter week.

Egypt took to the new religion with a fervor in tune with its millennial religious zeal. According to the Acts of the Apostles, Egyptians were present in Jerusalem on the day of Pentecost. These were either Egyptian Jews or Greek converts to the new syncretic doctrines of Philo of Alexandria. They would have returned to Egypt inflamed with the new faith. St. Mark is traditionally regarded as the first bishop of Alexandria, but the conception of "bishop" needs scrubbing to see him right. He was more like the cell leader of a modern seditious movement. A verse at the end of St. Peter's first epistle has been taken by some commentators to refer to a cell already existing in Babylon; the same verse includes a reference to St. Mark.[3]

Alexandria with a Hellenistic upper class and Babylon with an Egyptian lower class, accepted Christ in two distinct and separate ways.

The Greeks accepted the Word as the intellectual solution to a world of doubt. (Those Greeks who rejected him did so in favor of an etherealized philosophy refurbished to rival the moral purity of the new faith.) The Greeks were active in the wrangles that, over a few centuries, defined Christian doctrine. The creeds that remain the formal statements of Christian belief are the achievement of men who thought in Greek and lived in Egypt.

The Egyptians, whether fellahin or artisans, accepted Christ as an incarnate god showing a way to escape from sin. (Those Egyptians who rejected him did so in favor of magic.) Christ completed the Egyptian pattern of metaphysical development as much as he completed the patterns of the Greeks and the Jews.

From the beginning the Egyptians had been obsessed with the afterlife. The Pharaonic edifices which survive were nearly all concerned with death. The pyramids, far from being works of self-glory like the statues of Ramses II, were the chief statement of this obsession. The thousands who had labored to build them believed that in creating ladders to heaven for their god-kings, they were preparing ladders for themselves. They were present in their king as the congregation of a Catholic church are present in their priest.

With the development of Pharaonic civilization, ideas about the afterlife developed. Individuals began to hope for personal salvation, or survival. Important officials began to build their own houses for eternity; it was felt that only those who could afford embalming and the right mortuary ceremonies would live again. The poor were thus excluded, except as servants, from the cheerful Nilotic paradise portrayed on the walls of the rich men's tombs.

Toward the end of the Pharaonic period the god Osiris became not merely a magical guardian of the afterworld but a moral judge. To be properly embalmed, to have the correct spells written around your corpse, was not enough. You had also to make the "negative confession"—that you had not committed the major sins—to the dark powers of death.

Christ's promise that the sins of believers would be forgiven opened paradise to all. But the gloom of centuries still haunted the Egyptians. Salvation could not be easy. They looked in the new sacred texts and found proofs that they were right. Christ's offer of salvation was on severe moral terms. There had to be a rejection of the old, a rebirth of the new. The Egyptian Christians (who are called Copts [4]) were less tolerant of their pagan past than were the Greeks. While some Greek Christians continued to find merits in Plato, the Copts turned on their ancient religion with vengeful fury. History affords no parallel of a nation so radically rejecting its past. Descendants of the soldiers of Pharaoh emotionally identified themselves with the Children of Israel who had fled from their ancestors' power. They took biblical names; they fashioned a new, earthy art. Sometimes, as an afterthought, an ancient symbol would survive: the ankh of Akhnaton ♀ would be used as though it were a cross. But the spirit of Coptic art was totally removed from the tired art of the later Pharaohs. It was fresh, rustic, working-class. Realistic, at times humorous, it reflected plebeian or agricultural concerns. Both finicky and crude, it inspired attractive textiles, delicate carvings, and some moving religious art. The influence of Greece—more acceptable now that the Greeks were Christians too—was stronger than the influence of Pharaonic Egypt. The demotic alphabet of the Pharaohs was exchanged for an alphabet modeled on Greek; hundreds of Greek words were borrowed to express truths now shared by all men, not held as arcane secrets by a few.

The Copts contributed more to the disciplines than to the metaphysics of Christian life. Monasticism, their greatest contribution, was the response of Egyptian literalism to the gospel summons to perfection. St. Antony was an Upper Egyptian Copt who heard the command "If you would be perfect, sell all you have and give to the poor," and acted on it. He sold what he had, put his sister in a hostel for secluded women, and started a movement of withdrawal which in a short time crowded the Nile valley and its surrounding deserts with clusters of hermits' cells or barracklike monasteries where converted fellahin toiled and prayed under the stern lash of a spiritual praetorian in God. (A Coptic monastery still stands at the southern boundary of Cairo, on the banks of the Nile. It marks the spot where the Holy Family supposedly embarked on a felucca for Upper Egypt.)

In theory the Greeks and the Copts were brothers in Christ. In practice the Greeks gathered the taxes and ruled while the Copts produced the food and were taxed. Despite the claim of Constantinople to be a new, baptized Rome (it was inaugurated as such in A.D. 330), it remained a city where politicians practiced their fraudulent arts. The coming of the Gospel did not mean that there were

This ancient, gnarled "Virgin's Tree" is connected by tradition to the visit of the Holy Family to Egypt. The Virgin is reputed to have washed young Jesus' clothes in the trough in the foreground. (Costa Alifrangis)

no more prisons, no more extortions, no more judicial deaths. The Christianization of the empire by Constantine marked a watershed of disillusion for many Christians. The new dawn of grace was depressingly like the old evening of sin. It soon accentuated the rift between Greeks and Copts in Egypt. St. Antony, when over a hundred, had journeyed on foot from his Red Sea monastery to Alexandria, there to support Athanasius in his great contest with Arius over the nature of Christ. While Arius argued that "there had been a time when the Son was not," Antony agreed with Athanasius that both Son and Father were one, with the Spirit, co-eternal persons of one God. But after the fourth century relations between Greek and Copt were increasingly strained.

The upper-class view of the Copts is shown by Ammianus, the last important classical historian, a fourth-century Greek from Antioch. A military man, he knew all the eastern empire well. "The

Egyptian is ashamed if he cannot show his lean, brown body marked with welts upon welts received for his refusal to pay taxes. No physical torture has yet been discovered"—it sounds as though the Greeks needed modern help—"to make a hardened Egyptian robber acknowledge his name."

The Copts expressed their alienation from their Greek masters by exaggerating slight differences in metaphysical terms until a schism formed two mutually hostile communions: the Monophysite Coptic church headed by its own patriarch in Alexandria and the Byzantine (or Malikite) church with its patriarch in Constantinople.

By the early seventh century the Copts not only hated Byzantium but despised it, too. The emperor Heraklius was determined to force a new compromise variant of Christianity on all his subjects. At the same time he was unable to protect the Holy Places. In A.D. 619, for the second time since the conversion of Constantine, Jerusalem was occupied by those to whom Jesus was not a sacred person. Such occupations seemed destined to presage disasters to the occupiers. The first had been the emperor Julian. The Apostate had contemplated building a pagan temple on Mount Moriah and importing fanatical Jews to safeguard the city against a Christian return. Julian's death in battle against Persia led to the final defeat of the paganism he had loved. Now the king of Persia had occupied Jerusalem and carried off the Holy Cross. To the Copts Jerusalem, then as now, was the center of devotion. Its loss lowered Byzantine prestige as never before.

The Persian occupation of the Holy City coincided with unnoticed developments in backward Arabia. In 622 an Arabian called Muhammad abandoned Mecca, the holy city of pagan Arabia, in order to preach his monotheistic faith in greater freedom. The city to which he migrated was, as Medina, to be the capital of a suddenly expanding state; the year of his migration was to be the start of an era. The year before Muhammad died in A.D. 632, Heraklius managed to drive the Zoroastrian Persians back into their mountains. His triumph was short-lived. Within a few years the armed missionaries of Islam burst from an Arabia newly united in the faith of Muhammad. The Persian empire was to be destroyed, the Byzantine empire to be reduced by half.

The Arabians were by no means strangers to Egypt. The citizens of Babylon were used to the arrival of caravans bringing the spices of the south to the markets outside their walls. The Arabians also knew Egypt well. The man who was to conquer it for Islam—Amr ibn al-As—had himself visited Egypt, before his conversion, when he had been in charge of a commercial caravan.

But in A.D. 641 the Arabians arrived in greater numbers than before, and in a different spirit. The great gates of Babylon were closed as what looked like an armed camp sprang up outside the walls. This time the Arabians had come not as traders but as preachers. Their creed, the stronger for being short, rang out at the times of prayer: "No deity but God; Muhammad is the Prophet of God." The challenge brought by the Muslim leaders was equally simple: The people inside Babylon could submit to the doctrines revealed in the Koran (this "submission" is the primary meaning of Islam) or they could remain Christians (the Koran recognized them as well as Jews as "people of the Book") but pay a poll tax. The tax was

This crypt beneath a church in Old Cairo, which is often flooded when the Nile is high, is supposed to have been the lodging for the Holy Family during their sojourn in Egypt. (Costa Alifrangis)

significantly lower than the one they were already paying to their Greek overlords; men of religion were exempt from the tax altogether.

The tensions discussed in this chapter must have been in the minds of the men now besieged behind the stout Roman walls of Babylon. As they peeped over the parapets at the Bedouin camp on the empty plain to the north, as they heard the Call to Prayer, as they saw the massed soldiers prostrating themselves like one vast creature toward Mecca, they must have argued among themselves: Were these enemies, to be resisted in the name of Christian unity? Or were they saviors from a Christian disunity which had brought them misery?

The issue was not decided in one night. The Arabians had easily overrun the imperial forces at Heliopolis but it took them a seven-month siege before Babylon surrendered. Brilliant practitioners of desert warfare, the Arabians had yet to master the two techniques of fighting at sea and of investing fortified cities. During the protracted siege there were frequent probes from each side as to the intentions of the other.

The chroniclers have preserved an account of what the Egyptians found when they sent one embassy to the camp of Amr. "We found," they told the Byzantine governor, "a people who love death better than life, and set humility above pride; who have no desire or enjoyment in this world, who sit in the dust and eat upon their knees, but frequently and thoroughly wash, and humble themselves in prayer; a people in whom the stronger can scarce be distinguished from the weaker, or the master from the slave."

To many Copts these democratic Muslims must have seemed attractive; or if not attractive, then useful counterweights to the immemorial tyranny of Rome, whether old or new. (To later Muslims the description of their forebears just quoted must have made as ironic reading as early Christian history made to victims of Byzantine cruelty and court intrigue.)

In April 641, with incalculable results for the Copts and the world, the city of Babylon opened its gates to the representative of the Caliph in Medina. By the end of the summer the imperial capital of Alexandria had also surrendered and Egypt had become a province of Islam.

CHAPTER 4

Fustat:
City of the Tent

Amr was not a free agent in Egypt. He held his governorship on authority from Omar, the second successor (or caliph) of the Prophet. Amr himself had been captivated by an Alexandria whose Pharos still stood and whose two marbled streets still intersected at Alexander's tomb. In a report to Omar he had let himself go: it was, he wrote, a city with "4,000 palaces, 4,000 baths, 12,000 dealers in fresh oil, 12,000 gardeners, 40,000 Jews who pay tribute, 400 theaters or places of amusement." He did not mention (or burn) the great library; civil dissension and Christian dislike of pagan authors had long since scattered its 700,000 volumes. He cannot fail to have noticed the contrast between Cairo's torrid summer and the fresh breezes of the seaside town.

To Amr's enthusiastic dispatch, and his suggestion that Alexandria should be the capital of Muslim Egypt, the Caliph returned a chilly answer.

"In that case," Omar asked, "will there be water between me and the Muslim army?"

Amr had to admit there would be. Alexandria was a long narrow city, running east and west, cut off from Egypt by Lake Mariut but linked to the western branch of the Nile by a canal. At the time of the

Nile floods (which Amr had seen for himself) the delta became a lake and the city was isolated from the interior. Land communications with Arabia would be entirely cut. The sea which washed Alexandria on its northern side was also perilous to the Arabs, who at this time had no fleet. If the Byzantines were to counterattack, this would be the way they would come. (They did so a few years later when Amr was dismissed from his governorship by Omar's successor, Uthman; only the restoration of the respected Amr led to the recapture of the city for Islam.)

Amr, therefore, returned to Babylon-in-Egypt with the command to choose a new site in the vicinity of Memphis. But it would have to be on the east bank, the side nearer to Arabia. The building of a new capital was part of Omar's policy in all but one of the occupied territories. In Syria (which was already heavily impregnated with Arabian influences) the Muslims had taken over Damascus, at first sharing its great church with the Christians. In countries remoter from Arabian influence Omar planned to create separate barrack towns from which to administer provinces not converted to Islam but paying instead the poll tax provided for in all Muslim treaties. He did not wish his ardent soldiers to grow soft or to acquire land and settle down. The new Egyptian city would be similar in structure to Kufa and Basra in Iraq, or Kairouan in Tunisia.

As usual a picturesque tale accounts for the choice Amr made of a new site. He had left his military tent (in Arabic *fustat*) standing just to the north of Babylon, close to the Nile, when he had gone north to besiege Alexandria. On his return it was still standing; in a fold in its goat-hair hangings a dove had made its nest. Amr declared the site sacred and declared that the bird was to be left undisturbed. When her brood was raised he founded his mosque on this site and round it grew Misr-al-Fustat, City of the Tent.

Such a gentle gesture is not inconceivable. Amr was an impassioned Muslim and Muslims at this time glowed with the charisma of their revolutionary faith.

But Amr was also an astute general and a much traveled man. It was he who suggested the conquest of Egypt to Omar, on the basis of his own journeys to the country before the coming of Islam. He recognized the value of this particular site for his administrative capital. The area where he had encamped was on its west side defended (and watered) by the Nile; on the south there were the existing fortifications of Babylon-in-Egypt; to the north and east he could supplement the existing canal with a defensive ditch. (The Byzantine term for such a military ditch was *fossaton*—from a military viewpoint a more likely derivation for the name Fustat.) Once prop-

Greco-Roman painting of the wine god Dionysus, from the post-Christian period. To this day the Egyptian delta produces excellent wines. (Costa Alifrangis)

erly defended, this site would be an ideal position from which to control the country and to communicate with the Arabian headquarters of Islam. Caravan routes led east from Babylon to the Gulf of Suez; there they divided, one route going north to Palestine and Syria, the other south to western Arabia. The partly choked canal—known as the Amnis Traianus in Roman times, because of Trajan's efforts in keeping it clear—could easily be repaired. This would enable Egyptian agricultural surplus to be shipped home to the needy Arabian towns. The site was also bare. Except for a few scattered churches and convents, it consisted of fields and wasteland. It was also large. Size was important for Amr's purpose. He not only needed a barrack town, he needed a large barrack town in which the various Arabian tribes could be given separate regions; this was the only way to prevent those who had been feuding enemies before Islam from becoming enemies again.

The focus of the new city was its mosque.

Compared with modern notions of what a mosque should be—these notions being formed from awareness of an architectural development of more than thirteen centuries—it was a primitive affair. It reflected, indeed, the simplicity of the country from which Amr came. "It would appear that the pre-Islamic Arabs had but the crudest notions of building, that their principal sanctuary before 608 was nothing more than four walls the height of a man enclosing the sacred well Zemzem, and that in the early days of Islam they brought nothing architectural to the conquered countries beyond what would serve their simple ritual requirements." [1] Muhammad's own headquarters in Medina had consisted, according to an eyewitness, of "four houses of mud brick, with apartments partitioned off by palm branches plastered with mud, and five houses made of palm branches plastered with mud and not divided into rooms. Over the doors were curtains of black haircloth. Each curtain measured three by three cubits. One could touch the roof with the hand."

The building was put up during the winter of 640–641. It consisted of a rectangular room measuring about ninety-five by fifty-six feet. Its walls were of rough mud brick; palm-bole pillars probably supported a ceiling of palm planks, themselves supporting a roof made of palm leaves and daub. There was no courtyard, no minaret, no niche pointing the direction for prayer and no decorations. The floor was strewn with pebbles. It had two doors on each side except the side facing Mecca.

Amr himself led his soldiers in prayer and delivered a sermon:

The Nile floods have risen. The grazing will be good. There is milk for the lambs and kids. Go out with God's blessing and enjoy the land, its milk, its flocks and its herds, and take good care of your neighbors, the Copts, for the Prophet of God himself gave orders for us so to do.

The reference to the Copts as neighbors was not metaphorical. Fustat's flimsy buildings stretched in a great arc from the fortress and churches of Babylon up toward the Mokattam hills. Although the military town was deliberately kept distinct from the Coptic city, this did not prevent the Muslims from establishing friendly relations with its citizens. Markets sprang up between the tented town and Babylon. The Muslims depended on the local people for food as well as for clerical assistance in running the country. For more than a generation the administration was to be conducted in Coptic or Greek.

As the two groups tended to coalesce, so some Copts were converted to Islam. The fervent Muslim missionaries argued that in accepting Muhammad as God's Prophet the Copts would be accepting the Comforter promised by Christ himself. The traditional teaching of the Church was that the Comforter had already come, in the person of the Holy Ghost, the spirit that would lead men into truth. Some Copts may have doubted whether the wrangling disputes from which they had suffered could be the result of divine guidance. It was tempting to recognize the Comforter in a man recently alive, rather than in a spirit symbolized by a bird. The Koran confirmed, rather than refuted, much that the Copts believed and practiced. The daylong fasting prescribed for Ramadan resembled the penitential fasts of these Egyptian Christians. The Koran paid high honor to both Jesus and his mother, the latter the only woman to be mentioned by name in the new holy book.

There were other than theological arguments for accepting the new faith. In Muslim theory, anyone who recited the Islamic creed before witnesses became *ipso facto* a member of the Islamic nation. This nation, rapidly spreading throughout the world, enjoyed privileges denied to the tolerated but not entirely equal members of older monotheistic religions. By becoming a Muslim the convert would become, in theory at least, the equal of the Arabian rulers.

If practical motives tempted Copts to conversion, so opposite practical motives tempted Muslims to forget their basic principles.

45

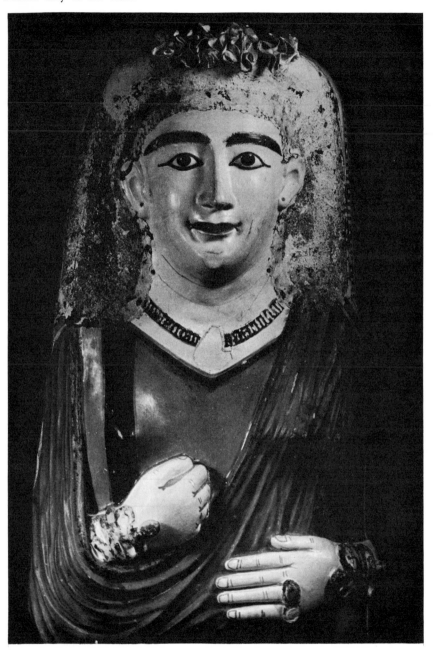

A portrait once attached to the mummified corpse of a Greco-Roman Egyptian aristocrat buried at Fayum. When converted to Christianity, this group adhered to the orthodoxy of Byzantium. (Costa Alifrangis)

The interests of the Islamic state warred with its doctrines. While its preachers urged all men to become Muslims, those running its exchequer preferred that Christians should remain what they were and pay the poll tax.

As the normal routine of politics took over from the first idealistic rush, as the needs of an expanding empire became more pressing, as the rulers of this empire tended to become the practical and the ambitious, not the pious and the austere, so the governors of Egypt required more money and more food—precisely the requirements of the Byzantine governors before them. For at least a century distinction was made between Arabian and non-Arabian Muslims, the latter suffering disabilities, the former constituting an effective elite.

For the Christians who remained faithful to their faith one immediate result of the Islamic conquest was the sudden efflorescence of a Coptic literature (admittedly restricted to works of a sacred nature) which began after the collapse of Byzantine power. Coptic artists in stone, wood, ivory, and textiles (already renowned under the Byzantines) found eager employers in the Muslim rulers, who increasingly wished to embellish their mosques and palaces. Coptic workmen found outlets outside Egypt. All over the Near East the new rulers were busy building.

In Fustat the mosque of Amr soon proved too small. Within a generation the Caliph Muawiya, reigning from Damascus, ordered the ninth governor of Egypt to enlarge it. What Amr had built was pulled down and a larger enclosure was made; this time its walls were covered with plaster, whereas rush matting took the place of pebbles on the floor. An open court was added to the northwest. At each corner of the enlarged mosque rudimentary minarets were recorded as having been built; these were either wooden platforms or short towers. The second mosque dated from 673.

Fustat grew fast as Islam became rooted in Egypt. In another generation the mosque needed to be enlarged once more. This third construction was made between 710 and 712. This time the mosque was given a prayer niche (or *mihrab*), inspired by the curved recesses in Coptic churches. Just a century later the mosque was again enlarged, this time being doubled in size. It now had thirteen doors. Instead of the primitive pillars of date boles, 378 columns supported those parts of the mosque which provided shade. The columns were not the work of contemporary stonemasons. They were purloined from the temples of Memphis, or from churches in disuse.

47

Again and again this first mosque of Cairo was to be rebuilt. After periodic lapses into disrepair it would be restored by some energetic ruler who felt the pull of its prestige. Enlarged and changed though it has been, the spirit of early Islam has stubbornly refused to be banished in any of its rebuildings. The large, ill-patronized mosque of the twentieth century, though in no concrete sense what it was when Amr built it, is in direct descent from the humble room in which the first Egyptian Muslims said their prayers, and in which the Copts were first invited to join the faith.

Outside the walls of this great mosque the two communities of Egypt, in the centuries after Amr, were to follow divergent paths. The Muslims, slowly expanding to their present ninety per cent, were to be the dominant community, though themselves dominated by rulers from outside Egypt. The Copts in their dark churches would continue offering prayers to Jesus and his mother as well as to the Father and Holy Spirit. Young men in each generation would forsake the world and become monks. But the Copts, under the Byzantines a suppressed majority, were to become, under the Muslims, a suppressed minority. The tolerance of Amr was at times to be denied them. These bad times depended on the whims of fanatical interpreters of the Islamic law; or they were the result of political tension between Islam and Christendom. When, for example, the Crusaders invaded Palestine, the chief victims were the eastern Christians. The Coptic neighbor was suspected as a secret ally of the bully with the cross.

It is a tribute to the spiritual wisdom of Egyptian Islam—a spirit that still seems to haunt the structure of Amr's much changed mosque —that despite these tensions Christianity was never eradicated from Egypt as it has been from the rest of Muslim North Africa. The Coptic Easter has become the national spring holiday of *sham al-nesseem* —literally "smelling the breeze"—shared by Egyptians of all faiths. It is a tribute to the tenacity of the Copts that even now a daily liturgy embodying passages in the language of the Pharaohs is recited all over Egypt. There are probably as many Easter communicants in Egypt as Catholic communicants in New York.

48

CHAPTER *5*

Ibn Tulun:
First Independent
Ruler of Egypt
Since Cleopatra

For two hundred years Egypt was ruled as a governorate of the Muslim caliphate. As this religious empire evolved, Egypt's affairs were controlled successively from Medina in Arabia, Damascus in Syria, and Baghdad in Iraq. As part of this early Islamic empire Egypt experienced the same metaphysical winds as Iraq, Persia, and Spain.

One bitter eastern wind was a sense of disillusion not dissimilar to that which had played an important role in "opening" (the Arabic metaphor for conquest) Egypt for Islam. The seventh-century Copts had resented an alien Byzantine government whose acts belied the Christian principles which it professed. By the ninth century a similar mood had built up toward a caliphate which had now become not the unknown rebel but the known authority.

In Islam political power proved as agonizing a trap as in Christendom. In a sense Christians were disillusioned less easily, not having been prepared for a kingdom of justice upon earth. In the first three centuries the Church had been an underground movement in the Roman empire. This buried time had served to impose on the Christian mind a bifocal vision which it was seldom to lose, a vision made easy for Christians by their master's differentiation between what belonged to Caesar and what belonged to God. Even when Caesar became a Christian emperor, an always articulate and often rebellious hierarchy maintained the dual vision. This distinction between secular and sacred (destined to sharpen in a Latin Europe split between Holy Roman Emperor and Pope) was something Christianity gained from its birth in a despised province of the Roman empire.

Islam had experienced an apparently easier birth in its wild Arabian cradle. Though persecuted by the upper-class polytheists of Mecca, Muhammad had managed to establish a state obedient to himself in the northern city of Medina. It was as though Christ, by some miraculous *coup d'état,* had seized and exercised the powers of the Sanhedrin and Pontius Pilate. Muhammad in the last ten years of his life was no mere visionary seer but the day-to-day ruler of a state having powers of life and death over all its members. This Islamic government made no distinction between the sacred and the secular. For instance, the paying of *zakat,* the alms commanded by the Koran, was a civic duty. It could be enforced by the law. A failure to fast in Ramadan could be punished by a governmental flogging. When Muhammad died in 632 his role of Prophet died with him; he bequeathed his other roles to his elderly friend and father-in-law, the pious Abu Bakr.

As caliph (that is, successor) Abu Bakr carried on the work of Muhammad. This was not simply to preach and practice a religion; it was to offer membership in a dynamic new community, a church lacking priests and sacraments but possessing an army and a collective missionary aim. Abu Bakr's greatest achievement in a two-year reign was his reimposition of Islam on a tribal Arabia which at first apostasized (thinking the bond between the tribes and Muhammad merely temporary) on the Prophet's death. The second caliph, Omar, propelled the missionary soldiers of this re-Islamized Arabia into Iraq, Syria, and Egypt.

Thus very early in its apostolic period Islam was forced to confront, and to try to solve, the problems of power. (These had remained theoretical for Christians until Constantine's conversion.) Within a very short time the apostolic charisma was stained with blood. Abu Bakr died in his bed; not so his three successors. The determined and scrupulous Omar was stabbed while at prayer in the Medina mosque; the dying caliph expressed himself happy that since the assassin was a Persian non-Muslim, he would go, as a martyr, straight to heaven. But the third caliph, the aristocratic Uthman, was

This Fayum portrait of a Greco-Roman woman strikingly recalls the features of the Levantines, who, in recent times, formed the Cairo aristocracy. (Costa Alifrangis)

murdered by fellow Muslims; they spilled his octogenarian blood over the Koran whose text he had codified. Egypt was involved with the motives of his murderers. The rather weak Uthman was accused of having replaced Amr with a time-serving relative who had adopted Islam only for the opportunities it offered for personal gain.

The fourth caliph, Ali, had the most tragic fate of all. No one had been closer to the Prophet. Ali's father, Abu Taleb, had brought up Muhammad in his own house, since Abdulla, Muhammad's father, had died before his birth and Amina, his mother, when he was a child. Ali was one of the first three male Muslims (the first Muslim of all had been Khadija, Muhammad's wife) and was married to Fatima, Muhammad's daughter by Khadija. Fatima bore him two sons, Hassan and Hussein.

Ali embodied to an outstanding degree the Arabian ideals of what a man should be: eloquent, open-handed, and brave. Yet his claim to the caliphate had been overlooked by the rough consensus of the Muslim community which elected the first three caliphs. Perhaps the Muslims sensed Ali's unfitness for the role of politician. When in 656 Ali was at last elected, those who had hoped that an intimate relative of the Prophet could reknit the fabric of Islam were to be disappointed.

Tragically, Ali owed his election to the murder of Uthman and Uthman belonged to the most powerful single family in Mecca, the Omayyads. This family, though kin to Muhammad, had persecuted Islam when it was struggling to birth and joined it when its cause was triumphant and profitable. Uthman had promoted Omayyads during his caliphate, tilting the balance from the revolutionary toward the conservative. His most brilliant relative was Muawiya, a politician in every fiber, whom he created governor of Damascus. On Uthman's death, Muawiya displayed his uncle's bloodstained robe in the mosque at Damascus and demanded vengeance. He would not recognize Ali as caliph until Ali had punished the murderers of Uthman; if Ali failed, then, Muawiya implied, he must be their accomplice.

Against the shrewd political skills of Muawiya and his ability to call on the support of men like Amr, Ali could at first count on the pious, the poor, and the non-Arabian converts, in particular the Persians. He was to lose much of this support when after the battle between his army and the Syrian army of his rival he submitted his claims to arbitration. Muawiya's army had been led by Amr who, facing apparent defeat, thought of a brilliant ruse: his soldiers hoisted copies of the Koran on their lances and called for the arbitrament of God.

Some of Ali's most fervent supporters—those who saw Islam as a community of the saved, not a political organism—attacked him for submitting something as sacred as the imamate (the headship of Islam) to human election. One group of such people planned to solve the problems of divided Islam by arranging three assassinations on one day: of Amr in Egypt, of Muawiya in Damascus, and of Ali in Kufa, his barrack city in Iraq. Only the assassination of Ali succeeded. Power was now firmly in the hands of Muawiya who moved the capital of Islam to Damascus. He founded a hereditary dynasty which in a century was to conquer a vast empire stretching from Spain in the west to Central Asia in the east. During this century Egypt was ruled from Damascus.

But behind the façade of Islamic triumph there was a fundamental split in the minds of Muslims. Many saw in the Omayyads worldly opportunists who simply used Islam to cement a kingdom hardly better than other kingdoms. The fate of Ali's descendants increased resentment. While Hassan renounced his claims to the caliphate in return for a princely stipend and a life of debauchery, Hussein waited for the death of Muawiya to lead an insurrection against Muawiya's son Yezid. Hussein and most of his family, lured to Iraq by misleading promises to support, were massacred after a long ordeal outside the town of Kerbela.

The tragic fate of the Prophet's nearest descendants stirred the imagination of Muslims. Ali had been killed on his way to prayer and the grandchild whom Muhammad had dandled on his knee had been decapitated by brother Muslims. As the bright hopes of early Islam were disappointed, as the dream of a new society became simply a new oppression, many Muslims saw in the treatment of Ali's family a basic sin which would continue to smear Islam until a new imam, or infallible guide, was accepted from his descendants. This Shia, or party, of Ali particularly attracted Persian Muslims who found that, despite their conversion, they were not treated as the equals of Arabians. The Shia formed a political movement embodying nostalgia for a lost charisma and the dream of a messianic age. Its basic tenet was that God would not leave his people without a guide. In every age a descendant of Ali would constitute a divinely inspired imam; when the visible descendants of Ali's line ran out, 53 pious fancy produced the attractive notion of a "hidden imam," a Messiah biding his time.

The Shia were to play an important role in molding the climate of opinion in which the Omayyad dynasty was destroyed in A.D. 750. Emissaries of another Meccan branch of the Prophet's wide-ranging clan, the descendants of his uncle Abbas, used the sympathies of the Shia as well as Persian nationalist resentment at Arabian supremacy to undermine Omayyad control.

The result of widespread disillusion with the Omayyad oligarchy was a military revolt in Khorasan led by Abu Muslim, a Persian soldier of genius. The last Omayyad caliph, Marwan, escaped to Egypt. After setting fire to Fustat and the wooden bridge which linked it to Roda Island, he took refuge on the west bank. But the Persian soldiers under an Abbasid general discovered his hiding place and paraded his lopped-off head round the ruined town before sending it back to army headquarters in Iraq. Marwan's fate was shared by nearly all his family. Ninety of his relatives, promised an amnesty by an uncle of the new Abbasid caliph, were invited to a banquet and treacherously slaughtered. The corpses were covered with leather mats and the planned banquet enjoyed on top of them. One Omayyad managed to reach Muslim Spain and there start an independent dynasty.

Though Islam was no longer coterminous with the caliphate, Egypt was now ruled by a caliph living in Iraq.

The first Abbasid caliph, al-Saffah ("the Slaughterer"), sent a governor to Egypt with instructions to rebuild the capital, but not on the site of Fustat, which was associated with the Omayyads. Known as Medinat al-Askar, or City of Cantonments, this new capital lay to the north of Amr's town. Its chief building was a large congregational mosque designed to rival Amr's. Each great Islamic city required one large mosque where all the male faithful could gather at noon on Friday to pray together and to hear a sermon from a leading member of the Muslim community. This kind of mosque, known in Arabic as *jami*, differed from a *masjid*, from which through Spanish the English word "mosque" derives, whose basic meaning was "a place for prostration"; a *masjid* could be large or small, a humble room in a hospital or barracks, or an impressive shrine. Later mosques were to be associated with education, healing, and death. Universities and schools, hospitals and tombs would enlarge the functions of a build-

54 ing originally intended for prayer.

In their Iraqi capital of Baghdad the Abbasids fused the religious tradition of Arabia with the cultures of ancient Greece and Persia to produce the richest compost of the medieval world. Al-Saffah's brother, al-Mansur, fathered a line of more than thirty caliphs, most of them to be begotton on non-Arabian, usually Persian, wives. Their effectiveness was steadily to diminish after the death of Harun al-Rashid (A.D. 809), the contemporary of Charlemagne and his superior in resources and culture. The Abbasids were not to banish the sense of disillusion which had brought them to power.

One reason for the gradual Abbasid decline was the way they treated their original supporters. Abu Muslim, who had put the Slaughterer on his throne, was murdered during an interview with his successor, al-Mansur. The Shia were persecuted even more thoroughly than under the Omayyads. Provinces of the empire were neglected.

In Cairo the canal that in Amr's time had ferried the cereals of Egypt to Arabia had fallen into disrepair, but it was still usable in late Omayyad times. Al-Mansur, the founder of Baghdad, closed it in A.D. 765 in order to spite some temporary enemies in Arabia. Thereafter the canal was merely to serve as an artery for the capital.

Abbasid treatment of their subjects—dictatorial and conspiratorial at once—undermined the bonds of trust between rulers and ruled. Arabian armies had already been discarded in favor of Persian; but since many Persians supported the Shia, they too were found unsuitable props for the Abbasid throne. Once again the problem of power, and once again an unsatisfactory solution.

This time the solution was a time bomb in the Arabic-speaking empire. To protect their interests the Abbasids relied on a new element in the Middle East: Turkish-speaking nomads who arrived in steady waves from central Asia. The Turks brought little but their ponies and ornamented saddles; their religion was an animism lightly overlaid by borrowings from the China on those western borders they had roamed. They were robustly built, devoted to fighting, and comparatively loyal. They were ready to sell their talents to whoever would pay. Absorbed into the culture of the caliphate, they became stalwart champions of orthodox—that is, non-Shiite—Islam. They were loyal to the Abbasid caliphs until, scenting their power, they preferred that the caliphs should be loyal to them. The slave became the master, the buyer the bought. The first large-scale buyer of Turks was the Caliph Motassim, Harun-al-Rashid's grandson. His burly praetorians began to quarrel with the citizens of Baghdad. The Caliph decided on a bold move: he would transfer his capital sixty miles upriver from Baghdad. At Samarra he founded the largest metropolis since imperial Rome. Once again Egypt had a new foreign capital.

The gigantic Friday mosque, the chief monument to have survived from Samarra, symbolized the new situation in the caliphate—a situation to be mirrored in the provinces. The mosque was constructed so that sixty thousand soldiers could pray at once. Samarra depended entirely on these Turkish guards. To pay them (their upkeep cost two hundred million dirhams a year, or twice the yield of the land tax) and to sate the ambitions of their officers, the Caliph and his weaker successors turned Islam into a feudal empire of farmed-out fiefs.

Egypt was one of these fiefs. It was offered, in 868, to a Turk named Bayikbey whom the Caliph feared and wished to remove. (He soon had him murdered, in a gallant but ineffectual effort to stem the Turkish flood.) To farm the fief Bayikbey sent his son-in-law, Ahmed, to govern Egypt. Ahmed was the son of Tulun, a Turkish slave who had been sold to Baghdad and had risen to a leading position in the military establishment; he had displayed an unusual passion for Islamic learning which he bequeathed to his son. Ahmed (known to history as Ibn Tulun, the son of Tulun) was thirty-three when he arrived in Egypt.

The country had changed in structure and spirit since Amr's days. Physically, there was the new provincial capital of Medinat al-Askar. In building this second Islamic capital the Abbasids had hit upon the rule of all who have built on the east bank of the Nile: new cities must always be constructed to the north of the old. Practical reasons prompted this instinctive policy. Since the dominant wind was from the north, whoever built on the northern side of inhabited areas avoided their smells and dust.[1] Fustat in any case had disadvantages. The nearby hills shut it off from eastern breezes; high floods submerged its low-lying land; giant mosquitoes haunted its marshes and pools.

More important than the physical changes were the spiritual.

The bright dawn of cooperation between the Muslims and their Coptic neighbors had soured in the tax collector's harsh noon light. The needs of the empire (in particular those of the Turkish praetorians) had made taxes onerous. Monks, for example, were no longer exempt from the poll tax; a man sworn to poverty found money hard to raise. The documents of state were now kept in Arabic; the administration of justice and the collection of taxes were largely in Muslim hands. Constant revolts by the still Coptic majority had inspired the Omayyads to encourage Arabian settlers to move into Egypt to strengthen the Muslim element. The Abbasids, more ruthless than the Omayyads, had resorted to periodic massacres.

Ibn Tulun, sensing the mood of disillusion, aware of the Caliph's weakness, decided to turn his fief into an independent state. (He was to wrest Syria from Abbasid control as well.) To show that his regime marked a decisive change he decided in his turn to build a new capital. He followed Abbasid precedent and chose a site a little to the north of Medinat al-Askar, extending from the hillock of Jebel Yashkur (where he planned his mosque) to the rocky spur of the Mokattam, on which he built his "Dome of the Air," a place in which to escape the stuffy atmosphere of the summer city. He built an aqueduct (the first of which we have record) to bring water to his palace from fresh springs south of the city. His city was known as al-Katai, or "the wards," since it was divided into separate areas for various military contingents.

Ibn Tulun's roots in central Asia contributed little except his physical stamina and appearance. His cultural formation had been in the grandiose metropolis of Samarra. Something of this vanished capital was transplanted from the banks of the Tigris to the proximity of the Nile; its aroma survives in the written reports of Ibn Tulun's capital:

The Meydan, where Ahmed and his captains played mall or polo, became the favorite resort of the town, and if one asked somebody where he was going the answer was sure to be "To the Meydan." It was entered by a number of gates, restricted to special classes, such as the Gate of the Nobles, the Gate of the Harim, or named after some peculiarity, as the Gate of Lions, which was surmounted by two lions in plaster, the Sag Gate, made of teak, the Gate of al-Darmun, so called because a huge black chamberlain of that name mounted guard there. Only Ahmed himself could ride through the central arch of the great triple gate: his 30,000 troops passed through the side arches.

With Ibn Tulun's passion for physical exercise went the administrative genius of the early Turks. (The Ottomans, more Balkan

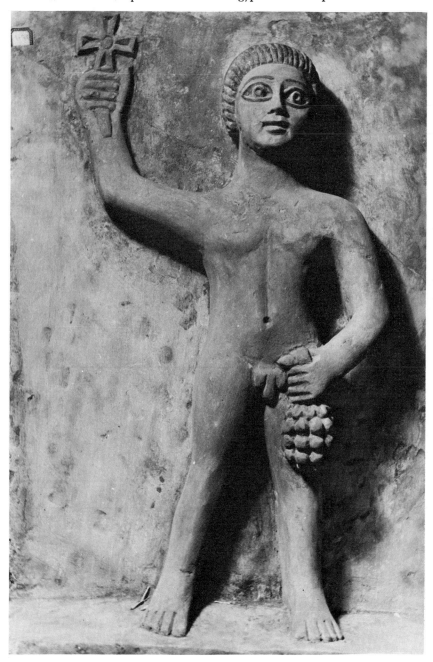

The cross and bunch of grapes are symbols of the Christian religion which the Copts adopted in place of the Pharaonic polytheism. (Costa Alifrangis)

than Turkish, were to distort the reputation of the Turks, who in Egypt and Anatolia left magnificent public buildings as traces of considerable states.) He ruled justly and reduced taxation. At the same time he had the ruthlessness of a despot. "In sickness the fierce emir was a terror to his doctors. He refused to follow their orders, flouted their prescribed diet, and when he found himself still sinking, he had their heads chopped off, or flogged them till they died."

His son Khomaruya had tastes of the kind which such eighteenth-century writers as Voltaire and Beckford were to evoke in their "Oriental" tales.

He enlarged the palace and turned the Meydan into a garden, which he planted with rare trees and exquisite roses. The stems of the trees were thought unsightly and he coated them with sheets of copper gilt, between which and the trunk leaden pipes supplied water, not only to the trees, but to the canals and fountains that irrigated the garden by means of water wheels. There were beds of basil carefully cut out to formal patterns, red, blue, and yellow water lilies and gilliflowers, exotic plants from all countries, apricots grafted upon almond trees, and various horticultural experiments. A pigeon tower in the midst was stocked with turtledoves, wood pigeons, and all sorts of birds of rich plumage or sweet song, who made a cheerful concert as they perched on the ladders set against the walls or skimmed over the ponds and rivulets. In the palace he adorned the walls of his "Golden House" with gold and ultramarine, and there set up his statue and those of his wives in heroic size, admirably carved in wood, and painted and dressed to the life with gold crowns and jeweled ears and turbans. In front of the palace he laid out a lake of quicksilver, by the advice of his physician who recommended it as a cure for his lord's insomnia. It was fifty cubits each way and cost immense sums. Here the prince lay on an air bed, linked by silk cords to silver columns at the margin, and as he rocked and courted sleep his blue-eyed lion Zureyk faithfully guarded his master.

Khomaruya was able to support these expenses on an empire (conceded to him as a viceroyalty by the Caliph) which stretched from Cyrenaica in the west to the Euphrates in the east. He married the Caliph's daughter with as much expense as pomp.

But Tulunid Egypt did not survive the third generation. Khomaruya died in 896 and was succeeded by his fourteen-year-old son, whose name meant "Father of the Soldiers of the Army." The soldiers did for their adolescent father after an incompetent reign of six months. His brother Harun lasted six years before he too was murdered. By 905 an Abbasid army had regained control of Egypt.

The extravagant palaces of Ibn Tulun and his family, flimsily built and unrespected, perished in the vengeful reconquest. What has survived to commemorate a man whose practical skill went with a love of learning and art is the largest mosque in the Egyptian capital. This building, being dedicated to God, survived the hammers of vandals.

Ibn Tulun's congregational mosque was the third to be built in Islamic Egypt. Of the first, the mosque of Amr, much survives, but it is not what Amr built. Of the second, the Abbasid mosque, nothing survives. Though the minaret has been remodeled and the great ablution fountain in the courtyard added,[2] Ibn Tulun's mosque is substantially the same as when he completed it.

Ibn Tulun was determined to endow his city with a mosque worthy of an independent capital. For this purpose he employed a Christian architect (probably from Samarra) and expended 120,000 gold dinars. He obtained the money by no longer sending tribute to the Caliph; he accounted for it to his people by claiming that he had discovered buried treasure—an excuse to be copied by later builders of costly buildings. The work was started in 877, according to one account, and was opened for prayers, as is shown by a commemorative inscription, in May 879.

The result is an architectural masterpiece which combines grandeur with tranquillity, majesty of conception with delicacy of detail. The influence of Iraq is pervasive. Ahmed and his father had worshiped in the Friday Mosque of Samarra, the grandiosity of whose containing walls looked back to the temples of the Babylonians. The first pre-Islamic feature of Ibn Tulun's mosque is the *ziyada,* or extension, which encloses external space on three sides of the mosque itself. (The fourth side, facing Mecca, was occupied by an administrative palace with a door giving onto the mosque.) This empty space removes the mosque from too close intimacy with the surrounding houses and corresponds to the sacred precincts of ancient Semitic sanctuaries. Ibn Tulun's cavalry may have used these vast enclosures to tether their steeds; the *ziyadas* were later used as bazaars; they are now cleared and provide an impressive approach to the mosque. "One mounts a slope to reach its doors, a few steps to enter the *ziyada,* and from the *ziyada* by another flight of steps to the mosque proper. This successive rise in levels recalls the Palace of Balkuwara at Sa-

A Coptic tapestry of praying saints. (Costa Alifrangis)

marra." [3] But the most vivid recollection of Iraq is the minaret. In Ibn Tulun's time the minaret was still a rudimentary form. The earliest minarets had probably been wooden platforms from which the muezzin summoned the faithful to their prayers; the pharos of Alexandria (which lasted until its destruction by an earthquake in the thirteenth century) may have suggested the tower form, since the Arabic word *minara* (the origin of minaret) means a place of flames, or lighthouse. The architects of the Samarra mosque had not imitated the pharos. They had instead created a giant spiral minaret which echoed, in a more elegant form, the tiered ziggurats (such as Aga Guf) which still puncture the Iraqi skyline and which in the ninth century were less eroded than they are today. A probably mythical tale accounts for the spiral shape of Ibn Tulun's minaret. The ruler, an impatient man who hated idle actions, was caught out in conference twisting a piece of paper into a spiral form. "Build me a minaret like that," he is supposed to have said, covering up his idle act. More likely he ordered his architect to build a helicoidal structure in the Samarra style. Later repairs have obscured the original design.

Echoes of Iraq haunt but do not distort a work of art which shows that Islamic architecture has come of age. The mosque proper consists of a courtyard, almost perfectly square, 302 feet long on each side, surrounded on all four sides by porticoes (or *riwaqs*), two aisles deep on three sides, five aisles deep on the side where the prayer niche

61

points toward Mecca. The aisles which provide the worshipers with shade (and places of study or rest for the students and ascetics who in mosques have always found a home) are not formed from purloined Pharaonic or Coptic pillars. The whole mosque is built of red brick[4] and this brickwork is covered with stucco that is, on the piers of the aisles, molded into pillar shapes, each surmounted with late Corinthian capitals (still in stucco) where vine leaves of Samarran decoration have replaced the classical acanthus. The soffits, or undersides of the arches, are decorated with exquisite friezes of formalized plant design.

That this great mosque has survived at all is one of the miracles of Cairo; that it has been so frequently restored but not reshaped has made it perhaps the greatest possession of a city that possesses so much. It is significant that this aesthetic achievement was the product of the first independent dynasty in Egypt since the death of Cleopatra.

CHAPTER 6

Fatimid Cairo:
Awe Returns to Egypt

Ibn Tulun, as an independent sovereign, contemporary with England's Alfred the Great, and as a Muslim, offering prayers in the name of the Abbasid Caliph, could in his lifetime reassure the people of Egypt that all was well. They admired his buildings; they watched his polo; they cheered the military victories that made the Tulunid capital the center of a considerable state. But the collapse of the dynasty, the restoration of Abbasid authority, did more than devastate the proud city of al-Katai. It revived the sense of disillusion which grew stronger as the Abbasid caliphate lost its spiritual appeal and its cultural vigor. At home in Iraq the rigid theologians had silenced the intellectual movements which had made ninth century Baghdad so brilliant; religious men turned more and more to the interior consolations of mysticism, or Sufism. Abroad, the caliphate again lost its grip on Egypt, farming it out this time to a dynasty known as the Ikshidites (from the term Ikshid meaning "king" in the founder's language, and conceded to him by the Caliph in return for tribute). This dynasty failed to revive the glories of Ibn Tulun and exacerbated popular discontent. It was unable to protect the country from foreign invasions; it taxed with severity.

The Shia exploited a feeling of world-weary disillusion by add-

63

ing to it a sense of milliennial hope. (Something of the same mood was shared by tenth-century Christendom, where many people neglected their work in the expectation that Christ would return in the year 1000.) The Shia offered, not a return of Ali, but the emergence of a mahdi, an infallible ruler who would repair the ruin of Islam.

Only four years after the temporary restoration of Abbasid authority in Egypt, a focus for Shiite hopes was established for the first time in the Muslim world. Its improbable site was the province known to the Arabs as Ifriqiya (from the Roman "Africa") and to the modern world as Tunisia.

How a descendant of Ali and Fatima (hence a Fatimid) survived the Abbasid secret police and created a kingdom for himself as the nucleus of an anticaliphate is one of history's great adventure stories. As in all true adventure stories—enacted in conditions of danger and double cross, maneuver and dissimulation—much of what happened is obscure. A brief outline can be given, but it must be remembered that each link in the chain may have been other than it seemed.

The man who headed the new dynasty was named Obaidallah. Of largely Persian extraction and culture he was accepted by the Shia as the great-grandson of Ismail, himself the undoubted descendant of Ali and Fatima. (Some branches of the Shia rejected Ismail because he had been known to drink. Those who accepted him replied that an imam was superior to man-made norms. By drinking he had not sinned but had shown that drinking was not sinful.) Obaidallah lived in prudent retirement in Syria, aware that he was the likely target of the Abbasid police. Just as the first Abbasid had owed everything to Abu Muslim, so the first Fatimid owed everything to another Persian energumen, a man surnamed al-Shi'i (the Shiite) for his devotion to the cause. Al-Shi'i must rank as one of the great propagandists of all time. Lacking modern means of communication, he used the best means available to him then: the annual pilgrimage to Mecca. He diffused Shiite ideas among the thousands of Persians, Egyptians, Arabs, and North Africans, who, having shown their sincerity by journeys of danger and cost, were inevitably men concerned with the deeper issues of the day. He had remarkable success with some fierce Berber tribesmen from what is now Algeria. (It is to be remarked that Shiite ideas have generally affected non-Semitic Muslims more than Arabs.) Al-Shi'i was invited to accompany their caravan back to North Africa, ostensibly to teach the

Koran but in reality to prepare the way for a Fatimid Messiah. No sooner had the Berbers got him back to their rugged mountains than they elected him their chief. To be a Berber chief meant something: almost singlehanded a small Berber army had accomplished the conquest of Spain. Al-Shi'i used his new authority to effect. After a brilliant manipulation of conspiracies and tribal wars, he found himself in a position to offer a base to Obaidallah. Outwitting the Abbasid authorities in Egypt, Obaidallah reached Tripoli in North Africa. Captured in a preliminary setback, the man of destiny was imprisoned for three years by the orthodox dynasty then ruling Tunisia. But after his period of "withdrawal" (so common in the lives of great men) he was rescued by the military élan of al-Shi'i who, on August 26, 909, presented him as the expected mahdi to a vast armed host. Al-Shi'i paid the normal price for his selfless zeal. The man he had enthroned put him to death less than two years later.

Like other founders of Muslim dynasties, Obaidallah disdained to occupy the capital of his predecessors. (This was Kairouan, the sister city of Amr's Fustat.) On a promontory off eastern Tunisia Obaidallah laid out a new city called Mahdia. This was a trial run for a new Egyptian capital which would be built toward the end of the century by the fourth ruler of Obaidallah's line.

Whether or not the original Fatimid had been a descendant of Ali or a masquerading Jew,* the Fatimid conquest of Egypt owes much to a Jewish convert to Islam named Yakub Ibn Killis. Disappointed by his treatment at the hands of the Ikshidite rulers, Ibn Killis fled to the Fatimid court. He gave the current ruler, al-Mo'izz, precise information on the state of public opinion inside Egypt, as well as the weakness of its military defense.

The Fatimids had never envisaged settling for a small North African kingdom. They were far more ambitious than men of the stamp of Ibn Tulun. Their ambition was to take over the caliphate of Islam and reverse all that had happened since the death of Ali. For the center of a new caliphate (after Syria and Iraq) Egypt was a tempting choice. They had in fact attacked Egypt several times already. As early as 914 their fleet had taken Alexandria and their soldiers had occupied the large oasis of Fayum just south of the delta. The information Ibn Killis brought confirmed that many Egyptians were now looking to a descendant of Ali for deliverance; Ibn Killis

---

* As Obaidallah's enemies had claimed.

65

assured the Fatimids that, unlike the other times they had probed at Egypt, this time they would not be resisted. The court astrologers, who greatly influenced the decisions of al-Mo'izz, affirmed that Ibn Killis had come at a propitious moment: the planet Jupiter had been in conjunction with Saturn in the sign of Aries when the Fatimids had taken over North Africa; it had now reverted to the same conjunction.

Prompted by military information and heavenly encouragement, al-Mo'izz put an army of 100,000 men at the disposal of a converted Greek called Gohar. His name meant "jewel"; it was to be auspicious for his master. Leaving Tunisia in February 969, Gohar had occupied Alexandria and reached the west-bank suburb of Giza by early July. The optimism of Ibn Killis was justified. Egypt was not only defenseless but weakened by a plague; in the neighborhood of Misr half a million had died. After some skirmishes on the west bank, Gohar forced the swollen Nile and the capital threw itself on his mercy. It did not do so in vain. Gohar gave the inhabitants a complete amnesty, forbade his soldiers to loot, and led them into camp some distance north of the town. The spot where he encamped was on a higher level than Fustat. He could see, as Herodotus had seen fourteen centuries before, how "when the Nile inundates the country, the cities are seen above its surface, very like the islands in the Aegean Sea; for all the rest of Egypt becomes a sea, and the cities alone are above the surface. When this happens, they navigate no longer by the channel, but sail across the plain."

That same night, Gohar determined to lay out a new palace city for his distant master. The site he chose lay immediately to the north of the existing inhabited area, called collectively Misr. Except for one Coptic convent[1] and a minor watchtower, it was empty ground; the actual experience of the flood showed its height above Nile level. In the scene described (in the first chapter) Gohar laid out a rectangle enclosing some 300 acres. Its southern wall would face the populous cities of Ibn Tulun and Amr; its western wall would give onto the canal; its eastern wall would run parallel with the Mokattam hills; open country would lie beyond its northern gates.

Gohar's city was new in conception as well as site. It would deserve its epithet of "the Guarded." Its walls were enormously thick, made of bricks that were, in the Persian style, nearly two feet long and fifteen inches broad. Two horsemen would be able to canter abreast along the top. Gohar's plan, according to the Arab writer Ibn

Duqmaq, was "to design palaces for his master to separate him and his friends and their armies from the general public." The new city was alien in spirit from democratic Fustat, where Amr had been a rough tribal leader among his soldiers, and alien too from al-Katai, where Ibn Tulun had reigned by the sword like some more civilized Anglo-Saxon king, enjoying the rough comradeship of his hedonistic knights. Gohar's sovereign was to reign mysteriously, as befitted an imam, from behind the curtain of awe. For Fatimid power was based on an idea: the sense that God allows an aspect of himself to be incarnate in an infallible ruler. Such a ruler must be hedged about with all that induces metaphysical and physical respect.

This palace city was to have a successor in the Forbidden City of Peking; it had had a predecessor in the Dalmatian city (now Split) where Diocletian had retired from public display. The shrewd and skeptical Roman emperor had deliberately tried to fabricate an awe-filled atmosphere, hoping that the cult of an emperor deified, while still alive, like the Persian kings, might provide an ideological cement for a divided empire. Diocletian had failed because most of his subjects had begun to believe in the divinity of Christ, while nobody, least of all himself, believed in his own. The Fatimids had a stronger idea and were to propagate it successfully for two centuries. At least one member of the dynasty was to credit his own myth.

Four years after Gohar had started work the new city was ready for its caliph. Leaving a viceroy in North Africa, al-Mo'izz sailed to Alexandria and then traveled up the western branch of the Nile to the tip of the delta. He arrived in the month after Ramadan. The various quarters of the old city were beflagged in his honor. Completely ignoring them, the Caliph drove solemnly into the palace enclosure. He was preceded by two elephants and the coffins of his ancestors. In Gohar's new congregational mosque, Al-Azhar (the Splendid), the Caliph preached the sermon and then retired into the palace prepared for him.

Al-Mo'izz reigned only two years in his new capital. They were years of active accomplishment. The Caliph was no palace parasite. He personally supervised every aspect of his government. He paid great attention to the army. Thanks to his sturdy North African troops, he was recognized as caliph in Mecca, Medina, Syria, and the whole of North Africa. Discovering that the old port of Babylon had silted up, he built a new one at Maks[2] farther north. This became the center of a lively shipbuilding industry.

67

It was probably al-Mo'izz who changed the capital's name from al-Mansuriya (after a city built by his father in Tunisia) to al-Qahira. The story of the raven and the bells was of the kind to impress his superstitious mind.[3]

At the same time al-Mo'izz set the sumptuous tone which was to characterize the whole Fatimid period, whose first century was probably the period of greatest Egyptian prosperity since the Pharaohs. Apart from having a caliph in their midst, the Cairenes had someone who ran the taxes in a far more centralized manner than the previous tax collectors. These taxes, paid in a new Fatimid currency, allowed the dynasty to build lavishly and to patronize the consumer arts. The fortunes left by two of the Caliph's daughters give a notion of Egypt's wealth. One bequeathed 2,700,000 gold dinars to her heirs; while the other's estate in gold, silver, embroideries, and precious stones required forty pounds of wax merely for seals.

Cairo's oldest mosque was built by Amr ibn al-As, who conquered Egypt for Islam in the seventh century A.D. The pillars were taken from Pharaonic or Greek temples and from Coptic churches. The mosque has been frequently restored. (Mary Eastman)

The fact that the ruler could now be Egyptocentric, no longer sending yearly tribute to the Abbasid caliph in Iraq, benefited the ordinary people. The money stayed at home.

The founder was succeeded by his son al-Aziz, who reigned from 975 to 996. Al-Aziz retained the energy of a soldier while indulging yet more lavish tastes than those of his father. He had a connoisseur's knowledge of gems and when riding used jeweled harnesses scented with ambergris. His vizir was Ibn Killis, the same man who had advised the Fatimids to invade Egypt. Ibn Killis recognized that the only way the Fatimids could establish their caliphate was through education, or propaganda. He suggested turning the congregational mosque designed by Gohar into something new: a teaching mosque which would be a powerhouse for Shiite ideas.

Al-Azhar was to remain for a thousand years the greatest teaching institution in the Muslim world, a religious university. But it was not to succeed in the task it was originally set. The majority of Muslims were not to accept the Shiite doctrines, which in Egypt itself made little headway.

The long-term failure of the Fatimids to convert the rest of Islam had important results.

On the international level, estranged from the Islamic East, which was loyal to the Caliph in Baghdad, the Fatimids opened Cairo to the West. This was not the first time that Muslims and Europeans had met each other, but it was almost the first time they had met as equals. Harun al-Rashid had received ambassadors from Charlemagne and given the Latin Church authority over the Holy Places in Palestine; but these had been contacts between a high civilization and a near barbarism. By the eleventh century Europe was recovering from its Dark Ages isolation. This recovery was facilitated by contacts with the world of Islam, itself the repository of so much pre-Islamic culture. Spain and Sicily were bridges between the Christian and Islamic shores of the Mediterranean. Sicily in particular enjoyed friendly relations with Fatimid Egypt, both under its Muslim rulers until 1060, and then, on its conquest by Roger de Hauteville, under a Norman dynasty which admired and encouraged Islamic civilization. Trade in the island remained largely in Muslim hands while Arabs introduced sugar cane, flax, olives, and the cultivation of the silkworm into Sicily. A particularly Egyptian contribution was the papyrus plant, whose fiber provided cordage for ships. The court of Palermo was more eastern than western; Frederick II (who later became Holy Roman Emperor) wore Muslim clothes, had a harem, and regarded the Fatimid Caliph as his closest ally. Encouraged by this symbiosis between Muslims and Christians in Norman Sicily, the merchants in the Italian city-states to the north traded eagerly with Egypt, a country not only rich in itself but the gateway to the yet greater riches of the Far East.

The isolation of the Fatimids from the rest of Islam had equally important results internally. The Fatimids could not trust their fellow Muslims. They felt safer using the services of Jews, Copts, Armenians, Greeks, and other minorities. The activities of these employees, many of them extremely able, enabled the dynasty long to survive the deterioration of its members. Again, their rejection by other Muslims as heretics emboldened the Fatimids to defy the rigid prohibitions of orthodox Islam. Most Fatimid rulers drank wine, often enjoying the hospitality of monks in their vine-growing monasteries. They enjoyed feasting. For the furnishings of their palaces and the utensils of their feasts they ignored the growing prejudice against representational art. This prejudice had not bothered the early Omayyads or even some of the caliphs of Baghdad; Ibn Tulun's son had decorated his palace with egoistic statues. But the scholar-jurists of Islam increasingly quoted a tradition of the Prophet (quite possibly false) to equate representation with idolatry. The Fatimids, arguing that the Koran made no mention of such a taboo, enlivened exquisite ceramics with lute players and animals. Their paintings, long since destroyed, are reported to have displayed the most lifelike semblances of secular and sacred scenes. In their public buildings that survive (such as the little mosque of al-Aqmar) there is an innovating freshness in decoration and design.

After fifteen years of Fatimid rule, Cairo had become the most impressive city in Islam, which meant, in the context of the tenth century, the world.

"Baghdad was in former time an illustrious city," wrote Maqdisi, the Arab traveler, in 985, "but it is now crumbling to decay and its glory has departed. I found neither pleasure nor aught worthy of admiration there. Cairo today is what Baghdad was in its prime, and I know no more illustrious city in Islam."

A road as wide as a parade ground separated the palace of al-Mo'izz from the smaller western palace of al-Aziz.[4] From afar these palaces loomed like mountains; near to, they could not be seen at all, so high were their walls. Giant black guards guarded an apparatus of state which revived the mystery of the Pharaohs. It struck echoes of awe even in those who disapproved of the Fatimid ideas: at least while it had power to command and be obeyed.

The effect of this city on those inside its walls was yet more striking than on those outside. To be at the still center of this hieratic ant heap, to know oneself the heir of charismatic blood, would have unsettled the most stable character. The effect on a neurotic does not need to be conjectured—it can be seen in the startling career of a son born to al-Aziz on August 14, 985, the very year that Maqdisi paid his compliment to the glowing city. The boy's mother was a Christian concubine of the Caliph; she was the sister of two Greek Orthodox bishops.

When the handsome child was a little more than eleven, his father died. The third Fatimid caliph was given a good tutor, a Slav called Burjuwan, and a sonorous official name: al-Hakim bi-amrillah, "he who rules at the command of God."

Al-Hakim has frequently been termed the Arab Caligula; the comparison with Nero is perhaps more striking. Paradoxically, there are also echoes of Akhnaton, the first Pharaoh to be known to us as an individual.

These echoes can be dealt with first. They are not religious: the monotheistic innovations of Akhnaton were profound, those of al-Hakim transient except for their garbled transference to a Levantine sect. The echoes resound in the quality of individuality shared by the two very different men inside a rigid and stylized tradition. The Pharaohs were traditionally presented as types, not as individuals; Akhnaton broke with this rule by inducing his sculptors to portray his epicene expression and giant female thighs. Arab historians of the Middle Ages worked in as rigid a tradition as the Pharaonic sculptors and painters; it was a tradition entirely different from that of Herodotus or Plutarch. They made little effort to evoke the contradictory traits of character which compose great men. Two categories existed for Muslim biographers: the good and the bad. If a ruler was good, he had the approved virtues of courage, generosity, sobriety, and patience. If the writer disapproved of him, he lacked no vice. This led to unconvincing biography. We feel intimate with few great Muslims. The accounts of their lives that survive recall the portraits of the Scottish kings which James VI commissioned for the empty walls of Holyrood Palace. Only a moral monster (as Akhnaton appears to have been a physical monster) could burst such a tradition.

71

At this point comparison with the pacific Akhnaton ceases. Those with Nero must take over.

Asked what had been the best period of the Roman empire, the "good emperor" Trajan named the first five years of Nero. It could be argued that al-Hakim's reign (during which revolts in Syria were crushed and an invasion from the west ably defeated) was the high-water mark of medieval Cairo.

The young Caliph was responsible for the embellishment and completion of a new great mosque which his father had started. It stood just outside the northern walls of Gohar's city. Now a haunted ruin, wrecked by misuse and earthquake, it retains enough vestiges to hint at an unrivaled elegance of taste. (Nothing comparable has survived of Nero's Golden House.)

Another comparison links al-Hakim with Nero. Just as Nero united against himself the pens of Christians he persecuted and of pagans he shocked, so al-Hakim's career outraged those who would write his obituaries. They were written without love. They bring him alive.

Al-Hakim wasted even less time than Nero in getting rid of his tutor. At the time he murdered Burjuwan he was a tall and power-fully built adolescent of fifteen. His actions were now entirely free. He showed signs of what would become an increasing obsession with night—an obsession shared by many lovers of Cairo—by insti-tuting a nocturnal council composed of his advisers and intimates. The council was short-lived as the Caliph soon tired of opinions other than his own. He now assumed total and meticulous control of the state and maintained this for the rest of his twenty-four-year reign. His entourage grew to dread his loud and resonant voice, to quail before his blue, dark-specked eyes. Those nearest him had most to fear. After Burjuwan he killed off other ministers of state. A victorious general who defeated the invading army of an Omayyad pretender from the west had the gratification of seeing the enemy leader paraded in a humiliating manner through the streets: he was buffeted from behind by an ape. Perhaps counting too much on the Caliph's gratitude (or not sensing the Caliph's interests in destroy-ing a successful general), the general penetrated the royal apart-ments without due notice. He came upon a scene worthy of Gilles de Rais. The Caliph was standing, his hands carmine with blood, over the disemboweled body of a handsome page. The general, of course, died.

Yet in his manic fashion al-Hakim came nearer to his subjects than many Islamic rulers. He dressed simply in a white woollen robe and disdained the panoply loved by less complex souls. On a favorite mule known as "the moon," he would patrol the streets of his capital inquiring into every aspect of public life. Sometimes he would summarily grant the petitions handed to him; sometimes, if these were wearisome, the petitioner would suffer. Caprice was the sole constant. Once an old woman was seen standing at a street corner with what looked like a petition. The Caliph seized what proved to be a lampoon upon himself. When he tried to vent his rage on the old woman he discovered that she was a dummy put there by unknown enemies.

A series of decrees embodied the Caliph's views. Many showed animus against women. At one time he tried to impose a twenty-four-hour curfew on the already secluded sex. He enforced this by imposing a ban on the manufacture of women's shoes; this he felt would be an effectual way of keeping them indoors since the streets were often dirty and manure-strewn (despite constant washing down by the army of water sellers). In the struggle against alcohol he even forbade the sale of raisins, since these could produce a fermented drink. He also forbade *malukhiya,* a slimy vegetable dish popular to this day with most Egyptians. One of his revolutionary proposals was that day should be used for enjoyment or sleep; that night was the time for work. The nocturnal Cairo which he loved now gleamed with candles and lamps.

The people of Cairo had been inured to the whims of rulers. (The first Ikshidite, for example, had increased his soldiers' pay so that they could afford to dye their hair.) When the Caliph sealed and parboiled a public bath full of rowdy women, some henpecked husbands may have nodded heads with sage approval. Even the Caliph's personal methods of administering justice would be approved by some. He took, for instance, a close interest in the markets of his capital, always the focus of Arab interest. On his rides through the narrow lanes of booths he was accompanied by a tall, well-built Negro called Masoud. If he found that a merchant was cheating he would command this swarthy slave to inflict what Victorian proconsuls described as "the worst indignity that one man can inflict upon another." Masoud would sodomize his victim openly in the man's shop; the Caliph did not disdain to assist by standing on the victim's head. Masoud entered into the folklore of Cairo. "If you

73

won't stop," a man would jokingly tell another, "I'll bring you Masoud."

Less tolerable was the drift of al-Hakim's thought.

It was a religious age and the Caliph brooded on religion. Although his own mother was a Christian, although his two uncles were patriarchs, al-Hakim became the first serious persecutor of Christians in Islam. Copts were placed under many indignities, such as having to wear a heavy cross if they went to a public bath. In 1010, as part of his mania against Christians, he first had the church of the Holy Sepulcher in Jerusalem destroyed and then gave the custody of the Holy Places to the Greek church of his mother instead of the Latin church of western Europe. This interference in ecclesiastical affairs was to be a remote cause of the First Crusade later in the century. Yet thanks to his alienation from the majority of his own community, he continued to rely on Christians and Jews, despite his attempts to organize the mass conversion of both these groups. His feverish attempt to promote the Shiite cause convinced few Egyptians. But as a by-product of his missionary aim, the Caliph achieved much for learning. He instituted a House of Science near his own palace where the learned could discuss every subject under the sun. It was probably the freest place of intellectual inquiry in the world at the time: the Shiites would open philosophical questions closed to the orthodox. Al-Hakim's library, planned as an intellectual arsenal, was one of the richest collections of Arabic manuscripts of all time. An observatory, intended to give astrological hints to the superstitious Caliph, was in its meticulous equipment the forerunner of the scientific observatories of today.

If the Egyptians were little moved by Shiite theories, this was not the case with himself.

Awe from the cradle, caliphal authority from the age of eleven, absolute power from the age of fifteen, made a mounting assault on whatever of modesty or restraint still lurked behind his terrifying eyes. All his life, al-Hakim had been imbued with extremist fancies. One of the best known Shiite stories related how when the Prophet of God was assumed into heaven—his Night Journey was supposed to have started from the Rock in Jerusalem—he entered a vast hall at one end of which was the Inscrutable's throne. On the Prophet's entry a veil slid across the throne alcove—but not before the Prophet had seen that the hand drawing the curtain was the hand of Ali.

74 Other Shiites argued that the Angel Gabriel had made a mistake of

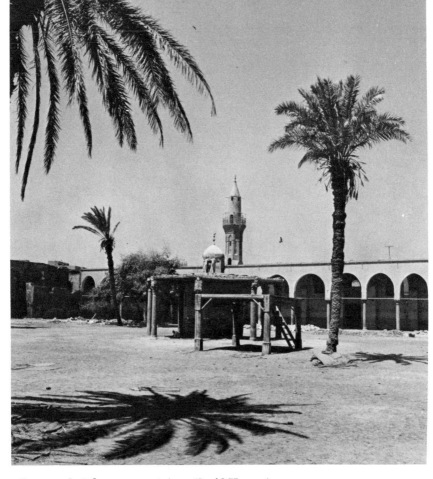

Courtyard of the mosque of Amr. (Sayid Hassan)

identification. Sent to summon Ali, he had summoned Muhammad to prophethood instead. Others argued that prophets were secondary to the avatars of deity whom they came to announce. As John the Baptist had announced his cousin Christ, so Muhammad had announced his cousin Ali.

The term avatar, derived from Aryan India, is used advisedly. Aryan Persia was to produce the greatest Muslim mystics and the most impassioned cultists of Ali. When al-Hakim's reason was tottering between prudence and insanity, two would-be prophets for an avatar arrived in Cairo. Both were Persians. They were to push an unreluctant Caliph towards self-deification.

The first enthusiast was an unsuccessful feltmaker named Hamza. He was drawn to Cairo by reports of the intellectual debates there raging. At first he contented himself with arguing for al-Hakim's divinity in private; by 1017 he was bold enough to proclaim it

75

openly. He made a forceful impact on a city crowded with genuine seekers after truth and plausible impostors greedy for caliphal subsidies. Hamza used a mosque for his pulpit. To growing cosmopolitan crowds he argued that al-Hakim, no ordinary man, was the incarnation of divinity. Hamza acquired the title "Savior of Those Who Respond" and a considerable following. In return he provided al-Hakim too with a new title: "The Maker of Time." Al-Hakim took to visiting the mosque, which lay to the north of his palace city, and discussing Hamza's ideas. Aware that the majority of native Egyptians were shocked by notions which contradicted the basic unitarianism of Islam, al-Hakim provided Hamza and his disciples with arms for their self-defense. The need for such precautions was shown when one of these disciples, al-Akhram, was murdered while riding in the Caliph's train. His murderer, an orthodox Muslim, was given a far larger funeral procession than the victim, despite the Caliph's orders.

The second great advocate of al-Hakim's divinity was Muhammad Ibn Ismail al-Durzi. Al-Durzi started as a disciple of Hamza but like many extremists soon turned on his master. Hamza's teachings were carried to yet wilder extremes. According to al-Durzi, the soul of the first Adam had been reborn in Ali; this same soul had now returned in al-Hakim, the worthiest of Ali's descendants. Al-Durzi was entitled by his followers "Supporter of God." This new version of the Shiite doctrine was taken up by the usual retinue of time servers and flatterers. They took to addressing the Caliph as "Our Sole Lord, Giver of Life and Giver of Death."

The anger of the ordinary people remained mute until the clash with what they had been taught in the Koran became too overt. A public scene roused the people to open rebellion.

One day in 1020 a group of Hamza's disciples entered Amr's mosque without dismounting—itself an impious and blasphemous act. The great courtyard was packed with people awaiting the chief judge of orthodox Islam. Three of the missionaries announced that they would take his place. They at once began expounding their thesis of the divine ruler sent from God. The people began to chant in reply the ancient battle cry: "God is greatest and He has no partners." At this moment the orthodox judge arrived with an escort of hundreds. The fervent Shiites handed him a paper to read. It opened with a parody of the usual *bismillah*: "In the Name of al-Hakim billah, the merciful, the compassionate." This was too much for orthodox sensibility. The three fanatics were done to death on the spot.

Al-Hakim's response was worthy of Nero. He ordered his black slaves as well as his Turkish and Berber troops to loot the city. The soldiers were torn between their religious prejudices (which were with the people) and their cravings for loot (which were not). For three days the southern city blazed. Al-Hakim watched the spectacle from the grandstand of the Mokattam hills. His mania was characterized by violent mood swings. One moment he was jubilant at the pyres of smoke and the screams of victims; the next moment he was struck with compassion for those whom God had cursed. The holocaust ended when the regular troops sided with the people and insisted they would burn down the palace city unless al-Hakim called off his slaves.

Al-Hakim's death was a mysterious aftermath of this event. He had always been fond of solitary rides on the Mokattam hills. From one of these he did not return. It was debated whether he was killed by his relatives, afraid that in his madness he might bequeath the caliphate outside their circle, or by subjects goaded beyond endurance by caliphal caprice. To al-Durzi the fact that the mule was found without its master was proof that the avatar had returned to heaven. He successfully preached this doctrine in Syria where to this day the Druzes perpetuate al-Durzi's name and in their secretive doctrines the cult of his master.

Even personalities as bizarre as al-Hakim could only to a limited extent affect the collective life of Egypt. Though al-Hakim's son was weak and his grandson weaker, the prosperity of the Fatimid state enabled it to support great burdens; though years of drought were accompanied by speculation in corn and followed by epidemics and civil disturbance, they were succeeded by periods of rapid recovery. The country's agricultural wealth enabled the destroyed to be rebuilt and the weak to be repaired.

As late as 1047 Cairo was able not merely to impress but to convert an outstanding visitor.

Nasir Khosrau, whose life (1004–1088) more or less spanned the eleventh century, was a Persian scholar of the kind which Islamic education at its best would sometimes produce. He had memorized the Koran (which is about as long as the New Testament) by the time he was nine; it had taken him the next five years to master classical Arabic grammar, lexicology, and poetry; his early ado-

77

lescence was devoted to astronomy and geometry, as well as to divining by sand and predicting by the stars. From fourteen to eighteen he studied the intricacies of Islamic law. His theoretical education was followed by a period of residence in India. Besides his native Persian and the official Arabic, the languages he knew included Turkish, Greek, the dialects of northwest India, and, in all probability, Hebrew.

Nasir visited Egypt in 1047. The caliph in power was al-Hakim's grandson, al-Mostansir. His capital was a double city: the northern palace city, al-Qahira, faced on its southern side the city of Misr, where the people lived and worked. Al-Qahira was impressive and Misr prosperous.

Nasir's account brings Fatimid Misr alive as a city bustling with life, its fifteen mosques maintained and crowded and its countless markets crammed with every form of produce. The caliph's insane grandfather had himself purchased both the two great mosques of Misr—the mosque of Amr and the mosque of Ibn Tulun—from the indigent descendants of their founders. (Mosques and other pious endowments could be inherited.) Al-Hakim had paid 30,000 dinars for the mosque of Ibn Tulun; he had added another 5,000 for the minaret when the family made as though they would otherwise pull it down. He paid a larger price—100,000 dinars—for the mosque of Amr. This mosque in particular was the focus of the spiritual and intellectual life of the city. There were seldom fewer than 5,000 people within its greatly expanded walls. On ordinary nights 100 lamps illuminated the mosque; on the nights of feasts no fewer than 700. The students, ascetics, travelers, and public writers who made it their haunt had aesthetic and intellectual distractions. Recitations of the Koran and religious discussions took place in the mosque's great courtyard; the eastern area roofed for prayer was now a forest of columns. The wall near the prayer niche was covered with white marble plaques on which the whole of the Koran had been inscribed in elegant calligraphy. The outside walls of the giant mosque were surrounded by *souqs,* or bazaars.

The vegetable variety sold in these *souqs* astounded the Persian visitor. On one single day—it can be precisely dated as December 18, 1048—Nasir recorded that he had seen in the market stalls: red roses, jasmine, water lilies, narcissi; bitter and sweet oranges, lemons, apples, melons, bananas, fresh cherry plums, fresh dates, raisins; sugar cane, aubergines, marrows, mangel-wurzels, turnips, celery, fresh broad beans, cucumbers, onions, garlic, beetroots, and carrots. It astonished Nasir that all these could be available on the same day in the same season.

The dwellings of Misr were no less impressive. Many were remarkably high. Nasir noticed that those which had seven stories were common, while some had as many as fourteen. There were terrace gardens on many roofs. One householder had solved the problem of watering his seventh-floor terrace in an ingenious manner. He had taken a young calf onto the roof, which had in due course grown into a bull; this stalwart creature turned an engine which raised the water required for a garden growing not only flowers and odorous shrubs, but orange trees and bananas.

Communications in the twin city were excellent. A bridge of thirty-six boats linked Roda Island to the east bank; from Roda a ferry service took the traveler to Giza on the west bank, where a famous Sunday market attracted huge crowds. Inside the city everyone rode mules or donkeys. Fifty thousand beasts which were available for a small fee were kept tethered all over the city. Only soldiers rode horses. The Nile was used for pleasure. Its banks were lined with kiosks and pavilions where one could sit drinking freshly drawn water, listening to music, and admiring the sunset. The Caliph himself kept a "stable" (Nasir's metaphor) of twenty-one boats on a lake near his palace.

The prosperity was buttressed by a sense of security. The merchants, jewelers, and money-changers of Misr did not bother to lock the doors of their shops when they left them for some purpose. A thin chain would be stretched in front and no one dared steal.

Nasir has left a detailed account of what was to be, till the twentieth century, the most colorful ceremony of the Cairo year. Each summer the rise of the Nile would be carefully watched. Throughout the country earth dams would hold back the swelling waters; in Cairo itself a similar dam would prevent the water from pouring into the city canal (which no longer linked the Nile with the Red Sea) until the propitious moment. Then simultaneously, throughout Egypt and in Cairo itself, the dams would be broken. In the valley and the delta the water would inundate the land; in Cairo the flood would fill the dry canal with fresh clean water.

When the time for the ceremony approaches [Nasir writes], they erect for the Caliph, at the head of the canal, a huge awning of Byzantine satin, covered with embroidery in gold and sown with precious stones. All the interior furnishings are similarly decked. A hundred horsemen can stand in the shade of this tent.

Before the ceremony, over a period of three days, kettledrums have been beaten in the royal stables and trumpets constantly blown; all this is to accustom the horses to a great din.

When the Caliph mounts his charger, there are in his procession 10,000 horses with saddles of gold, their harnesses enriched with precious stones. The saddle carpets are all of Byzantine satin and *bouqalemoun* which is woven expressly, neither cut nor sewn. An inscription bearing the name of the ruler of Egypt runs round these saddle cloths. Each steed is covered with a coat of mail or armour. A helmet is placed on the pommel and other arms are affixed to the saddle itself.

This day all the soldiers of the Caliph are afoot: arranged in companies and distinct detachments. The first is that of Ketami, who came from Tunisia with al-Mo'izz; I am told there are 20,000 of them. The second is that of the Bathili; these are people from North Africa installed in Egypt before the arrival of al-Mo'izz. They are mounted and consist of around 15,000. The third are the Masmoudi; they are black and come from Masmoud: 20,000. The "Easterners," so called because,

The first Arab city on the site of Cairo was Fustat, "the Tent." It is now largely the ruins and potteries shown here. In the background are the walls of Cairo's oldest mosque, Amr ibn al-As. (Sayid Hassan)

Egyptian-born, they are mostly of Turkish or Persian origin, not Arabs, number about 10,000, and have an imposing aspect. Then come a corps of slaves bought for money: roughly 30,000. Another corps consists of Bedouin from the Hijaz: 50,000 horsemen all armed with the lance. There is another corps of 30,000 slaves bought for various services. There is also a troop composed from the sons of foreign rulers who have come to Egypt; they are not considered as forming part of the army. These princes come from North Africa, Yemen, Byzantium, the Slav lands, Nubia and Ethiopia. Also in the procession can be observed men of letters, scholars, a fair number of poets, all stipendiaries of the Caliph. Not one of these princes of whom I have just spoken gets less than five hundred dinars as his stipend; some receive as much as two thousand Maghrabi dinars. They have no duty to fulfil but that of attending the Vizir's audience, of saluting him and then of returning to their homes.

The morning of the ceremony 10,000 men are engaged to lead by the bridle the horses of which first I spoke. Preceded by men beating drums and blowing trumpets and bugles they move forward in groups of a hundred. A company of soldiers marches behind them. For this service each man gets three dirhams. Then come camels, charged with palanquins and litters. At a great distance behind the horses and soldiers advances the Caliph. He is a young man of imposing appearance and pleasing expression, as befits a descendant of Hussein, the Prince of the Faithful, the son of Ali. He has a shaved head and rides a mule whose bridle and saddle are of the utmost simplicity, unadorned by silver or gold. His white jubba covers a long full tunic, as is the fashion in Arab lands: its value at least ten thousand dinars. The Caliph's turban is a length of white material rolled round his head; in his hand he holds a riding whip of high price. Just in front of him go three hundred Persians, all on foot, dressed in Byzantine brocade, belted at the waist. Their sleeves are long in the Egyptian manner. They carry short spades and mattocks; their legs are girt with lengths of cloth. The man who carries the Caliph's parasol keeps close to him. He wears a turban of cloth of gold enriched with gems; his costume is worth ten thousand Maghrabi dinars. The parasol itself is of the utmost splendour. This officer is the only person near the Caliph who is mounted. To the right and to the left eunuchs carry pots burning amber and aloes. As the Caliph approaches it is customary for the people to prostrate themselves upon the ground and call down heavenly blessings upon him.

The Vizir, the chief religious judges, and a large throng of doctors and functionaries follow the Caliph. This great ruler thus reaches the head of the Canal, the place, that is, where it will take water from the Nile. He stays on horseback under the awning for the space of an hour. Then he is handed a short spade which he hurls against the dam. This done, the ordinary folk attack the dam with shovels and picks until it yields to the pressure of the water which then floods into the canal.

The first boat launched on the canal is filled with deaf mutes. These are believed to exert an auspicious influence; the Sultan sees that they are given alms.

The whole population of Misr and al-Qahira throng to watch this spectacle and to take part in innumerable amusements.

Fatimid Egypt seemed to Nasir the noblest embodiment of Islam. Everyone, he wrote, trusted the ruler; no one feared arbitrary actions from the Caliph or denunciation by informers; everyone was assured of the safety of what he owned. In some cases what Egyptians did own was astonishing. Nasir met one Christian whose number of boats and general wealth seemed incalculable. In one year of poor harvest this merchant had told the Caliph that his reserves of flour could, if need be, feed the people of Misr for five years.

Nasir was lucky to have seen Fatimid Egypt at the zenith of its power, in a year when food was abundant at home and when abroad the caliphal writ ran in North Africa, Sicily, western Arabia, Palestine, and Syria. Nasir took away with him a glowing vision of how a descendant of Ali could transform a state. He devoted many of his remaining years to writing poetry which expressed ideas deriving from his stay in Cairo. The authorities in his Persian homeland did not take kindly to this poetic propaganda, and he died as a hermit in the remote mountains of Badakshan. Nevertheless, this one-sided vision of the glories of al-Mostansir's reign was to have a long-maturing fruit. In the sixteenth century, an independent dynasty, the Safawids, were to make Persia the one lastingly Shiite state in the Muslim world. Public opinion in Persia had been formed by Nasir, the first didactic poet in the Persian tongue.

Yet Nasir Khosrau's vision of eleventh-century Cairo was incomplete. The latter part of the handsome young Caliph's reign marked the decline of Fatimid power and the start of radical changes in the appearance of the twin cities which composed its capital.

At the time of Nasir's visit the caliphal armies were successfully challenging the Abbasid Caliph of Baghdad and the independent Seljuk-Turkish sultanate (which nevertheless recognized the spiritual authority of the Abbasid Caliph) ruled by Tughrul Beg. Al-Mostansir's armies did not remain united. The Caliph's mother had been an African, and the Caliph's sympathies were said to lie with his Negro guards. There were therefore constant disturbances between his black soldiers and his white. These weakened the defenses of the state and did much to disorganize the urban prosperity which Nasir had described. In 1068 a Turkish army invaded Egypt and captured Cairo. The great library which al-Hakim had endowed, as well as the Caliph's palace, went up in flames. In a moment al-Mostansir and his family were powerless and destitute. If the Turkish general had not been assassinated the Abbasid Caliph's name would have replaced the Fatimid's in public prayers and the dynasty would have collapsed. Al-Mostansir was saved, not merely by the assassin's dagger, but by the timely arrival in Egypt— an arrival which illustrates the extreme mobility of the Middle Ages —of Badr al-Jamali, a gifted Armenian who put himself and his Armenian followers at the Caliph's disposal. He was made commander of the Egyptian armies; the Arabic word for armies was *jyush,* or in the Egyptian pronunciation, *gyush,* and this gave him the name by which he is known: al-Gyushi. Though Syria was permanently lost to the Seljuks, al-Gyushi reconquered Egypt for the Caliph.

The form and spirit of Cairo were profoundly affected by al-Gyushi.

He altered Cairo's form by rebuilding the walls of Gohar in a manner which owed much to his knowledge of Byzantine fortifications. He also made significant additions. In the north he extended the walls so as to bring the great extramural mosque of al-Hakim within their protection. The two great gates which still stand are his work: Bab al-Futuh (the Gate of Conquests) and Bab al-Nasr (the Gate of Victory). A memorial of Shiite doctrine was inscribed over the Gate of Victory. To the Muslim creed "No deity but God; Muhammad is the Prophet of God" was added the controversial sentence: "And Ali is the Deputy of God." (Al-Gyushi's own memorial was a lonely mosque on the Mokattam hills; even in ruin it shows the Fatimid elegance.) To the south he increased the palace city by about 200,000 square yards by pushing the walls a hundred yards toward Misr.

In the spirit of the palace city al-Gyushi started a transformation which was to be completed only with the collapse of the Fatimid dynasty which he had done so much to buttress. By encouraging some of the Caliph's most trusted troops to build themselves private houses inside the walls of the city he altered the quasi-sacred nature

83

of al-Qahira. By encouraging them to scrounge their building materials from abandoned houses in Fustat he accelerated the decline of that large region of the southern city.

Many factors contributed to the decline of Fustat. The disturbances in the city, the Turkish invasion, had emphasized the defenseless character of its houses. Centuries of experience had shown the climatic and geographic disadvantages of Amr's city. The level of health was notoriously worse in the southern town than farther north. The main port of the capital had moved north to Maks, as the old port of Fustat silted up; the branch of the Nile between Fustat and Roda island was frequently blocked. In summer evenings dust (raised by the hoofs of mules and camels) would merge with smoke (raised by the furnaces of public baths) to form a smog encompassing the city like a cloud; passers-by choked and regular residents suffered from chest disease.

As people began to migrate nearer al-Qahira, or to build houses within its once exclusive walls, so Fustat sank into progressive neglect. From the reign of al-Mostansir dates a new Cairo phenomenon: the existence of vast areas of ruined and abandoned streets.

Known as *Kharab,* these derelict quarters spread like a cancer. Even in the time of al-Gyushi such insalubrious quarters, haunts of thieves and prostitutes, extended in a great swath between the Roda bridge and the mosque of Ibn Tulun. Al-Gyushi's concentration on rebuilding and strengthening al-Qahira doomed the older southern city. It was left to its own devices. Its ruins grew more extensive. By the early twelfth century the derelict areas extended virtually from the mosque of Amr to the southern gates of the walled city. From time to time efforts were made to repair what was reparable. In particular, the area between Bab Zuweyla, the southern gate of the walled city, and the Rumeyla square at the foot of the Mokattam (near Ibn Tulun's polo Meydan) was put into some kind of shape. But deep in Fustat, lane after lane, street after street, had to be walled off as its condition became dangerous. Only two motives would induce the Caliph to visit Fustat: to pray in the prestigious mosque of Amr, or to preside at the festivities concerned with the summer flood. To facilitate such journeys a road called al-Azam was cleared through the ruins. Its sides were lined by high walls which shut out the depressing vista of collapsing houses. This high wall, which hid decay but did nothing to arrest it, was symbolic of the last stage of Fatimid power—or impotence.

84

CHAPTER 7

Saladin:
A Muslim Idealist

The son of a Kurdish chief was to do for Egypt's capital what Menes had done for Egypt itself: link the north with the south in a new unity. While Menes had united the valley with the delta on the linchpin of Memphis, Saladin opened the palace city of the caliphs to aristocracy and plebs alike and joined it in a comprehensive fortified unity with ruined Misr to the south. The linchpin was a new fortress city built on the spur of the Mokattam hills where Ibn Tulun had built his Dome of the Air. Only after Saladin can the Egyptian capital as a whole be referred to as "Cairo."

How Saladin took over Egypt deserves recounting in some detail.

The Fatimid dynasty had amply justified—in part inspired—the later analysis of the great medieval student of politics Ibn Khaldun.[1] The passage of three generations, according to this acute Tunisian analyst, sufficed to reduce an innovating dynasty to exhaustion. Ibn Khaldun wrote from a vast experience of medieval Islam; the states he knew well stretched from Spain through North Africa to the Middle East. He saw the history of his age in terms of dynasties arising from sturdy desert stock and degenerating under urban temptation into palace parasites incapable of taking those actions which might have prolonged their rule.

Although the Fatimids had ruled Egypt for two centuries, not two generations, the family had produced no effective ruler after the death of al-Hakim. Their weakness had affected their internal power and the extent of their domains abroad. At home the constant riots between soldiers of different race had caused anguish and loss to the people of Cairo; only the stupendous riches of the Egyptian soil could make good the losses.

Abroad the Fatimids lost effective control of North Africa and Syria. Thus weakened, they had to confront a major challenge from Western Europe.

The actions of al-Hakim in destroying the church of the Holy Sepulcher, his support for Byzantine Christians as against the Latins, had alienated the Christians of western Europe (to the Muslims known collectively as Franks) who were in 1095 to launch the First Crusade. Their motives were, of course, more complex than a simple desire to repossess the tomb of Christ. Younger sons of powerful families wanted to possess themselves of estates or kingdoms; ordinary Europeans wanted to see the world while earning merit. By 1099 the Franks had seized Jerusalem and massacred 70,000 Muslims, to say nothing of Jews and eastern Christians. The expansion of the Crusader state during the twelfth century was as rapid as that of Israel in the twentieth. In 1109 the Franks occupied the north Lebanese port of Tripoli; in 1124 Tyre had fallen to their arms; by 1153 Ascalon, the last Fatimid toehold on the Palestinian coast, was theirs.

Muslim disunity played as large a role in facilitating twelfth-century Christian Zionism as Arab disunity did in facilitating Jewish Zionism eight centuries later. Because the Fatimids were Shiite, they were regarded as heretics by the orthodox caliphate; the Fatimids themselves disapproved of the orthodox tenets of the Seljuk Turks, who in Syria offered the only nucleus of resistance to the invasion from the west. The caliphate itself was too preoccupied with its own troubles (the Mongol invasion which was to destroy it in 1258 was only the last in a series of Turkic invasions from the east) to bother about events on the Levantine coast.

But Egypt could not be indifferent to the loss of Palestine and holy places sacred to Islam. Throughout Egyptian history the possession of Palestine, or the existence there of a friendly power, had been important. The earliest settlement on the site of Jerusalem, long before the reign of David, had been Egyptian.

Egypt was equally important—as an enemy, friend, or vassal—to the kingdom of Jerusalem, which saw itself as being there to stay. If either of the contestants in the Levant—the crusading Franks or the Seljuks of Damascus—were to win Egypt to its side, the gain might be decisive. Each side had ground for hopes.

The Franks understood the doctrinal schism which separated Seljuk Damascus under Nureddin the Turk from Fatimid Cairo. Just as Queen Elizabeth of Protestant England could argue that a dislike of popery linked her country to the Ottomans, so the king of Jerusalem could argue that in the Fatimid regime, dependent as it was on so many Christian ministers, he had a natural ally.

The hopes of the Damascus Muslims were more firmly based. They knew that the Shiite doctrines meant nothing to the Egyptian masses; the Islamic bond between Damascus and Cairo was heightened by a shared resentment at the Frankish occupation of Jerusalem, after Mecca and Medina Islam's most sacred city.

This double pull from the outside reflected itself within the sagging Fatimid state. There were those who, against the orthodox Muslims of Damascus, would side with the Frankish devil (to whom

Cairo's largest mosque, the mosque of Ibn Tulun, was built of brick and stucco in the ninth century. The spiral minaret may have been inspired by the tiered ziggurats in Iraq, where Ibn Tulun was born. (Mary Eastman)

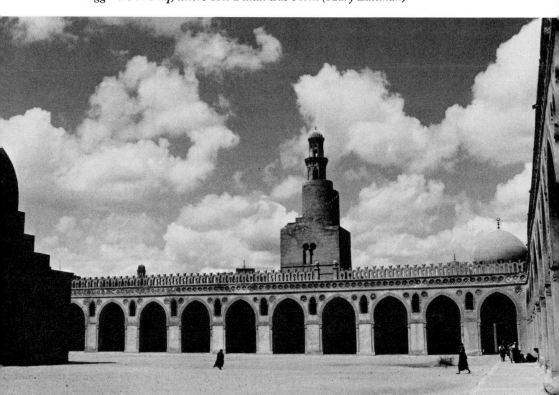

they were already paying a yearly tribute); and there were the majority who wished to be done with sectarian squabbles and to deal a Muslim counterblow to the foreign settlers.

Two vizirs, Dirgham and Shawar, disputed the remains of Fatimid power.

Dirgham, with sectarian courage, made friends with Almaric, the king of Jerusalem. He expelled his rival, Shawar, who took refuge at the court of Nureddin in Damascus. In 1164 Shawar returned with the backing of a Syrian army led by a Kurdish warrior, Shirkoh. On Shirkoh's staff was his nephew Saladin. The invading Muslims defeated Dirgham, who in his desperation pillaged the pious foundations of Islam (or *awqaf*) to pay for his army. Despite this sacrilege, or because of it, his army melted and he was lynched by the mob. (Dirgham's readiness to collude with the Franks against Islam, as much as his laying hands on the awqaf, accounted for this outburst of violence.) In a short-lived stalemate, both armies, Frank and Syrian, withdrew; each was now aware of the weakness of Fatimid defense.

Soon Almaric was in touch with Shawar, who shared his predecessor's delusion that he could use the Franks for his own ends. William of Tyre, a leading Crusader, recounts an embassy of 1167. The palace gates were still guarded by Ethiopians; inside, large courtyards still glittered with marble; there were enchanting gardens, shady pools, menageries of exotic beasts. Behind the luxurious façade was evident debility. Soon an army, half Frank, half Arab under Shawar's son, took possession of Cairo.

This fraternization between Franks and Fatimids exasperated Nureddin, who decided on the conquest of Egypt. His deputy Shirkoh occupied Upper Egypt while his nephew Saladin took possession of Alexandria. After another truce the Frankish king in his turn decided the time had come to take over Egypt. This time there would be no question of an alliance with local supporters. He would rule alone.

Fatimid weakness in face of this Frankish threat gave the old southern city its *coup de grâce*.

Al-Qahira was protected by al-Gyushi's walls; Fustat had no protection whatsoever. In a desperate attempt to prevent the Franks from occupying and using this *terrain vague*—whose ramshackle dwellings of reed or palm leaf squatted among the ruined mansions Nasir had admired—the last caliph ordered the city to be burned in

88

1168. The thousands who still inhabited its ruined quarters fled like doomsday dead arising from their tombs. The evacuation was disorderly; in the general terror it was each man for himself. The owners of mounts took advantage of the panic. They charged ten dinars, instead of the usual pennies, for a ride from doomed Fustat to the gates of the walled city. Twenty thousand barrels of naphtha and ten thousand torches were used to ignite what remained of the capitals of Amr and Ibn Tulun. The fire flared, smoldered, and flared again for fifty-four days.

The people of Fustat, an Arab historian tells us, remembered a somber verse in the Koran: "These towns, We have destroyed them when they have sinned and for them We have appointed a time of destruction."

What was destroyed even more finally than Fustat was the hieratic spirit of the palace city. The refugees from the fire were lodged in the mosques, schools, and baths of the royal enclave. They were never to leave the once exclusive city. They were instead to make it their capital. The bazaars of goldsmiths and coppersmiths would stand where an avatar of God had withdrawn from his people. The grandiose palace blocks, the superb parade grounds, the tree-surrounded villas, became the ground plan of twisting narrow lanes, of mysterious cul-de-sacs, which remains the nucleus of Cairo to this day. It was a city which would often put up with monsters but which would never make them gods as well.

Having burned his southern capital, having prepared the transformation of his northern capital, the Caliph sent tresses of his wives' hair to stir the hearts of the orthodox rulers in Syria. This time Shirkoh and his nephew arrived in Egypt to stay; the Franks withdrew. The volatile Shawar was put to death and his office assumed by Shirkoh. He enjoyed it for two months only, dying in March 1169. Saladin now became vizir of two contradictory faiths: of orthodox Islam in Damascus and of Shiite Islam in Cairo. This balancing act was difficult in an age of faith. Saladin performed it for two years. But when, on September 10, 1171, it was clear that the last Fatimid caliph was on his deathbed, prayers were offered in the Cairo mosques in the name of the caliph in Baghdad. The dying Fatimid was not informed.

With very little stir Shiite rule had ended in Egypt. The people of Cairo, never convinced by the teachings of their North African master, went about their business as usual.

Although of his twenty-four-year reign Saladin was to spend only eight in Cairo and to die in Damascus (1193), and although his main achievement was in defeating the Crusader state, he was to leave a more lasting impression on Cairo than any of his predecessors.

As a personality as much as a ruler and town planner, Saladin impressed his contemporaries, whether Christian or Muslim, and for the people of Cairo became a legend. If al-Hakim could be compared to Nero, Saladin could be compared to the second and greatest caliph, Omar. "Himself neither warrior nor governor by training or inclination, he took on both roles because he realised that the cause of his religion required someone who could revive the selfless determination of the early Muslim caliphs. Unselfish, humble, generous, he provided a new version of the Islamic ruler which struck echoes in his contemporaries. . . . He was no simpleton, but for all that an utterly simple and transparently honest man. He baffled his enemies, internal and external, because they expected to find him animated by the same motives as they were, and playing the political game as they played it." [2]

The political game in Saladin's time can be briefly summarized. As in most ages, its goal was the possession of power, either for its own satisfaction or for the pleasures it could bring. Its means were

The enclosure of the mosque of Ibn Tulun. (Mary Eastman)

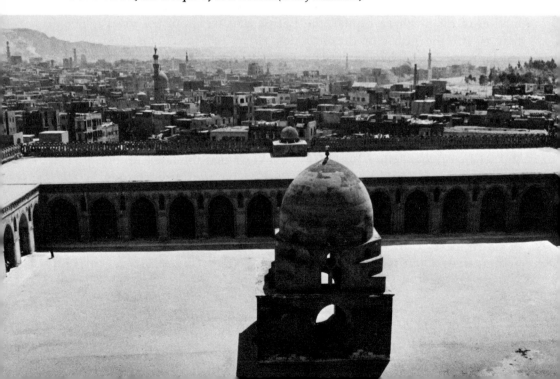

not the manipulation of voters but physical control based on a standing force of devoted mercenaries. "Mercenaries," in the context of the twelfth century, needs qualification. These men differed in some respects from the riffraff of later ages who would sell their killing power on contract. They were known as mamelukes. The word, which in Arabic means owned or possessed, explains their situation. Boys, usually Turks, were purchased from their conquerors or parents and trained to be professional cavalry. In due course, having been converted to Islam, they would often be freed and given estates on which to support themselves and dependents of their own. The mamelukes gave their loyalty to their owner so long as he treated them well. They would follow him into rebellion or new alliances without any moral considerations. They would loosen their loyalty if mistreated or underpaid. As they were opportunists, soldiers fighting for professional not idealistic motives, their loyalty was costly to maintain. Their tastes were expensive; they liked jewels and extravagant clothes. A small fief could maintain but a small number. One of the motives for the constant warfare of those days was the acquisition of more territory to support larger forces.

Saladin's repudiation of this anarchic system was shown in his every action. He had restored the name of the Abbasid caliph in public worship because he wished thereby to reunite Islam. He reigned not as caliph, but as *al-sultan,* "the power"; he had no pretensions to religious leadership. He refused to move into one of the Fatimid palaces and lived in a modest residence outside the city walls until his new fortress on the Mokattam was built.

The inspiration for his city—a departure from the work of preceding town planners—came from his life as a young man in Seljuk service. Syria and southern Anatolia were dominated by military citadels on projecting spurs of rock. The form of these defensible high places occurred to him when he pondered the problem of guarding his Egyptian capital against further inroads from the north. The spur of the Mokattam which he chose was preferable to the Mokattam itself (where only the tomb mosque of al-Gyushi stood in lonely silence, wheeled round by hawks) since this plateau was completely waterless. Inside Saladin's fortress deep wells led to drinkable water.

Saladin's citadel differed from the citadel of today. The northern portion was a veritable town whose narrow lanes contained stables, workshops, even cattle pens. It was a practical place.

91

The ruler's administrative nucleus, bustling with the activities of state, was to be linked with all the existing east-bank settlements in one huge fortified *enceinte*. The city planned by Saladin thus resembled a giant inverted triangle whose southern tip was at the Castle of Babylon [3] and whose northern base was al-Gyushi's city wall extended considerably to the west, past the canal, to Maks. At this time the Nile silt had added about a mile of terra firma to the east bank; the channel of the Nile ran more or less where the railroad station stands today. The area enclosed by Saladin's walls was about 3,500 acres, or ten times as large as the Fatimid palace city.

On the spirit of Cairo Saladin left the impress of another Seljuk institution: the *madrasa,* or teaching mosque. Saladin recognized that the fragmentation of Islam was due to the decline of its spirit. The best way to revive this spirit was by extending education, particularly religious education, to the masses of the people. After Saladin's time the schooling of boys began to form a main purpose in many mosques.

We have contemporary eyewitnesses for the Cairo of Saladin's day.

One was Ibn Jubayr, a pious Muslim who worked as secretary to the Moorish governor of Granada. Offered wine by his employer (the date of the temptation was 1182), he refused, whereupon the angry governor forced him to drink seven cups of the forbidden liquid. Seized by remorse, the governor atoned by filling the seven cups with gold coins. Ibn Jubayr used the gold to finance a visit to the Near East. He arrived when Saladin's citadel was being built:

> We also looked upon the building of the Citadel [he wrote], an impregnable fortress adjoining Cairo which the Sultan thinks to take as his residence, extending its walls until it enfolds the two cities of Misr and Cairo. The forced labourers on this construction, and those executing all the skilled services and vast preparations such as sizing the marble, cutting the huge stones, and digging the fosse that girdles the walls noted above—a fosse hollowed out with pick-axes from the rock to be a wonder amongst wonders of which trace may remain—were the foreign Christian[4] prisoners whose numbers were beyond computation.

A hospital endowed by Saladin also impresses the Moorish visitor:

> The maristan is a palace, goodly for its beauty and spaciousness. This benefaction he made so that he might deserve a heavenly reward,

and to acquire merit. He appointed as intendant a man of science with whom he placed a store of drugs and whom he empowered to use the potions and apply them in their various forms. In the rooms of this palace were placed beds, fully appointed, for lying patients. At the dis-

The al-Aqmar mosque provides the first instance of a decorated stone façade on a Cairo mosque. Built on the site of a Coptic convent in the twelfth century, it is one of the few remaining Fatimid buildings. The minaret is of later date. (Sayid Hassan)

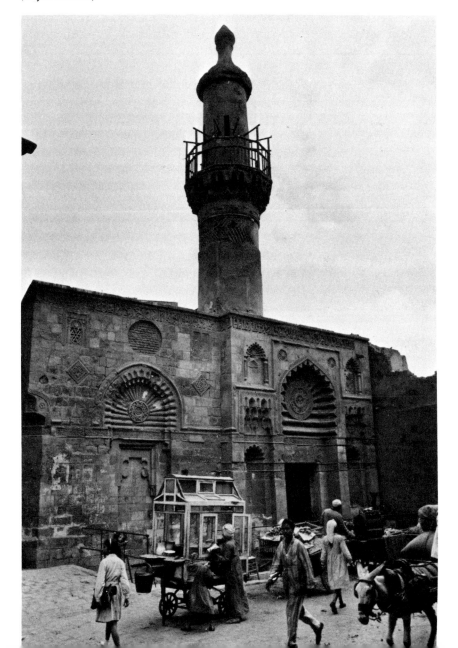

posal of the intendant are servants whose duty it is, morning and evening, to examine the conditions of the sick, and to bring them the food and potions that befit them. Facing this establishment is another specially for women, and they also have persons to attend them. A third, which adjoins them, a large place, has rooms with iron windows, and it has been taken as a place of confinement for the insane. They also have persons who daily examine their conditions and give them what is fitting for them.

Like other tourists, Ibn Jubayr was even more impressed by "the ancient pyramids, of miraculous construction and wonderful to look upon, four-sided, like huge pavilions rearing into the skies; two in particular shock the firmament. The length of one of them from one angle to another is three hundred and sixty-six paces. They have been built with immense hewn rocks, arranged above each other in an awesome fashion and wonderfully joined having nothing between them that, like cement, would serve to bind them. Their tips seem to the eye to be pointed, but it may be that the ascent to them is possible with danger and difficulty, and that their pointed tips may be found to be broad and level . . ." There was dispute what the pyramids were. Some thought they were tombs of early prophets mentioned in the Koran, others that they were the granaries of Joseph. Ibn Jubayr's conclusion: "To be short, none but Great and Glorious God can know their story."

As much as by the modernities and antiquities of Saladin's capital, Ibn Jubayr was pleased by its atmosphere of order and justice. The desperate Fatimids had imposed a tax on the pilgrims who had to pass through their territory on the way to Mecca. Those who could not pay it were cruelly punished. "Among the various inflictions devised was hanging by the testicles, or such foul acts. May God protect us from the abuse of His decrees." Saladin had abolished all such "foul acts." The subsequent revival of prosperity was extending the city even beyond his walls. We hear again of Giza. "On the west bank of the Nile . . . is a large and important burgh with fine buildings called Giza. Every Sunday it holds a large market where many congregate. Between it and Misr is an island, Roda, with fine houses and a commanding belvedere, which is a resort for entertainment and diversion."

Another visitor to the Cairo transformed by Saladin came from the eastern extremity of the Arab world. Abdul Latif was a physician from Baghdad who won the friendship of Saladin and his sons. Like Nasir Khosrau, he was a man of science in the Islamic tradition; that is, though specializing in medicine, he also had a thorough grounding in language, literature, and theology. In Cairo Abdul Latif was, toward the end of his stay, to make the one advance from Greek medical theory achieved until the advent of modern medicine in seventeenth-century Europe.

Like Ibn Jubayr, Abdul Latif was fascinated by the pyramids of Giza. Their number had already diminished by the time of his visit. The smallest ones had been quarried for the citadel. "Their ruin was effected by Karakush,[5] a Greek eunuch, one of the emirs, and a man of genius. To him was entrusted the superintendence of the buildings of the capital, and he it was who built the stone wall which surrounds Fustat and Cairo, the space between the two towns and the citadel on Mount Mokattam. He likewise constructed this citadel, and dug the two wells which are found today. These wells themselves are reckoned among the wonders of Egypt. They were descended by a staircase of nearly three hundred steps."

But the main pyramids remained. The two great ones of Cheops and Chefren were compared by poets, we are told, "to two large breasts rising from the bosom of Egypt."

The third pyramid of Mycerinus is described by Abdul Latif as being of red granite; it seems to have been his favorite; its external covering was apparently still intact in the early thirteenth century. Abdul Latif gives a scientific explanation for the shape of the pyramids: [6]

The single most remarkable fact presented by these monuments is the pyramidal form in which they were built; this form begins with a square base and culminates in a point. One of the advantages of this form is that the centre of gravity is the centre of the building itself. Since it presses on itself, since itself supports the whole pressure of this mass, all its parts bear respectively one upon the other, and it does not press on any external point.

The Abbasid Caliph Mamoun, son of Harun al-Rashid, had gashed an opening in the great pyramid in the hopes of discovering gold. All that had been discovered was an empty sarcophagus. Robbers had been working long before the Arabs.

Like modern tourists, those who went with Abdul Latif wanted to see inside.   **95**

The Fatimid mosque of al-Gyushi is claimed as the tomb of the Armenian convert to Islam who rebuilt and extended the walls of the caliphal al-Qahira. From near this mosque on the Mokattam hills, Napoleon shelled the city when its people revolted against French rule. (Mary Eastman)

Most of our party clambered through the opening and mounted to the chamber in the upper part of the pyramid. On their return they talked of the wonderful things they had seen, that the passage was so full of bats and bat dung as to be almost blocked, that the bats were as big as pigeons, and that, high up, openings were visible and windows, constructed, it seems, to let in air and light.

Despite this rather unappetizing account, Abdul Latif summoned the courage, on a second visit, to go in himself.

With several others I entered the interior passage and penetrated about two-thirds of its length. But fainting from the terror I experienced as I climbed, I returned half dead.

Saladin's son, who inherited his kingdom and reigned from 1193 until 1198, was persuaded by his courtiers to demolish the pyramids. He began with the red pyramid, the last and smallest of the three. The Sultan sent drillers, stone cutters, and ropers, under the supervision of some of the principal officers and emirs of his court, with orders for its destruction. They pitched camp near the pyramid, and

mustered from every quarter an army of workmen whose mainte-
nance cost a fortune. They and their horses stayed on the job eight
months. With all their efforts they were able to remove each day at
most but one or two stones, and this at the cost of tiring themselves
utterly. Some were charged to move the stones forward with wedges
and levers; others tugged at them from below with cords and cables.
When at last one of the stones fell, it made a tremendous noise
which reverberated far off, shaking the very earth, and making the
hills tremble. In its fall the stone would bury itself in the sand,
thus requiring extraordinary efforts to free it. By means of wedges
the stones were split into several pieces; each single piece required
a cart to carry it to the foot of the escarpment, where it was left.

After remaining long in camp, and expending all their money, they
saw that their labour increased while their resolve diminished; in
chagrin and shame the men who had been entrusted with the task con-
fessed themselves beaten. So far from accomplishing what they had set
out to do, they had merely spoilt the pyramid and shown themselves
incapable. These events took place in the year 593 of the Hejira.[7]

Just as no two tourists take the same photograph, so these two
observers—Ibn Jubayr and Abdul Latif—left different descriptions
of the Sphinx.

Ibn Jubayr, the Moor, writes of "a strange figure of stone rising
up like a minaret in the form of a man of fearsome aspect. Its face
is towards the pyramids."

This account contains one error of fact and two dubious judg-
ments. The Sphinx, so far from facing towards the pyramids, faces
directly away from them, staring toward the rising sun. To justify
the comparison with a minaret at all we must remember two things;
that the Sphinx was buried up to its neck in the sand (the sand was
not to be cleared away till the nineteenth century) and that minarets had not yet reached their later slimness. Even so the comparison
seems poor. In describing the Sphinx's expression as fearsome, Ibn
Jubayr was almost certainly moved by verbal rather than visual
impressions. The Arabic name for the creature was Abu'l-Hol,
which means "Father of Terror." The Arabs who first named it so
were probably themselves confusing the ancient name of Horus, the
beneficent god the Sphinx represented, with their word for terror;
r and l being consonants that are frequently exchanged.   **97**

Abdul Latif gives a different description of the thirteenth-century Sphinx:

A little more than a bowshot from these pyramids is a colossal figure of a head and neck projecting from the earth. The name of this is Abu'l-Hol and the body to which the head belongs is said to be buried under the earth. If the dimensions of the head are a clue to those of the body, it must be more than seventy cubits long. On the face is a reddish tint, and a red varnish as bright as if freshly put on. The face is remarkably beautiful; the mouth in particular has a charming expression; it seems to be smiling gently.

When Abdul Latif was later asked what had most impressed him in Egypt, he replied: the excellence of proportion in the Sphinx's head.

It was as an anatomist—in a season tragic for Cairo—that Abdul Latif made the chief discovery of his Egyptian journey. He also experienced the effects of a constant older than the pyramids or their guardian Horus: the Nile.

In 1200, when Abdul Latif was lodging in Cairo, the river rose no higher than twelve cubits and twenty-one fingers. Although it had started to rise at the proper time, by September 9 it had reached its peak and this was far too low to promise anything but dearth. The resultant state of the unflooded earth was called by the Egyptians *sheraqi,* an adjective which might have one of two possible meanings: either it might mean "of the east wind," referring to the wind which scorches the earth; or it might be derived from a verb connected with drying meat in the sun, like pemmican. Either way Abdul Latif and the populace took the omens as sinister. (In describing the all-important progress of their river the Egyptians still used the old Coptic months. The Nile usually began to rise in Epiphi, which started on June 25; was at its strongest in Tot, which began in late August; and then declined in Paopi, which marked late September and early October.) This ill-omened year the watchful Cairenes had noticed a greenish tint in the water similar in color to the leaves of the white beet. This tint grew steadily more marked; it was accompanied by a fetid smell which resembled sour beet juice. People began to prefer the brackish water from the Cairo wells. Abdul Latif, as eager to experiment as Sir Francis Bacon four centuries later, collected some of the water in a vial. A green cloud formed on the surface which he removed and dried. It was recognizably an aquatic moss. The water which remained was clear, but it still tasted and smelled foul. Abdul Latif tried boiling the water; this merely intensified its unpleasant attributes.

Despite the impending catastrophe, Abdul Latif, a true scientist, was fascinated by his aquatic moss. He knew of the ways in which the Copts claimed to foretell whether the flood would be high or low. In Upper Egypt they would put a lump of clay in the open on a particular night; in the morning they would weigh it and from the amount of moisture it had absorbed would predict the flood. Others linked the flood with the amount of dates on the palms, or the amount of honey in the hives. Still others—and Abdul Latif was not prepared to contradict them—believed that the study of the stars could be a useful guide. But his moss, Abdul Latif was sure, gave the clearest sign. This moss must form in puddles and pools situated near the headwaters of the Nile. When the rains in central Africa were weak, then the moss would dominate the river, as it had done that particular year; only when the rains were turbulent could they wash away the moss. In this one particular the Nile was inferior to the two great rivers of Abdul Latif's homeland. The Tigris and the Euphrates pelted southward from the highlands of Anatolia; they flowed fast and clean to the Persian Gulf. The Nile, on the other hand, moved from a region of stagnant swamp.

Having made his scientific analysis, Abdul Latif now observed the effects of a Cairo famine.

Once it was clear that the Nile would not flood, food prices soared. Those who could afford to leave Egypt did so. Whole families—another reminder of how mobile medieval man could be—set off for Syria, Yemen, Arabia, and even Morocco. Country people swarmed into Cairo. When the cool winter had passed and the sun had entered Aries (the first sign of the new astrological year), the effects of dearth began to show. The poor, always indigent, were forced to eat carrion, dogs, corpses, and even the excrement of beasts. (An alarming diet anywhere, but to pious Muslims particularly objectionable.) Far worse was in store. The sight of unprotected waifs began to tempt the hungry. The government had to issue a decree that those who killed children or ate their flesh would be burned at the stake. The edict was ineffective. "I myself saw a small roasted child in a basket. They carried it to the Emir and led in at the same time the mother and father of the child. The Emir sentenced them both to be burnt alive."

Shock and disapproval soon turned into acquiescence in what became an everyday staple. "I saw one day a woman wounded in the head, whom ruffians dragged across a souq. They had arrested her while she was eating a roasted infant they found in her possession." What struck Abdul Latif about this gruesome scene was the indifference of the onlookers. They had become as inured to cannibalism as twentiety-century readers to accounts of air raids. Gourmets began to discuss what recipes got the best out of human flesh.

As the famine advanced, so gangs of hunters began to supply the market. Country orphans, driven into Cairo by the death of their parents, became the prey of men and women alike. Not many offenders were caught, though women had less skill at avoiding arrest than men. In the course of a few days thirty women were burned at Misr after confessing to eating children. "I saw them lead one before the Governor, having a roasted child suspended from her neck. They gave her more than two hundred lashes to make her confess her crime, but in vain. She seemed to have lost all the faculties which characterize human nature." The guilty were burned. Their flesh, having been already cooked, was swiftly put on sale.

Adults, as well as children, soon had cause to fear. Physicians would be called out to lonely, ruined houses, and then attacked. A frightened midwife told the Emir a ghastly tale. She had been summoned to a house and on arrival had been invited to partake of a strange-looking stew.

"What meat is this?" she whispered to a little girl of the household.

"Oh, a fat lady came to visit us," the mite replied. "My father killed her and she's in there, strung up." Through a half-open door the midwife glimpsed a butcher's shop of human cadavers. On this occasion the cannibal, being rich, escaped with a bribe of three hundred dinars.

Fat old men went in particular peril. One portly bookseller only just eluded the nets of a gang who hunted round the area of Ibn Tulun's mosque. Another gang practiced near the mosque of Amr.

Children, women, men: finally it was the turn of relations. The tenderest bond of all became, not a barrier, but an inducement to appetite. A woman discovered nibbling a thigh retorted: "Why not? It's my husband." And an old woman argued that as the child she was eating was her grandchild, there was nothing wrong: it was better for her to eat it than an outsider.

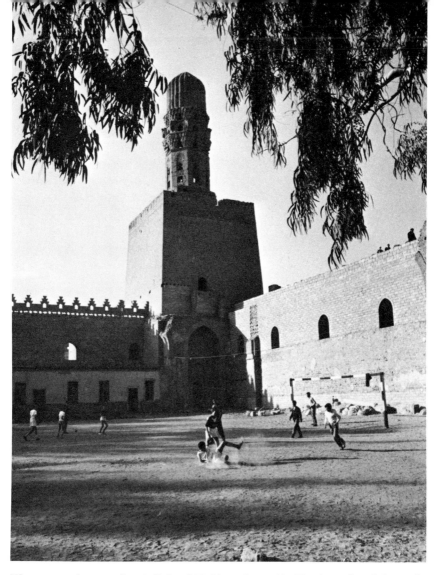

The reputation of the Caliph al-Hakim, the Fatimid Nero, has led to the neglect of the congregational mosque he built. The northern minaret is shown here. (Sayid Hassan)

What devastated Cairo assisted science.

As a physician Abdul Latif had been trained in the tradition of Galen. His education had consisted originally of memorizing a vast number of the second-century Greek's treatises. Galen himself had never been able to practice anatomy because of the Greek belief (so well exemplified in the story of Antigone and her dead brother) that the soul could find rest only if the body was buried. The Greek taboo against dissection of corpses was shared by Islam.

The Cairo famine now provided an observer with thousands of rotting bodies. Abdul Latif took advantage of his luck. He inspected a pile of 20,000 corpses near Maks. "The witness of our senses is better than reading Galen, who is often evasive," he could now declare in a startling declaration of medical independence. He was able to refute the master on a point of anatomy. All medieval physicians, following Galen, concurred in saying that the "jaw-bone is composed of two bones which are firmly joined near the chin. What I saw of this part of the corpses convinced me that the bone of the lower jaw is all one, with no joint or suture. I repeated the observation a great number of times, in over two thousand heads. I employed all kinds of means to assure myself of its truth, and I never saw anything but a single bone."

To defy tradition, to place observation over the authority of Galen, required courage. This act of courage—one step forward in the struggle for the disinterested investigation of physical phenomena—was one result of the famine which in 1200 reduced urban areas to empty wastes. In the heart of Cairo a tenement which had lodged fifty families would now house only the four watchmen of the street.

This disaster shows two constants in Cairo's history: the recurrence of famine and, more important, the extraordinary ability of the city to recover from this repeated disaster. It is not as though the famine described by Abdul Latif were unusual. To quote the researches of Marcel Clerget: [8] in one half century—which might seem exceptional, but was not—there were brutal famines in 1179, 1181, 1193, 1195, 1199–1202, 1206, 1220, 1226, 1229, and 1231. But again and again the Nile, whose penury in one year had caused the damage, repaired it with next year's plenty. This cycle of dearth and plenty profoundly affected the character of the city. The constant deaths in the city (such as were described by Abdul Latif) both increased the area of ruin, or *Kharab*, and encouraged new settlers to move into the vacant houses. Cairo was a magnet to its hinterland. This included not only the Nile valley and delta, but all Muslim countries. For now that Saladin had reopened Egypt to orthodox Islam, "foreign students began again to frequent the mosques of Cairo. . . . Professors from remote cities of Persia or even from beyond the Oxus met the learned men of Cordova and Seville." [9] Such scholars married Egyptian women; as a result the population of the city was constantly enriched with alien blood.

CHAPTER 8

Tree of Pearls:
The First Woman
to Rule Egypt
Since Cleopatra

Like a Victorian family squabbling over a will, the descendants of Saladin disputed his power. The objects they coveted were provinces and their arguments were swords.

The last princeling of this weakened state had the imposing name of Malik al-Salih Nejm al-Din Ayyub. This "pious king, star of religion," as his name meant, had imprisoned his brother in the Citadel and then fought the Crusaders in Syria. To strengthen his power base, Ayyub had purchased a formidable body of stalwart young Kipchak slaves from a Turkish-speaking area between the Urals and the Caspian. These mamelukes quarreled with the townsfolk of Cairo in the same manner as the Caliph's mercenaries had done with the people of Baghdad. Ayyub solved the problem less radically. Instead of moving his capital, he moved his mamelukes. He lodged them in barracks on Roda Island, thus keeping them some distance from the built-up areas. Though of Kurdish origin himself, Ayyub seems to have been a Turcophile. For his second wife he took a slave girl of Turkish origin whose pretty name, Shajrat al-Durr, meant Tree of Pearls.

Ayyub and his mamelukes were finally challenged at home in Egypt by the Seventh Crusade. The leader of this crusade was Louis

IX of France, a man inspired by militant piety; but the crusading kings who accompanied him were making a last desperate attempt to seize the land bridge to the East. They wished to undo the commercial effects of Saladin's achievement—the isolation of Western Europe from the East—and make it possible for Europeans to

Bab Zuweyla, the southern gate to the Fatimid city. The spirit of the saint al-Mutwalli is believed to haunt the doorway. The minarets were added later. (Sayid Hassan)

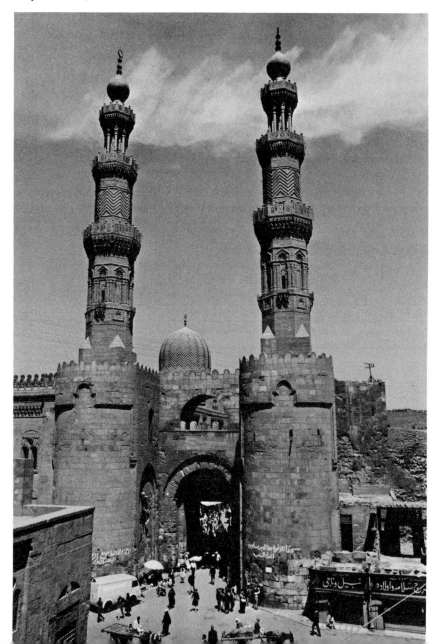

import Far-Eastern spices without paying enormous dues to Muslim Egypt.

In 1247 the Franks occupied the port of Damietta. Ayyub, by this time dying of a mixture of cancer and tuberculosis, was unable to repel the invaders. His death left the whole delta open to the Franks. His elder son, Turan Shah, was off fighting in Iraq; his son by his second wife, Khalil, was still a baby.

Tree of Pearls derived from a nomadic society in which women rode unveiled and had equal standing with men. (The Turks adopted the harem, and its symbol, the veil, after their contact with the more civilized countries to the south.) Her energy and strength of will were now to make her the first woman to rule from Cairo as her capital. To give herself time, she spirited her husband's corpse from near the delta battlefield and concealed it in the mameluke barracks on Roda Island. Meanwhile, she gave out that his majesty was on an invalid's diet, which she conspicuously prepared. Her ailing husband wished, she furthermore announced, to delegate his powers to a generalissimo who would play the role of viceroy until his son Turan should return from the East. This generalissimo would be one of Turan's mamelukes.

At this moment the balance in Egypt hung between some form of hereditary monarchy and a state overtly ruled by whoever could muster military power.

The French launched an attack in the delta which surprised the generalissimo in his bath. He was killed in it. Another slave-soldier, Bibars, then showed his mettle by launching a brilliant counterattack. The Egyptian countryside assisted his success. A diet of corpse-fed fish gave the Crusaders stomach pains and scurvy; these were followed by the plague. Louis IX was imprisoned in a house in Mansoura.

Turan Shah had now returned to his Egyptian inheritance. His stepmother gracefully conceded it. She may have guessed that his vicious and intemperate character—so typical of the third generation in these active houses—would soon destroy him. This time the redoubtable Bibars distinguished himself by striking the first blow at Ayyub's son. The terrified debauchee tried, in vain, to escape by plunging into the Nile. One of the murderers misjudged the temper of the imprisoned French king (to be canonized by his church) by bursting into his prison to display the bleeding heart of Turan Shah.

The monarchy was effectively destroyed. Egypt was without a **105** sovereign. Now sensing their power, but making an unusual choice, the mamelukes called on Tree of Pearls, widow of the late king and mother of his surviving son Khalil, to assume the royal power. They agreed to her proposal that her mameluke lover, the Emir Aibek, should act as viceroy. To placate Islamic prejudice against the rule of women, she would reign, not as Shajrat al-Durr, but as Um-Khalil, Mother of Khalil. As such she would strike her coins.

But because of the loyalty to the Abbasid caliphate renewed by Saladin, Egypt was not entirely independent. Its ruler owed spiritual allegiance to Baghdad. When the mameluke emirs asked the Caliph, Mostassim billah, for formal permission to appoint Um-Khalil as their ruler, they got an angry answer: the Prophet of God had said "Woe to the nations ruled by women." If the mamelukes could not produce a man themselves, the Caliph would send one.

The mamelukes thereupon appointed Emir Aibek as sultan, while leaving the exercise of power to Tree of Pearls, who was now his wife. Being interested in power, not its trappings, she was pleased with this solution. She was prepared to rule the state from behind a curtain. This hung in front of her special seat in the Citadel's Hall of Columns, the great reception building where the affairs of state were discussed and managed. From behind her modest screen she received ambassadors and commanded subordinates. In the Citadel, too, she instituted nightly concerts of military music.

The beneficent interlude between monarchy and a new form of despotism lasted until Aibek betrayed, not the queen, but the woman. Islamic law allowed a man to have four wives at once. The queen was aware that Aibek's control of Syria might be made less precarious if he married the daughters of powerful men in that dissident province. Her jealousy forbade her acceptance of such a scheme.

From his side, Aibek had begun to resent his wife's monopoly of his masculine attentions. Like many men of action he was superstitious. A court astrologer had warned that he would die at the hands of a woman. He prepared a plan to lessen his dependence on Tree of Pearls. An alliance with the Emir of Mosul, who had a beautiful daughter, was his simple scheme.

The queen found him out. The way she did so gives the flavor of a system in which the minute hand was intrigue and the hour hand treason.

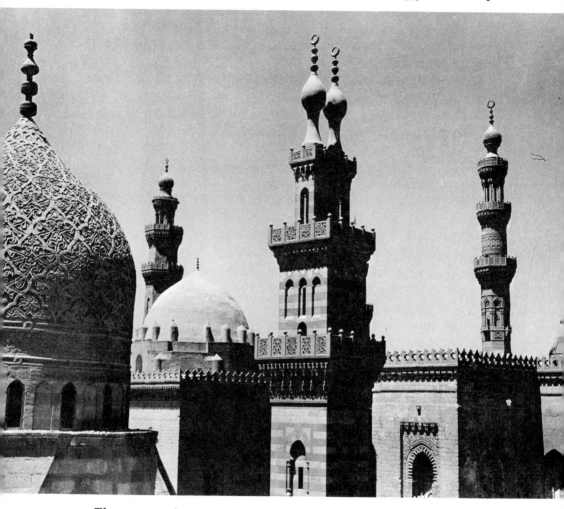

These stone minarets are typical of the religious architecture patronized by the mamelukes, a self-perpetuating caste of military despots. (Costa Alifrangis)

A group of refractory mameluke youths had been sent by Aibek to the Citadel to await his chastisement. One of them knew the queen and her jealous temper. As they stood, bound, in the hot courtyard, he recognized the window above; in its alcove the queen often sat. Suspecting she might be there, behind its meshrebiyeh grille, he whispered in the Turkish which the queen knew from her childhood:

"I am the mameluke Idekin; I carry the slippers of the Sultan. I   **107** swear, Princess, we know not why we are held. But when his Majesty ordered us to go to Mosul to ask for the hand of the Princess, we expressed our indignation on your behalf. For to you and your late husband we owe all we have."

The fluttering of a handkerchief told the cunning youth that his mistress had listened and understood. As the mamelukes were led off to their noisome dungeon, Idekin reassured his friends. "The Sultan has contrived our imprisonment; but we have contrived his doom."

The queen was decisive. She posted a letter to one of Aibek's enemies in Syria. "Learn this: after putting the Sultan to death, I intend to marry you and place you on the throne of Egypt."

The men in this story were less brave and more garrulous than the women. The Syrian emir either feared that the proposal concealed a trap, or felt that the queen's proposals were those of a praying mantis. In his alarm he consulted the Emir of Mosul, who in turn warned Aibek. A royal dowshah raged between husband and wife, reflecting the affection that still linked them both. Aibek left his quarters in the Citadel for a small pavilion near the polo ground of al-Luk. This was a flat area of silt-formed land to the west of the city. He vented his anger on the ball. A few days later, after a vigorous chukka, he received an overture from Tree of Pearls. He was ready to make peace. Grubby from the game, he decided to ride to the Citadel and wash off the grime before appeasing his queen. As he entered the bath five concealed assassins rushed at him with swords. Like Racine's Hermione, Tree of Pearls could not support her own decision. Seeing her lover helpless, naked, hearing his piteous cries, she entreated the assassins to spare his life. With murderer's logic, one replied: "If we stop, Madame, half way through our job, he will kill you and us." They got on with the job.

The guilt-stricken queen was terrified. When her offer to marry the new chief mameluke was declined, she put it about that Aibek had died of natural causes. But palaces were gossipy places; murders were not easy to conceal. Aibek's personal mamelukes learned the truth from the queen's serving-women whom they briskly tortured. The queen was shut up with her jewels in a Citadel strong room. Somehow she obtained a mortar and pestle and in the brief time left ground her jewels to dust.

The mamelukes now recognized their power to make and unmake their ruler. For the next sultan they chose Aibek's son by a previous wife. The young man emerged from retirement to the delights of power. His first thoughts were to reward his injured mother, who had been divorced at the queen's command. The dutiful youth offered her the queen to do with as she wished. The woman's revenge was commonplace but painful. Having insulted and stripped Tree of Pearls, she handed her over to her women. These angry dames beat the former queen to death in the bath; the tools they used were the heavy wooden clogs used in the *hammam*. Her battered corpse was then flung over the Citadel wall to feed the pariah dogs which haunt the desert parts of eastern towns. With that compassion which no less haunts the East, the queen's remains were collected in a basket and buried in the small mausoleum she had built for herself during her brief personal reign. It still survives. It has, in its prayer niche, the earliest example in Cairo of the use of golden and dark-hued Byzantine mosaic. Popular prejudice against a woman ruler—as in the case of Queen Hatshepsut three thousand years earlier—caused the deliberate defacing of inscriptions that recorded her rule.

The queen's short reign was memorable for more than the singularity or her funerary mosque.

Tree of Pearls had made the pilgrimage to Mecca in royal state. She had traveled, concealed, in a richly ornamented howdah. Too busy with problems of power to make the pilgrimage again, she had sent the howdah, or *mahmal,* empty of herself but containing the aura of royal power. The symbolism of the gesture caught the imagination of the people and their rulers. In its solemn procession it echoed both the Hebrew Ark of the Covenant and the ritual boats of the Pharaohs borne above the heads of the people. Later rulers, beginning with Bibars, maintained the custom and the departure of the *mahmal* for Mecca became an annual event. The *mahmal*'s shape was traditional. It was described six centuries later by Edward Lane:[1]

It is a square skeleton-frame of wood, with a pyramidal top; and has a covering of black brocade richly worked with inscriptions and ornamental embroidery in gold, in some parts upon a ground of green or red silk, with tassels surmounted by silver balls. Its covering is not always made after the same pattern, with regard to the decorations; but in every cover that I have seen, I have remarked, on the upper part of the front, a view of the Temple of Mecca, worked in gold; and, over it, **109** the Sultan's cipher. It contains nothing; but has two mus-hafs (or copies of the Koran), one on a small scroll, and the other in the usual form of a book, also small, each enclosed in a case of gilt silver, attached externally at the top.

A specially tall and handsome camel was chosen each year for the sacred burden; his reward would be retirement from all menial labor for the rest of his days. Those who saw the *mahmal* pass would rush to kiss its hanging fringes. In popular belief, to kiss these fringes was the equivalent of kissing the Prophet's hand.[2]

This peculiar custom would be enough to preserve the memory of Tree of Pearls.[3] More tragically, her reign marked a historical transition of somber import. Monarchy, in its various traditional forms, gave way to mameluke rule—to the despotism of white slaves who depended on other white slaves for their power. Mamelukes were to provide the sovereign rulers of Egypt from the death of Tree of Pearls in 1257 until the Ottoman conquest of Egypt in 1517; thereafter the mamelukes were to provide the country's ruling caste until they were destroyed by Muhammad Ali, himself a mameluke writ large, in 1811. In one sense Tree of Pearls was a mameluke herself: a Turkish slave, the paramour of the mameluke emir, Aibek. Yet she was also the widow of a free king. More important she had been a woman. A woman's caprice was not to rule Cairo again. The whims of men, no gentler, as capricious, were from now on in charge.

CHAPTER 9

Platonic Republic
Without Philosophy

Classical writers such as Aristotle had thought to define the possible systems of government under which men could live. Experts on aristocracy, oligarchy, and democracy, they never envisaged a system as strange as that whereby white-skinned slaves ruled a dark-skinned Egypt.

The Egyptians wrote about their muscular lords, retailing their foreign expeditions, their victories, their defeats; they described the coming to power of a fresh sultan, his donation to the troops, or the death of a tired one, no more able to donate. The feasts of a triumphant mameluke, the burial of a failure, bejeweled their pages. They made no attempt to analyze the system, nor did European travelers. These described the externals of what was, until the seventeenth century, "the greatest city on earth." They were fascinated by the recurrent spectacles of this mysterious place: the noisy departure for the pilgrimage, the joyous summer morning when the canal was breached. Like the Egyptians, the Europeans accepted the mamelukes as a fact of political life, hardly more to be analyzed than the weather.

After the mamelukes' extinction, European scholars such as Dr. Weil [1] or Sir William Muir [2] made efforts to preserve what Arab

111

historians had written. But both were Victorian. At a time when western Europe and America seemed to be nudging the world toward liberal democracy, when habeas corpus was as exportable as top hats and railways, the underlying pattern of the mameluke system seemed irrational and absurd: something that had occurred once and would not occur again. Except for its details, of color or cruelty, of excess or blight, it was as pointless as the history of Scotland before its union with England: a sequence of power changes important to those who took part in them, but insignificant as part of the progress toward liberty and peace.

To a historian like Muir the mamelukes offered repugnant problems, too. "Of their habits and inner life we have scarcely anything as our guide. To one dark feature we can but distantly allude." Muir published this in 1896, when Oscar Wilde had just been jailed.

The twentieth-century writer has a melancholy new freedom which allows him to mention sodomy by name; his experience also persuades him that mameluke rule was far less transient than his grandparents supposed. A widespread rejection of the liberal dream, the rule of the muscle-bound under different titles, the erosion of constitutional freedoms, the revival of torture—such signs of modern progress make the mamelukes seem our contemporaries. We know what they were about.

The mameluke system was never worked out theoretically and then applied. Like other systems, it was the response to a complex of needs.

Islamic societies, distrustful of the loyalty or prowess of their peasants, needed reliable defenders. The caliphate based on Baghdad and Samarra had initiated the system. It was to find its perfect field in Egypt whose covetable wealth required protection.

Need equally inspired the nomads who protected, then took over, the fragments of a formerly Arab empire. The Arabians themselves had migrated from their deserts impelled in part by need. The migrant tribes which moved west out of eastern Asia—tribes belonging for the most part to the Turkic race—were inspired by need alone. They brought no religion, no culture with them: only themselves. As they traveled through the uncivilized areas on the northern boundaries of Islam they were—again like the Arabians before Islam—equipped for a career as soldiers by constant strife among themselves. They had no experience of settled family life;

112

they despised (again like the Arabians) the settled, food-growing man. They saw humanity in two terms: the warrior nomad and the pacific farmer. The farmer should toil for the warrior or die at his hands.

From the thirteenth to the nineteenth century there seems to have been a steady overproduction of babies by these migrant parents. The pasturage of Asia, the pickings from intertribal war, seemed suddenly lean as travelers by their dung fires spoke of fertile Egypt with its many crops. They were inspired by tales of how

In the mid-thirteenth century, the Mongols destroyed Baghdad, capital of the Abbasid caliphate. The last Abbasids escaped to Cairo, where the caliphate continued in a shadowy form until the Ottoman conquest of Egypt in 1517. The tombs of the Abbasid caliphs are shown here. (Sayid Hassan)

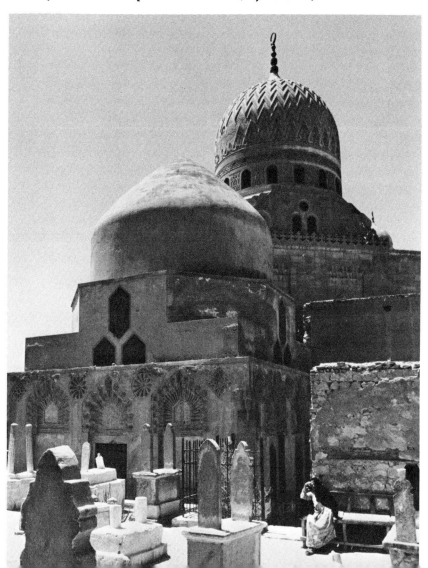

Turks like themselves had become sultans or emirs. The supply of boy slaves became as spontaneous as it was abundant. No longer was it necessary for slaves to be acquired in war; parents were eager to sell their children into a chance of limitless wealth.

The spirit of Islam in two senses boosted the slave fighter's self-respect. God had ordained everything and every relationship, however servile. At the same time the relationship between God and man was that between master and slave. The *abd* prefixed to so many Muslim names emphasizes this bond: "Abd-Allah" means, for example, "the slave of God." In colloquial Arabic, *abd* came to mean a Negro slave; the white mamelukes were not so described. Nevertheless, like the Negro slave, the mameluke was someone who had been bought by a master, for a certain task. It mattered very much to the mameluke's pride that he had been bought at a high price. Those who had cost a lot were proud of it; they often used their price in their title.

Bibars, the mameluke so prominent in the reign of Tree of Pearls, had been originally sold at Damascus for 800 silver pieces, "but returned to the broker for a filmy defect in one of his blue eyes." The only mameluke to establish a substantial hereditary line was Kilawun. He took as one of his titles "al-Alfi," or the Thousander, from the heavy price paid for him when he had been a handsome youth. (A great sultan was sometimes bought cheap. Qait Bey cost only fifty dinars.)

The system which grew up as though by hazard answered the needs of a society menaced by invaders from the north and east; it fitted into a society where the native people had long resigned themselves to being ruled by others.

The mamelukes were bought for the task of fighting, though the darker purposes alluded to by Muir must be discussed in due course. As cavalry they proved good investments to those anxious to maintain and, if possible, expand their kingly power. To the people of Egypt they were a less good bargain. But even for them they secured one advantage: when the Mongols devastated so much of the Middle East, under Genghis Khan and then under Tamerlane, Egypt was saved by its slave-rulers from the fate of Iraq. That Cairo has survived as it has survived—unlike Baghdad, whose memories of greatness are haunting fragments—was due to the mamelukes.

114   Much of what the mamelukes preserved was also their work.

The most generous and persistent patrons of art that Egypt had known since Ptolemaic times, they were to create the distinctive skyline of Cairo, with its delicate minarets and tomb-protectintg domes.

Liberal Arabists were long puzzled by what seemed a mysterious contradiction: How was it possible that such undesirable ruffians should have presided over an efflorescence of the arts that six centuries after its prime evoked astonishment? Stanley Lane-Poole [3] put it neatly in 1893:

A band of lawless adventurers, slaves in origin, butchers by choice, turbulent, bloodthirsty, and too often treacherous, these slave kings had a keen appreciation for the arts which would have done credit to the most civilized ruler that ever sat on a constitutional throne.

Lane-Poole looked backward from his Cairo hotel to an England then at its apogee of greatness. On the British throne sat a dumpy yet civilized empress. What edifices inspired by Victoria or her late husband could be put against the buildings inspired by the mamelukes? "Their morals were indifferent, their conduct was violent and unscrupulous, yet they show in their buildings, their decoration, their dress and their furniture, a taste which it would be hard to parallel in Western countries even in the present aesthetic age."

The nearest Lane-Poole came to a solution of this puzzle was a passing reference to "the passion of the barbarian for display." Barbarians, however, were as plentiful as sand; only in Cairo had they commissioned such consistent masterpieces.

Other answers to the problem would have come, in the ninteenth century, from the exponents of the fashionable doctrine of race: men like the French Count Gobineau, or the English, later natu-ralized German, Houston Stewart Chamberlain. Such theoreticians would have argued that the migrants from central Asia, in particu-lar the Caucasians, were a more creative race than the peoples they ruled. This theory encounters several hurdles. Neither the Turks nor the Circassians were precisely Indo-European (the race usually favored by the racists); the artisans who did the building and decorating of the mosques were the permanent Egyptians, who re-discovered, under mameluke prodding, the dexterity and taste which had distinguished the work of their Pharaonic forebears.

115

The mystery of the mameluke achievement in art is a mystery of taste, not a mystery of construction. The mamelukes were themselves uncreative soldiers; they evoked from others patterns in stone, glass, and wood which are humane in proportion and inspiring in effect.

Art and the love of art are deeply involved with man's emotional life. A solution to this mystery of taste may be connected with that "dark feature" which disturbed Sir William Muir.

The nearest Muir comes to confronting the dark feature is in such sentences as the following where he talks of the jealous dislike of one sultan (Nasser, the son of Kilawun) for his offspring: "Ahmed, the eldest, a wretched specimen of slavery to the lowest form

The hospital and mosque of Kilawun, a mameluke ruler, stands on the west side of the street called "Between the Two Palaces." In Fatimid times, this street divided the two main caliphal palaces. (Sayid Hassan)

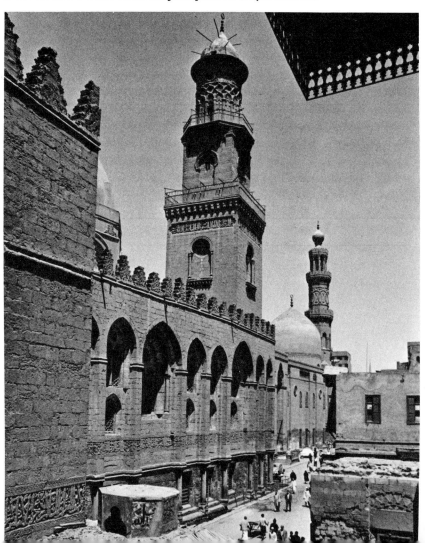

of vice, was banished to Kerak as his father failed to sever him from the company of a mameluke youth."

The eighteenth century had been less tongue-tied.

The great French traveler Volney visited Egypt just before the French Revolution, when a mameluke caste ruled Egypt under nominal Ottoman sovereignty. At that time its area of recruitment had moved from central Asia to the border provinces of the Ottoman empire, in particular the Balkans. Most mamelukes were the children of Christians; their parents had sold them for profit. Volney was himself a domestic outsider. He had been born a bastard and had changed his given name to an amalgam whose first syllable commemorates Voltaire and whose second commemorates the philosopher's residence at Ferney. From the standpoint of a rationalist, Volney describes the mamelukes:

> Strangers among themselves, they are not bound by the bonds that bind other men. Without parents or children, the past has done nothing for them; they do nothing for the future. Ignorant and superstitious by upbringing, they become fierce through murders, mutinous through tumults, deceitful through intrigues, cowards through dissimulation and corrupt through every species of debauch. Above all they are addicts of that shameful custom that has been from time immemorial the vice of Greeks and Tartars: it is the first lesson they learn from their master of arms.

As a pre-Freudian Frenchman, Volney found it hard to account for this queer taste. The mamelukes were rich enough to afford women; indeed, they possessed them. He could only account for their vice by the supposition that a voluptuary lusts to experience from his own sex what he has inflicted on the other. But the vice was universal. "There is not one mameluke without this stain. Their contagion has infected the whole population of Cairo, including the Syrian Christians who dwell in the city."

In one respect at least—the fact that they were strangers among themselves, not bound by the normal human bonds—one is reminded of another institution which has patronized great art: the Roman Catholic Church. There the comparison must almost cease. The detachment of the Western cleric was effected by celibacy. The detachment of the mameluke from the usual concern for posterity was effected by two extraneous facts: the constant destruction of young

117

men in deeds of violence, and the apparent inability of the mamelukes to found families which would last. This puzzled Volney. What prevented, he wondered, men of magnificent physique, married to sturdy women of their own race, from "adapting a blood formed at the feet of the Caucasus to the banks of the Nile?" He quoted an ancient Greek treatise (Hippocrates' *On Air, Places and Water*) to argue that Egypt was one of the two lands (the other was Scythia) where all the individuals were alike and where the race was quite separate from any other. Plants and men could not adapt themselves to such an idiosyncratic climate. This explained, for Volney, why instead of begetting replenishments, the mamelukes sent constantly abroad, to the slave markets, to keep up their numbers. (The mameluke indifference to the bonds of kinship is illustrated by a laconic paragraph in the biography of a sultan. "A little child was brought from the Caucasus who was said to be the sultan's brother; also another said to be the brother of the Secretary of State. They were both put in barracks.")

The caste's need for replenishment kept the slave markets of the eastern Mediterranean and the Levant busy. An account of the business was left by Emmanuel Piloti, a Venetian merchant from Crete who settled in Cairo around 1400 (it was he who styled it "the greatest city on earth") and lived there for forty years:

> There are in parts of Turkey and at the court of the Great Turk, as at Adrianople and Galipoli, several great heathen merchants who deal in no other merchandise than little male and female slaves of the right age to suit the sultan and to be brought to Cairo. When they have one hundred or two hundred souls, they take them to Galipoli and put them on shipboard; some are born from heathens, some from bad or ill-disposed Christians. They bring them, sometimes by way of Damietta, sometimes by way of Alexandria, and thence to Cairo. When they are brought into the presence of the sultan in Cairo, there are old practised valuers who are expert in judging a boy's appearance. They make great distinctions between one nation and another. Tartars are the most highly prized; they fetch between 130 and 140 ducats apiece. A Circassian goes for between 110 and 120 ducats, a Greek for ninety ducats, while Slavs and Albanians fetch between fifty and eighty ducats depending on quality.

Piloti puts the number of young slaves at the sultan's palace at between five and six thousand.

If the detachment of the mamelukes from family life parodied the Latin priesthood, their open practice of pederasty parodied Platonic ideals. Inspired by the 300-strong Theban "Sacred Band," Plato had proposed a Whitmanesque male friendship as a cement between the rulers of his republic. Plato himself lived in a society where most males had experienced, without guilt, attachment to members of their own sex. Without having the benefit of twentieth-century anthropological research—which tends to prove that practically any emotional pattern can exist in organized groups—Plato had foreseen one aspect of the mameluke system; the mameluke's indulgence in the love of boys Plato might have condoned; but while condoning he would have sought in vain for the philosophy which he commended as its accompaniment; he would probably have been indifferent (since, like Tolstoy, he disapproved of art) to the informed intelligence shown by unphilosophic soldiers where architecture and the arts were concerned. Twentieth-century psychology has given a clue which Plato lacked.

Latent feminity in a man—or masculinity in a woman—is often linked with an interest in art, or an ability to excel in it. A society in which men glide quickly from puberty to marriage, a society in which fatherhood is the main concern of males, tends to erode or conceal the feminine in a man. A society on the other hand where the first lesson a recruit must learn is to submit, in the feminine role, to another man, is a society where even the roughest develop whatever of the feminine exists in embryo within them. The mamelukes, for all their warlike mustaches and rowdy manners, were a caste deeply responsive to the arts which make life beautiful.

This is not to suggest that the mamelukes resembled pupils at progressive schools whose dream is an avant-garde canvas and its exhibition at a public gallery. The mamelukes were not artists themselves. While sensitive to beauty, they were more susceptible to the lure of power.

Most of the six thousand young slaves could hope for no more than a commonplace existence. The few who stood out could hope for a glittering if perilous career; there would be opportunities for acquiring splendid clothes, magnificent weapons, and handsome slaves. If a recruit caught the sultan's eye, if one of the emirs bought him for his own use or to offer to the sultan as a gift, he could rise through such menial roles as page, cupbearer, valet, or slipper-bearer to formal emancipation and a position of trust. He could be made an Emir of Ten, then an Emir of a Hundred, and best of all, an Emir of a Thousand. He would then be in the running for supreme power himself, when his master died, if he belonged to the sultan, or, if he belonged to somebody else, when a sultan's debility or death opened the jousts to the cleverest intriguer or the toughest swordsman. As a senior emir his security would lessen as his prestige grew. Great wealth would in itself tempt enemies (including the sultan) to contrive his overthrow. If he rose to the supreme power, he could expect, as sultan, an average reign of five years and a few months.

No one has better described the mameluke mentality than Volney; though he diagnosed the caste in its decrepitude, his analysis of its motives and their calamitous results is as true of the fourteenth or fifteenth century as of the eighteenth:

The young peasant sold in Mingrelia or Georgia no sooner sets foot in Egypt than his ideas undergo a revolutionary change. A boundless career opens before his eyes. Everything combines to stimulate his daring and ambition; still slave, he feels destined to be lord, and already he adopts the spirit of his future state. He assesses his master's need of him and sells dearly his service and his zeal; he weighs them against the salary he gets, or the salary he expects. And since this society knows no other incentive than money, the main preoccupation of masters is to gain the loyalty of their servants by appeasing their cupidity. Hence the profligate extravagance of the beys, so ruinous to the Egypt they despoil; hence this insubordination of the mamelukes, so fatal to the chiefs whom they exploit; hence the intrigues which never cease to agitate big and small. No sooner freed than a slave has his eyes on the highest posts; those who hold these posts have no moral superiority to inspire his respect. He sees nothing but soldiers like himself, whose power depends on the edicts of the strong; if the strong wish, he can arrive too. Nor will he be less skilled in the art of ruling, since this art consists solely in giving sabre cuts and taking money.

Power gained expressed itself in cruelty as much as in art. Two punishments in common use, according to the Arabic historians, were *al-tawsit*, in which the victim was cut in two at his belly, and *al-khazuq*, or impaling. "They stick a sharpened pale in the ground like a ship's mast. They lift the naked man onto the pale, whose point enters the rectum. They leave him for an hour or so, then finish him off by pulling him forcibly down." Flogging, manual strangulation, drowning in the Nile were simple punishments com-

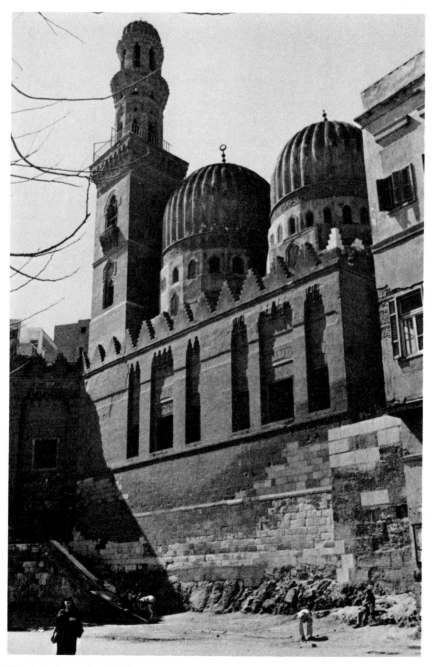

The double tomb of Selar and Sangar al-Gawli, two mameluke princes. (Sayid Hassan)

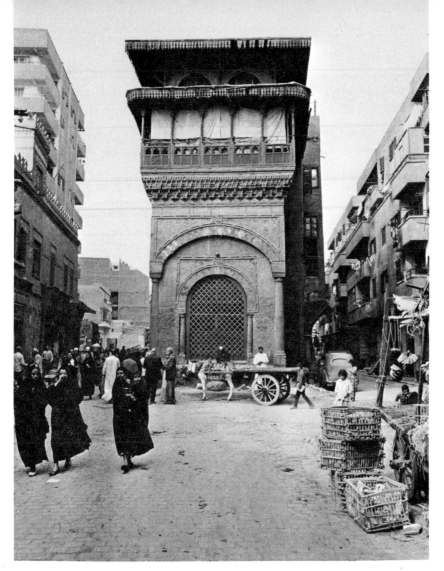

To attain virtue, wealthy Muslims endowed either schools or sebeels—cisterns where the poor could obtain free water. This building houses a school on top of the sebeel on the ground floor. It stands in the middle of the road "Between the Two Palaces." (Sayid Hassan)

pared with the adfixture to a man's head of a metal helmet heated redhot. Though executioners usually undertook these gruesome tasks, an occasional sultan would intervene himself. Faraj, the son of Barkuk, for instance, spent a whole night killing mamelukes who annoyed him. One after another he cut their throats, and then dishonored their corpses with urine or wine. A man nailed to a board and paraded through the streets on camelback was a common sight.

Such tortures (no worse than those inflicted in Christendom of the same date) reminded the emir that while art might delight posterity, only power could preserve his posterior from the agonizing pale.

For the great majority of mamelukes life revolved round the material pleasures available to men who lived in barracks, men who were brilliantly and briefly young, then obscurely middle-aged. They dreamed of acquiring enough money when they were in their youth to tide them through the years when no one feared them. The pay of mamelukes decreased as they aged.

Yet the white slaves were not untouched by the spiritual aspects of the culture which they served. Piloti recounts what happened to the young barbarians after they had been bought. They were lodged in a great training establishment several stories high. Here, in airy dormitories, the pupils slept on rush mats. The school was under the control of respected eunuchs, each of whom had a class of twenty-five boys under his control. Before the mamelukes were submitted to the sultan—who would have his pick of the new generation on the occasion of the Nile flood—they were put through an exacting catechism in the religion of the Prophet.

There is no reason to doubt the sincerity of the mamelukes' attachment to Islam. Through it they subtilized their nomadic attitudes. Their undoubted passion for display was devoted to pious works as much as to jewels, furniture, and costly clothes. Though they still respected the profession of arms more than any other, though they still regarded merchants and farmers as inferior breeds, the Koran, which proclaimed that God had created men in degrees, gave them a sense of an overall pattern in human existence. This fusion of atavistic attitudes with the stately vision of the Prophet produced, under their swords, a caste system in Islam. It was a system that worked. It was a system that was accepted by those inside it. It was a system that resembled in some ways the feudal system of the West.

In this system, the Turks constituted the class that governed and fought. The cosmopolitan citizens of Cairo engaged in trade. The fellahin—for the most part Copts or the descendants of Copts—were those who produced food. The Bedouin were those who ferried cargoes across desert seas; they were also respected as fighting irregulars.

An important second class—immediately below the Turks—was the result of the mameluke belief in Islam. The sultan did not see himself as a man ruling on his own account; he held his power under

123

God; over him and his subjects stood the Holy Law. As Islam made no distinction between the law of God and the law of the state, the purpose of the sultan was to effect what God had revealed through the Koran, the Prophet, and the consensus of Islam. This second important class was that of the *ulema,* or scholar jurists. They expounded and interpreted the Holy Law.

The mamelukes were orthodox in their Islam; they generally disapproved of the Sufi mystics; they actively persecuted the Shia of Ali. But to the four orthodox schools they gave public approval: the Hanifites, Hanbalites, Malikites, and Shafiyites. These schools were tendencies rather than sects. The differences between them were of nuance and tradition, more like the differences between various Catholic orders than like the differences between Protestant sects. A Hanifite would have no objection to praying in the mosque of a Shafiyite. One great mameluke mosque [4] was to have a schoolroom for each of the schools at the four corners of its central court. Each school was headed by its chief cadi, or judge; these four dignitaries played an important role in the public life of the mameluke state. Though the cadis and scholar jurists suffered, as a class, from timidity, though they were subservient more often than rebellious, they embodied an important reminder that the sultan's authority was not absolute. Even more important, as native-born Egyptians, they embodied a reminder to their foreign rulers of the potential dignity of those they ruled.

CHAPTER 10

Mameluke Day

The mameluke system was made firm by the same Bibars who had been rejected by his first purchaser for an eye flaw, who had counterattacked the Frankish soldiers in the Seventh Crusade, and who had taken a leading role in assassinating the last Ayyubid sovereign. Bibars was assisted by the greatest disaster in Islamic history: the sack of Baghdad by Hulagu in 1258. The Mongol victor, by murdering the thirty-seventh Abbasid caliph and his family, removed any spiritual overlord from the mamelukes of Egypt: by destroying the Iraqi canal system he turned the home province of the caliphate into a frontier waste of crumbling towns and neglected agriculture. Bibars led (under Kotuz, viceroy for Aibek's son) an army that defeated the Mongols and saved Syria and Egypt from the fate of Iraq. Bibars rewarded himself for his victory by murdering Kotuz; he then returned in triumph to Cairo, where he was unanimously elected sultan. His electors were the mamelukes whom King Ayyub had barracked on Roda Island. Bibars was to control their allegiance for a reign of seventeen years. His energy as a military man and his justice as an administrator atoned for much of the violence that had put him on the throne.

Bibars was also a constitutionalist of vision. He was responsible   **125** for a legalistic innovation which made mameluke rule seem a right as well as a fact. He recognized that a slave sultan unsupported by any legal bulwark would be at the mercy of the first cabal among his fellow mamelukes or of any well-laid plot by those who would have liked to restore the Fatimids. Bibars hit on the ingenious notion of restoring the Abbasid dynasty of caliphs in his own capital.

The operation was conducted in two phases. "Hearing, therefore, that an Abbasid still survived the Mongol massacre, Bibars had him brought in triumph from Syria to Cairo. At his approach, the Sultan with his Court went forth in state to meet him, while even the Jews and Christians carrying aloft the Law and Gospel followed in his train. He was then installed as caliph, Bibars and the officers of state swearing fealty to him; while he in turn conferred on Bibars the sovereign title. At public worship, after the established ritual of reading the Koran and invocation of blessing on the Prophet and on the lineage of Abbas, the Caliph offered prayer for the welfare of the Sultan. Some weeks passed, and the royal party, having witnessed a festive combat on the Nile, assembled in a garden outside Cairo where the Caliph invested Bibars with a robe of honour and the glittering badge of Imperial State." [1]

This was only the first phase. The intended puppet showed no understanding of the Sultan's motives. Believing that his restoration was real, the Caliph took Bibars with him to Syria with the intention of reconquering Iraq. Bibars knew that the Caliph's gratitude might evaporate once he had secured a power base of his own; Islamic history provided too many examples of kingmakers being destroyed by their kings. Bibars therefore dispatched the dazzled Caliph to Baghdad with a calculatedly inadequate force of Bedouin and Turks. The Mongol governor did the rest.

Bibars now moved into the second stage. A replacement for the dead Caliph was produced who lacked his pretensions. A pensioner of the mameluke state, he embodied a shadowy continuity with the Islamic past. He had less real power than the Archbishop of Canterbury today. With the four cadis of the orthodox schools he formed part of the religious hierarchy of the mameluke state.

This state was effectively run. Bibars eradicated the remaining Frankish settlers from all of Palestine but the sea fort of Acre; having reaffirmed his defeat of the Mongols, he established mameluke authority deep in Anatolia. His imperial communications were fast. Letters between Cairo and Damascus took sixty hours—a speed not

These houses, part of the Dead City, are largely tombs, though a sparse population lives, as in the past, among them. In the background are the Mokattam hills (left), the Citadel of Muhammad Ali (center), and the mosque of Sultan Hassan (right). (Sayid Hassan)

to be rivaled by the republican posts of the 1960's. The Sultan himself was always on the move—"one day in Egypt, the next in Arabia; here in Syria, now in Aleppo." Under Bibars the empire of Saladin was pushed farther south. The Nubians of the Upper Nile valley were induced into Islam. Hitherto this dignified and honest people had belonged to the Coptic church.

Bibars bequeathed his system to a mameluke posterity; he could not bequeath it to his own. His son Said was "cruel and treacherous like his father, but utterly devoid of his father's ability"; he soon gave way to his father-in-law, Kilawun, the one mameluke to establish a line of descendants for a considerable time. Kilawun briefly posed as guardian of a younger son of Bibars, when Said was deposed; dropping the pose, he reigned as sultan from 1279; his last descendant was not deposed until 1382.

Kilawun spent much of his eleven-year reign in war. He possessed no fewer than twelve thousand mamelukes whom he regarded as a modern general regards his armored cars or tanks. He disposed a third of this armor, mostly Circassian, in a new barracks by the Citadel; the other two thirds remained on Roda Island. (The Arabic terms were *Bahri*—of the river, or the Nile—for those quartered in   **127**

Roda; *Burji*—of the tower, or citadel—for those quartered at the foot of the Mokattam hills. The dynasty of Bibars and Kilawun is known as *Bahri*; its successors, who were largely Circassians from the Citadel, are known as *Burji*. The terms "Nile Mamelukes" and "Citadel Mamelukes" give the sense.)

In Cairo, Kilawun was to be remembered for the quantity of useful and beautiful building which he sponsored. One huge edifice, built by forced labor and with materials cannibalized from the pyramids and previous buildings, was designed to be college, hospital, and mausoleum all at once. As an educational establishment it included a library open to the public and staffed with librarians. Public lectures for adults were sponsored by each of the four orthodox schools. For children there was an orphanage, a children's religious school, and a species of kindergarten. As a medical establishment it had large rooms equipped with beds for the sick, whether rich or poor, male or female. There were well-stocked laboratories provided with every sort of medical appliance. The needs of the soul were not neglected: fifty readers chanted the Koran in the mausoleum.[2]

Kilawun's younger son Nasser, begotten when his father was in his sixties, reigned after his brother from 1293 to 1341, but not continuously. He was called to the throne on three separate occasions.

His first reign, as a child of nine, was very brief. After one year he was deposed by a Mongol mameluke, Katbogha, then kept deposed by a Greek mameluke, Lajin. The former was detested for introducing a tribe of horse-eating Tartars into Syria; the latter, married to a daughter of Bibars, and deserving well for his architectural works,[3] was despised for his passive submission to his minion, Menkutimur. He died by violence.

Nasser's second reign started when he was fourteen. Two great ministers—Salar and a second Bibars—now overshadowed him. Salar, a short, thickset Tartar with piercing eyes and swarthy skin, was his energetic regent; Bibars, a fair-skinned Circassian, was his economical majordomo. The young Nasser fared badly when he personally took to the field against a new incursion of Mongols into Syria. "The Egyptian troops, casting aside their arms and uniform, had fled from the battlefield in utter confusion past Damascus to Cairo, which the young Sultan reached with hardly a follower about him."[4] He showed his mettle by taking rapid steps to undo the reverse. Egyptian counterattacks destroyed the Mongol power in Syria, pushed north into Armenia, and in the south crushed Bedouin revolts in Upper Egypt.

But closer to Cairo than forays on distant horizons was the devastating earthquake of 1302. It came in the middle of public rejoicing for one of Nasser's victories against the Mongols; the pious took it as a punishment for the drunkenness which had enlivened the feast. Suddenly the walls of the mosques began to tremble, houses to fall in upon themselves, minarets to sag like factory chimneys. Without their veils women rushed into the streets; the river hurled boats fifty yards onto the banks. After the earthquake the city looked as though it had been sacked.

Nasser's majordomo restored the mosque of al-Hakim; his polo master restored the last Fatimid mosque of al-Salih; Salar, his regent, restored the two great mosques of Amr and al-Azhar. None of the emirs spared expense. Salar in particular could afford to spend. His life of luxury, his love of extravagant clothes, were notorious. His daughter's dowry had been 160,000 gold dinars. His restoration of the ruined shrines reflected the complexity of mameluke rule: the coexistence of cruelty with piety, of barbaric display with exquisite taste.

Salar's chief monument commemorates a mameluke friendship which was lifelong and noble. His friend Sangar al-Gawly shared with him the cost and planning of a double mausoleum for them both which would include a school.

As though to show that loyal friendship could redeem even the power struggles of slaves, this tomb-mosque with its twin domes stands against a cliff which is all that remains of Ibn Tulun's military base.

Salar moved into this mausoleum when his brilliant career met a hungry end. In 1310 Nasser was able to enter into his full inheritance. In this third period of his reign he determined to destroy his two self-willed ministers, one of whom had reigned as virtual sovereign for a year. His experience of reversal had made him crueler. Jealous, suspicious, and avaricious, Nasser seems to have had an obsession with eating. He found it more difficult to forgive a remembered denial of food by Bibars, as superintendent of the palace kitchen, than his insubordination. Having made the usual promises of an amnesty, he had his niggardly majordomo brought before him in irons.

"Do you recall your answer when I once asked for a roast goose? **129**

You said: 'What will he do with a whole roast goose? Does he want to dine twenty times a day?' "

Bibars was first flogged, then carried to the execution room to be half strangled, then revived for one last scolding, then wholly strangled before Nasser's gaze. His property and slaves were divided among the rising mameluke emirs.

It was now Salar's turn to experience the vengeance of his phagomanic king. Trapped by the unwitting complicity of his dear friend Sangar, the mameluke millionaire (whose property, valued at 800 million gold coins, was not remote from Nasser's aim) was

In medieval times Sharia Saliba was the main thoroughfare from the Citadel to the Nile. It is frequently mentioned in the chronicles. (Sayid Hassan)

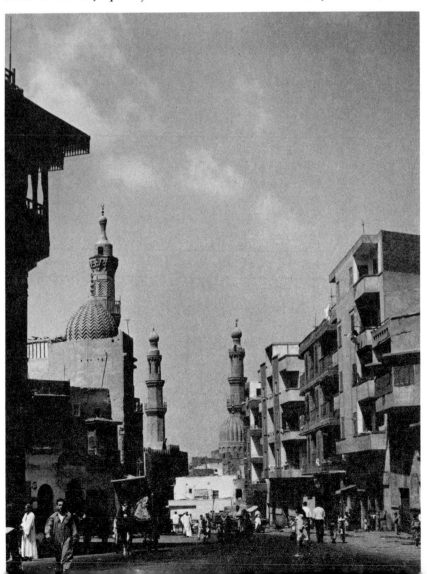

thrown into a dungeon. Enraged at the way he had been tricked, Salar refused a tray of prison fare sent down to him at Nasser's command. According to one account, Nasser retaliated by serving him a chilling diet: dishes of gold coins, silver coins, and precious stones were borne into the dungeons on sumptuous trays, under covers, as though to keep them hot. Salar died of starvation, having tried to eat his boots.

But unlike Bibars, whose body had been thrown into a sty, the body of Salar was lovingly washed and buried by his friend Sangar under one of the two domes in their joint mausoleum. Sangar would take his place under the adjoining dome twenty-four years later, having in the meantime governed Palestine, where he built monuments in Gaza and Hebron.

This concern with a fitting dwelling place for death linked the mamelukes and their subjects. The Pharaonic ancestors of the Egyptians had labored on their "houses for eternity"; the Egyptians still buried their dead under the floors of what parodied ordinary houses. This concern with tombs was not Arabian. The Prophet's dictum, "the best grave is one you can rub away with the hand," was in tune with practice. Muhammad himself had been buried under the floor in his wife's hut; it is recorded of Abdul Aziz Ibn Saud, founder of modern Saudi Arabia, that ten years after the king's death no one in Riyadh knew where he was buried.

The mameluke concern with mausoleums may derive from Turkish awareness of the Chinese cult of ancestors. It is not likely to have been derived from Egyptian practice. For in India and Anatolia as much as in Egypt, rulers of Turkish origin built splendid mausoleums, of which the Taj Mahal and the early Ottoman tombs at Bursa are the most famous.

The Turkish obsession with tombs shows in the development of Cairo mosques.

The great early mosques of Amr, Ibn Tulun, and the Fatimids had been places for congregational prayer, for the hearing of sermons, for religious discussions. Al-Azhar had assumed the functions of a great college where scholars would lecture to groups of students by the pillars of the mosque; dormitories were added in which students from all over Islam would lodge, nation by nation, near their place of study. Saladin had introduced the Seljuk madrasa, or the mosque which was also a school.

Only as the Turkish element began to govern did the conception

131

of the mosque as a tomb begin to dominate. This did not dissociate it from education. A school could still be attached to a tomb; the teaching of God's word could hallow the resting place of a man who needed forgiveness.

But there is an evident turning inward in these beautiful, melancholy mosques; the melancholy and the beauty go hand in hand. These mosques mirror an interiorization of Islam as Muslim ideals less and less affected communal life, as below the level of consciousness Islam recognized that the age when it held the future was no more. Mysticism, the contemplation of an inner landscape where the facts of history cast no shadow, was the consolation of the pious. A tomb became the consolation of the powerful. The greatest of all such tombs, built for Sultan Hassan, the seventh of Nasser's eight reigning sons, mirrors the mameluke puzzle. No shrine on earth is more calmly majestic. Four vast naves open onto a central court which rivals for religious awe the greatest of Pharaonic monuments; the chastity of its decoration—a great Kufic frieze of Koranic verses runs on a background of floral arabesques, the marble prayer niche is flanked by Gothic pillars from Crusader churches—makes the later Pharaonic temples seem vulgar by contrast. Yet the tomb chamber holds a cenotaph. Hassan packed into a six-year reign (from 1354 to 1361) the usual quota of third-generation debauch. He died in prison and his body disappeared. The Citadel Mamelukes, who ruled Egypt from 1382 to 1517, sited their tombs at some distance from the city of the living. These mamelukes concentrated their buildings in the desolate region to the northeast and southeast of Cairo. In the northern cemetery, Barkuk, the first great Circassian sultan, is buried in a tomb built for him by his brutal son. It is even more remarkable than his mosque, built near the mosque of Kilawun. It stands in a khaki landscape, where no grass grows and where the wind whips dust against the stone of slowly eroding tombs. Barkuk's tomb-mosque is on the same pattern as Ibn Tulun's but the piers that support the cloisters are slender and the cloisters themselves are roofed with shallow domes. This mosque was not entirely abandoned to death. It was meant to be prayed in by congregations; attached to it was a retreat for scholars and holy men, one of whom is reputed to have been the historian Maqrizi; it also contained a school.

A short walk from this mosque is the greatest monument of the later mamelukes, the tomb of Qait Bey, himself the last impressive

Although the Ottoman occupation of Egypt led to a general decline in the arts and architecture, this Ottoman mosque indicates that they did not entirely disappear. It stands on Bulak, an island which later became connected to the east bank and then grew prosperous as the port of Cairo. (Sayid Hassan)

sultan. Painted by Bellini, he was described by Meshullam ben Menahem, a Jew from Tuscany, in 1481: "On Friday 22 June I saw the Sultan close to. He is an old man of about eighty, but tall, handsome and as upright as a reed. Dressed in white, he was on horseback, accompanied by more than two thousand mameluke soldiers. . . . Whoever wishes can have access to the Sultan: there is in the town a great and splendid fortress at the entrance of which he sits publicly on Mondays and Thursdays, accompanied by the governor of the city and his interpreters who stand at his side; a guard of more than three hundred mamelukes surrounds him. Whoever has been manhandled or robbed by one of the mameluke princes or emirs can there complain. Thus the nobles refrain from actions that might carry condemnation." A great builder, Qait Bey designed his tomb as a uniquely tall and solemn chamber set next to a small mosque for prayer. The minaret has the intricate, slim simplicity developed in mameluke times. But now that no Sufi ascetics live nearby, it calls only to the dead and those who live among the tombs.

For the ordinary Egyptians who were not yet dead and who planned no lavish tombs, life in mameluke Cairo was intermittently prosperous. Egypt was at the center of the trade routes of the world. While the mamelukes took much of the percentage, some filtered down to the merchants in the souqs. Despite the religious barriers between Islam and other faiths, Jews and Christians were politely welcomed. There could be exceptions to this easy policy. In 1335, during Nasser's third reign, Father Jacobus of Verona, a pilgrim who had already visited Palestine, Gaza, and Sinai, came to Cairo. His visit only lasted two days. There were rumors (unjustified) of a new Crusade. He had no time for more than superficial impressions:

There are in Cairo and Babylon[5] numerous Christians known as Christians of the Belt; this is from the fact that they wear a belt while the Muslims do not. The Christians also wear black turbans, while the Muslims wear white ones. Otherwise they dress alike . . . I saw a number of churches in Cairo, and would willingly have stayed several days to visit the marvels of the town had not rumours of war—people believed that a new crusade was imminent—made people suspect that Italian or Latin Christians might be spies. I was very frightened and only stayed two days. With God's help and the assistance of some Christian slaves I escaped to Damietta by boat.

Other foreigners, such as Leonardo Frescobaldi of Florence, might get their facts wrong—he thought that the pyramids were Joseph's granaries and that the Citadel was the place where Moses had been reared—but could calmly describe the customs and costumes of the people. "It is necessary to know," he wrote after a visit during the reign of Barkuk, "that Cairo has twelve governors, of which two are the principal. The town is divided into twelve quarters, as Florence is into four; each emir governs his particular quarter and for his purpose has a large number of armed men."

Frescobaldi described the manner in which the women were veiled: "They are veiled in such a way that you can only see their eyes; the most distinguished women cover even their eyes with a transparent cloth through which they can see without being seen." The men wore white turbans and white clothes which could be of silk, cotton, or linen. They never wore boots, always a kind of slipper.

The city in whose houses people lived—except for a horde of the homeless who slept in the streets or in ruined buildings—had changed physically since Fatimid times. The most spectacular change was the work of the Nile. Its bed had moved steadily toward the west; its agglutinative silt had formed two important new islands, which in turn had become attached to the eastern bank.

The first was Bulak, which appeared as an island around the beginning of the fifteenth century, when Maqrizi, who tells of it, was

Muhammad Ali Pasha, the early nineteenth-century ruler who made Egypt an autonomous state, built this Palace on Shubra, a second island which had become part of east-bank Cairo.

probably living in the mausoleum of Barkuk. It was then joined by a causeway to the old bank near Maks. The causeway soon became solid earth. The attached island grew. As Maks had replaced the silted-up port of Fustat, so Bulak replaced Maks. Maks itself became silted up in the expansion of the east bank. By the end of the fourteenth century the hinterland of Bulak had become so large and so developed that a new canal, the Khalig-al-Nasri, was dug to bring water to plantations and farms.

A little to the northeast, a ship called the *Elephant* had been wrecked in late Fatimid times. Never salvaged, its skeleton attracted silt, sand, and debris which formed the nucleus of an island. By Saladin's time this second new island was under cultivation; by Kilawun's its revenues were considerable enough for the Sultan to direct them to the upkeep of his college and hospital. By the end of the fourteenth century the island merged with Bulak and became an outlying agricultural suburb. The city of Cairo was now a considerable walk, or even donkey ride, from its source of fresh water and main artery to the outside world.

CHAPTER **11**

Mameluke
Twilight

The end of a dynasty, from a distant viewpoint, seems inevitable and fast. To those living through the years concerned the result is hazardous; the doomed seems at moments likely to survive.

The reign of the last effective sultan is easily summarized. Kansuh al-Ghuri was the forty-sixth mameluke sultan and the twentieth of the Citadel Mamelukes. A contemporary of Caesar Borgia and the young Henry VIII, he reigned from 1501 to 1516. Starting life as a page to Qait Bey, he rose by slow degrees. He was over forty when made an Emir of Ten. By the time he came to the throne at sixty he had governed Tarsus, Aleppo, and Malatya. His reign was three times longer than average; his sins were less than those of many; his greed and need for money made him unpopular; he left behind an elegant mosque and college which still stand;[1] he died in battle resisting the Ottoman Turks. He was not to occupy his tomb. He left an adopted son who reigned but a few months.

But rather than abstract the sixteen years which reduced Cairo from the capital of an empire to a city bolting its doors at a new conqueror's approach, it is possible to slow time down and see, through the details of daily life and recurring incident, the texture of human existence in this twilit reign.

route home from the India they now controlled. In 1779 some enterprising British officers organized a convoy to England by way of Suez, Cairo, and Alexandria instead of by sea round the Cape of Good Hope. Two shiploads reached Suez safely; with them they brought some French prisoners of war. The Bedouin of Tor decided to pillage the hopeful travelers. Five leagues from Suez (on a road which takes a twentieth-century motorist around an hour) the party were attacked. Stripped of everything they had, half of them returned to Suez while the others, who had lost their wits with their greatcoats, tried to struggle on to Cairo. The combination of January cold by night and fierce sun by day killed all but one, a French prisoner—"his only shade a thorny bush in which he plunged his head, his only drink his urine." Rescued by an Egyptian fellah who appeared from nowhere on a camel, this M. de Saint-Germain rested three days in the peasant's hut and then continued his journey to Cairo.

One result of this catastrophe was to reduce the importance of the English trading post in Cairo—it specialized in selling small arms and cloth. Volney even hints that the marauding Bedouin had been put up to the attack by officials of the British East India Company in Constantinople. This suggestion is not entirely farfetched. After the recent loss of her North American colonies, Britain's ambitions were largely centered on her new empire in India; the East India Company, a private company with governmental support, had invested vast sums in a trade which went round Africa; the Company was likely to be suspicious of a new short cut to the East which was not under its control. When in the coming century a French entrepreneur, Ferdinand de Lesseps, was to undertake the project of a canal through the Isthmus of Suez, British officials in their embassy in Constantinople were to endeavor to get the Ottoman sultan to suppress it. When the short cut to India had finally been made, Britain was to buy a dominant holding in Suez Canal Company shares and then to station troops alongside its investment. The loss of British interests in eighteenth-century Cairo—where the Venetians continued to sell silk and mirrors and the French to sell goods cheaper than those of their rivals—would have seemed a small price to pay for the continuance of a monopoly in Indian trading.

Volney's concluding impression was that the Egyptians should be pitied, not despised. The fellahin were tough, hard-working people, enduring hardships with great resistance. Rightly directed, their

169

energies could create a much better society. But the major obstacle to progress was a general and total ignorance.

A young French officer, Napoleon Bonaparte, was to be Volney's most attentive and influential reader. Decades later, when his meteoric career was over, when the exiled Emperor of the French could look back on conquests unrivaled since the age of Alexander, "in his first interview with the Governor of St. Helena, Napoleon said emphatically: 'Egypt is the most important country in the world.' " [8]

CHAPTER 13

Napoleon
Through
Cairo Eyes

To the people of Cairo June 15, 1798, marked the start of the 1213th year since Muhammad migrated from Mecca to Medina and in so doing initiated the Islamic era.

To the peoples of Europe 1798 marked the fifth year since the execution of Louis XVI of France had confronted the Old World with a militant new republic. In the previous year the twenty-eight-year-old Corsican general Napoleon Bonaparte, armed with proconsular authority from the Directory which now ruled France, had completed the conquest of an Italy which included the Papal States and the half-oriental Venetian republic. It now expected that France would strike a blow against England, the prime enemy of its republic as it had been the prime rival of its monarchy.

To Napoleon 1798 marked a year of challenge. If he was to do in France what Julius Caesar had done in ancient Rome, he needed some spectacular triumph from which he would return with the means to impose his will. Public opinion believed that Napoleon's equivalent of Caesar's Gaul would be England itself. But Napoleon, who had read Volney's account of Egypt and who in Venice had sniffed the first aromas of the mysterious East, believed that a nation of shopkeepers who were also a nation of brilliant seamen might be

171

perilous to attack at home. He concurred with Talleyrand, the defrocked bishop who directed French foreign policy, that the shrewdest way to injure England would be by an invasion of Egypt. An almost defenseless province of a ramshackle Ottoman empire, Egypt was halfway to an India where the East India Company had numerous enemies (the chief was Tippoo Sahib of Mysore) only waiting for arms and encouragement to rise against the British. Such rational aims were, as so often in Napoleon's case, confused with visionary dreams. "I saw myself founding a religion, marching into Asia, riding an elephant, a turban on my head and in my hand the new Koran that I would have composed to suit my needs." He would break the power of the mamelukes in Egypt as he had broken the power of the priests in Italy. Alexandria would be made the new capital, not only of Egypt, but of a French empire guiding the three continents of the Old World into a future based on the principles of the Revolution. The Emperor of this new polity would be, of course, Napoleon.

"The time I spent in Egypt," Napoleon was later to say, "was

A sheikh at the al-Azhar University lectures on Islamic teaching in a corner of the mosque before the afternoon prayer. (Sayid Hassan)

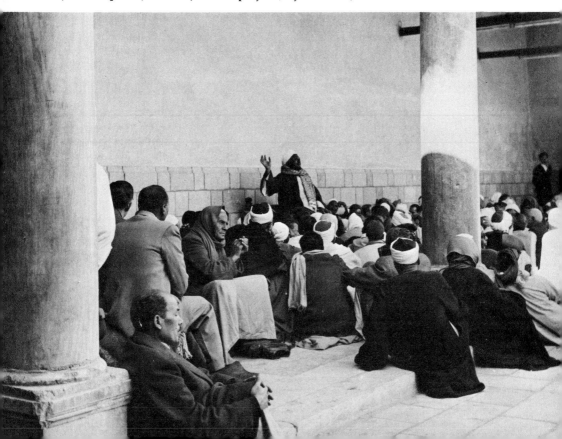

the most beautiful in my life, because it was the most ideal." The year he landed in Egypt was described by a Cairo diarist as "the start . . . of a period of great battles, of ghastly events, of disastrous facts, of frightful calamities, of constantly growing evils, of upsets, of reversal, of continual terror, of revolution, of administrative disorder, of catastrophe, of general devastation: in one word, the start of a whole series of great misfortunes." For once, Arabic hyperbole was almost justified. The writer, Abdul Rahman al-Jabarti, an Azharite graduate of Somali origin, lived through the greatest crisis in Cairo's history since the Ottoman conquest: the arrival in Egypt of the enthusiastic young soldiers of Revolutionary France.

On Sunday, 10th Muharram, messengers from Alexandria brought news that on Friday, the 8th of the same month, ten English vessels had sailed close enough to the shore to be visible from the town. A little later, fifteen further ships had arrived. The inhabitants of the town were wondering what was afoot when a pinnace put ashore with a party of ten. These presented themselves to the notables of Alexandria, including the governor, Sayid Mohammad Korayim. The strangers declared themselves to be English. They were pursuing, they said, a body of Frenchmen who had sailed, with a considerable fleet, for a destination unknown. They feared the French purpose might be a sudden attack on Egypt since the Egyptians could neither repel such an attack nor prevent a disembarkation.

Distrusting their words, fearing a trap, the governor gave no ground. The strangers continued: "We shall content ourselves with guarding the city and protecting the coastline; all we ask is food and water, for which we will pay."

"This country belongs to the Sultan," the Alexandrines answered. "Neither Frenchmen nor others have concern here. Be so kind as to leave us in peace."

On these words the Englishmen returned to their ships and went elsewhere for their provisions, that "God might achieve the work decreed in his destiny." [1]

This news caused a stir in Cairo. Everyone discussed it, exaggerating greatly.

Three days later it was learnt that the English had sailed away. People calmed down. The self-confident Emirs were not worried by these reports. All the Europeans put together could not stand an instant before the mameluke horse, but would be trampled underfoot. On Wednesday, the 20th of the same month, letters from Alexandria, Ro-

173

setta and Damanhour announced that two days earlier a very large French fleet had anchored off Alexandria. Some Frenchmen had rowed ashore to contact their consul and other persons. As night fell, some ships moved into Agami where they disembarked men and war matériel. The next morning saw French soldiers as thick as locusts in the city. The Alexandrines, helped by Bedouin, tried in vain to repulse the invaders. They could not. The Bedouin fled while the people locked themselves in their houses. Though they tried to continue the resistance, their lack of preparations and of arms made this a vain attempt. The French then hoisted their flag and summoned the notables. They demanded the surrender of all the arms remaining in the city. Furthermore they insisted that everyone should wear the cockade on his chest. This cockade consists of three pieces of cloth, blue, red and white, worn together in concentric circles.

Al-Jabarti, who was in Cairo throughout these events, describes the consternation in the capital. The two chief emirs, Ibrahim Bey and Murad Bey, reported in haste to Constantinople. Murad Bey was entrusted with organizing an army to defeat the French. While Murad moved north, his cavalry on the ground, his foot soldiers on the Nile, he ordered the construction of an enormous chain to block the river to French ships.

In the city, directly threatened for the first time since 1517, and by an enemy who was not of the same faith, there was a general panic. The streets were abandoned to thieves and cutthroats. As a countermeasure, to preserve confidence, authorities ordered cafés to stay open and citizens to light lamps in front of their houses and shops.

The first contact with the French came through a written proclamation clandestinely distributed by North African Christians, assembled for this purpose, al-Jabarti believed, in Malta.

It began with the Islamic *bismillah*: "In the name of God, the Merciful, the Compassionate! On behalf of the French nation, founded on liberty and equality, Bonaparte, the great general and commander-in-chief of the French army, proclaims to the entire population of Egypt that for far too long the Emirs who rule the country have insulted the French nation and outraged its merchants. The hour of their chastisement has struck. For long centuries this riffraff of slaves purchased in the Caucasus or Georgia have tyrannized the most beautiful country in the world. But God, Master of the Universe and the All-Powerful, has decreed that their reign

174

should cease. People of Egypt! You have been told that I have come here to destroy your religion. It is a lie. Don't believe it. Say to such liars that I am only come among you to seize your rights from the hands of tyrants and restore them to you and that, more than do the mamelukes, I adore God and respect his Prophet and the Koran."

Attached to the rest of this preamble—which continued in the same vein, with the added claim that the French were true Muslims —were certain stipulations: Any village that resisted would be burned; and "the flag of our friend the Ottoman Sultan" should be flown beside the tricolor of France.

As in 1517, the Cairenes were spectators of their fate. No one thought to organize them to defend their land. All they could do was pray.

Since the departure of Murad Bey from Cairo the learned men assembled daily in the mosque of Al-Azhar to recite the book of Bokhari[2] for the success of the Egyptians. The sheikhs of all the religious sects also assembled and offered prayers. So did the pupils in the schools . . . Groups of ascetics and dervishes processed with flags, making music and praying for victory. Omar effendi, chief of the descendants of the Prophet, issued from the Citadel holding a great flag which the people called the standard of the Prophet and so traversed the city as far as Bulak. He was surrounded by thousands of individuals carrying clubs, making music and shouting prayers.

After this exodus to Bulak, the only people left in Cairo were women, children, and weak old men. They hid themselves in their houses. The streets were empty and dirty, since no one swept or sprayed them any more.

But neither religious faith nor mameluke self-confidence availed against the superior fire power and military training of the French. The mamelukes were routed at Imbaba and "on Tuesday the French entered Cairo and Bonaparte moved into the palace of Mohammad Bey al-Alfi, situated at Ezbekia, in the quarter of al-Sakit. The Emir had built this palace, at great expense, the previous year; it was richly furnished." As for the French soldiers, "they chatted good-humouredly with the people and bought at exorbitant prices the things they needed." The cafés and shops reopened. All seemed well.

But as other occupiers of Muslim cities have found on other   **175** occasions, resistance soon takes the place of cooperation. The people of Cairo would not long sit quiet under their infidel masters. The inevitable French reprisals destroyed forever the initial harmony between the old Muslims of Muhammad and the new Muslims of European deism. After the first major revolt,

bands of Frenchmen entered the city at night and penetrated every part. They tore down all barricades they found and assured that everyone was quiet. They then entered Al-Azhar mosque with their horses, which they tethered to the prayer-niche; they smashed lamps as well as the night-lights and desks of the students. They looted everything they found in the cupboards; they threw books and the Koran on the ground and trampled them with their boots. They urinated and spat inside the mosque; they drank wine; they smashed bottles which they threw all over the place. They stripped all the people they found there to steal their clothes.

On Friday some of their soldiers stood guard before the entrance to the mosque. The faithful who came to pray fled on seeing them. Other French soldiers patrolled the quarter near the mosque. This quarter, long the most highly regarded in the city, had been avoided by the French during the first days of their occupation. Now it was avoided by Egyptians as the French surged through it by the hundred.

To the unarmed Egyptians the French seemed omnipotent. In fact, since August 1798 they had been in the precarious position of an expeditionary force cut off from their home base. The enormous French invasion fleet (which on open sea covered between two and four square miles) had been told, Napoleon was to argue later, either to put into harbor at Alexandria or return to Adriatic safety in French-occupied Corfu. Instead, Admiral Brueys kept the vast armada anchored in Aboukir Bay, near the site of the ancient Canopic mouth of the Nile. (This mouth had long silted up and as a result Alexandria's importance had decreased while Rosetta, some distance to the east, had become the main port of Egypt.) Nelson's fleet, with better ships, better captains, and better crews had missed the French armada in Malta (where the French knights had surrendered to Napoleon) and had pursued it across the Mediterranean. They caught up with the anchored French ships on the evening of August 1 and at once attacked. By 2 P.M. next day the English fleet was celebrating the total destruction of their enemy's ships. Napoleon's expedition to the Middle East was thus doomed to strategic failure. The Ottoman sultan, instead of welcoming Napoleon's destruction of the mamelukes, declared war on the French republic. Napoleon spent another twelve months in Egypt and Syria, months in which his brutality was displayed in the siege of Acre and in which his idealism was expressed in his schemes for reforming Egyptian society. As a disciple of Volney, Napoleon believed that the native-born men of religion, the *ulema,* could provide a basis for social revitalization. Modern engineering would do the rest. "What could be made of that beautiful country in fifty years of prosperity and good government? One's imagination delights in the enchanting vistas. A thousand irrigation sluices would tame and distribute the overflow of the Nile over every part of the territory. The eight to ten billion cubic yards of water now lost every year to the sea would be channelled to the lower parts of the desert . . . all the way to the oases and even farther west." [3]

But neither savagery in war nor idealism in peace could make the Egyptian campaign more than a sideshow in the war against England and the struggle for power in Paris. In August 1789 Napoleon returned secretly to France. The army he left behind was embittered. Its leaders lacked Napoleon's vision of cooperation with the Muslim majority and began to patronize Syrian Christians and Greeks. During the remainder of the French stay in Egypt—their evacuation was negotiated with the British and the Ottomans in the summer of 1801—the Greek executioner Barthélemy was to be kept busy.

The eighteenth century finished badly. In April 1800 the Muslims got their own back on the Christian collaborators when the French general Kléber, Napoleon's successor, went out to defeat an Ottoman force at Mattariya. Kléber regained the city by shelling first Bulak, then Cairo. On June 14 a young Syrian Muslim, Suliman al-Halabi, assassinated Kléber in his garden near Ezbekiah. His motives have been ascribed to fanaticism; more probably they were due to a feeling of Islamic solidarity with a country overrun by infidels. Suliman involved against their will three sheikhs of al-Azhar in his plot. The sentences on the four men adjudged guilty showed a curious departure from the professed aims of the Revolution. The three men of religion were beheaded, while Suliman himself was to have his offending right arm burnt off to the elbow, after which operation he was to be impaled. (The missionaries of the Revolution, which in France had introduced the supposedly humane guillo-   177 tine, argued that only the traditional punishments would teach the requisite lesson.) Barthélemy (who normally sold glass knickknacks in a bazaar near Khan al-Khalili) let some of the burning tar fall on the young man's forearm. With extraordinary presence Suliman pointed out that he was exceeding the penalty. During his subsequent impalement, he cried out that he thirsted. A French officer, unable to stand the sight, rushed forward with a glass of water. The executioner dashed it to the ground. "Don't do that, sir," he shouted. "The first sip, and he'll be dead." His death took several hours to accomplish.

Kléber's successor, General Menou, tried to placate the Muslims by announcing his own conversion to Islam and removing all local Christians from the government. At the same time he announced that Egypt would become a French protectorate.

The collision of Cairo with the forces of France shows what was to be a continuing pattern. The first effect, it is evident, was opposition to an outside force which could impose its will through superior force.

The second force, however, was no less lasting. This was admiration.

Muslims recognized that at least in its ability to defend itself Islam had fallen behind Europe. Al-Jabarti was an intelligent member of the class which Napoleon had considered the most hopeful in Egypt. He had been educated in the traditional disciplines, unchanged since the days of Nasir Khosrau. The effect of what he saw, as he mixed with the crowds watching the French launch a balloon in Ezbekiah, or as he visited the savants of the Institut d'Egypte, was as decisive as his disgust at the behavior of the soldiers.

In reading his diary it is hard to say which events are the most important; sometimes a trivial incident could be as challenging as something obviously important. The French workers designing the orderly boulevards which Volney had craved used wheelbarrows instead of the primitive carrying bags employed by Egyptians. Windmills were established for grinding corn. "Among other things the French constructed near Ezbekiah a building where ladies and gentlemen met at a certain hour to pass the time and amuse themselves. The spectator paid on going in and needed a ticket to enter." This was "the first service club in history, named *Le Tivoli* after a popular amusement spot in Paris. It offered a dance band (though few partners), billiard tables and other games,

Women were not permitted to dance by Islamic tradition. In their place, male dancers performed in women's clothing and long hair. These transvestite but mustachioed dancers are still occasionally hired for ceremonies and old-style weddings. (Costa Alifrangis)

a library, the two newspapers published by the army, coffee, European food, a pleasure garden, and similar comforts of home. At the grand opening, the *Courrier de l'Egypte* reports, what 'produced the most agreeable sensation . . . was the presence of fifteen or twenty women dressed with some splendour—an absolutely novel sight in Egypt.' "[4]

But striking though this was in an Egypt where the sexes were so strictly segregated that at weddings it was considered seemly for

179

boys to dance disguised as women, what impressed al-Jabarti most was a French library. In the mansion belonging to the mameluke emir Hasan Kashif,

The French established a large library with librarians to look after the books and to issue them to those who wanted them. This library opened daily at ten in the morning. The readers assembled in a large room adjoining the room where the books were kept; they sat on chairs round big tables and got down to work. Simple soldiers used to work in this library. If a Muslim wanted to come in, he was in no sense prevented; on the contrary, he was greeted with great friendliness. The French were particularly happy when a Muslim visitor showed himself interested in the sciences; they at once got into discussion with him and showed him all sorts of printed books, with pictures representing different regions of the world, as well as plants and animals.

This library represented the most explosive contribution of the French, not only to Egypt, but the whole Levant. Unlike any conqueror before, Napoleon had taken with him a corps of learned men; these savants produced a lasting memorial in their encyclopedic *Déscription d'Egypte*. He had also brought with him fonts for printing Greek and Arabic, the two ancient languages of the Middle East. The use of printed books, which even common soldiers could read, was to do more to combat the senescence of centuries than the mameluke defeat.

The French had given the Muslims a tool with which slowly but with increasing momentum they would repair their stagnant society. It would be a tool that would often be used against the French themselves. But a grateful respect for French culture was to be part of most educated Egyptian minds. The fact that French culture came in a lay, not a religious, form made it the more acceptable. The French occupation of Egypt had not lasted long in terms of time. The pattern of love-hate toward the West which it bequeathed would last two centuries at least.

CHAPTER 14

Muhammad Ali & Company

Egypt had been the background of a youthful triumph to Napoleon; as well as memories he took back to Paris new motifs for chair legs derived from the Pharaohs. To Egypt Napoleon had been the first boulder in an avalanche of change. Other rocks, stones, and pebbles in this avalanche were the members, and enemies, of a dynasty which for better or worse would transform Cairo more radically than any ruler since Saladin.

The founder of this dynasty (whose last representative, the infant son of Farouk I, was deposed in 1953) was Muhammad Ali, the son of a yeoman farmer in what is now northern Greece. He spent a humdrum youth as a tobacco dealer and minor official. In 1798 at the age of twenty-nine he was sent to Egypt as second-in-command of a regiment of volunteers recruited from the Muslims of his district. This district, halfway between Macedonia and Thrace, was the same fringe land between the Aegean Sea and the Balkan mountains which had given birth to Alexander and the Ptolemies. Europeans have usually referred to Muhammad Ali as an Albanian; Egyptians often referred to him as a Turk; he can probably be best described as a Macedonian. The question is unimportant. A man's national status meant less than his religious affiliation in the cosmopolitan Ottoman empire. Muhammad Ali went to Egypt as a Muslim owing allegiance to the Ottoman sultan in Constantinople. Narrowly saved from drowning at the battle of Aboukir by the British admiral's gig, Muhammad Ali did nothing to defeat the French invaders. The next time he stepped on the dry land of Egypt was as Ottoman-appointed Pasha in 1801, the year of the French evacuation. The Ottomans were anxious to reassert their control over Egypt now that the French had shot to pieces the mameluke myth. The young man's ambitious nostrils picked up the same scent of possibility as had excited the young slaves from Mingrelia and Georgia. The mameluke beys, divided as ever among themselves, were determined to resist an Ottoman attempt to deprive them of control. Muhammad Ali would introduce into a decade of anarchy two steely constants: his regiment of soldiers and his own ambition. (Loyalty was a constant of no one.) He now sided with the Ottomans (whose writ was his only authority for being in Egypt) and now with the local beys.

At some time between 1801 and 1805 he formulated an ambition which must have been the secret dream of the more ruthless sultans and beys of the past: the total destruction of all rivals and the concentration in his own hands of everything in Egypt. Such an imperious monopoly had been impossible under the Ottoman system. Unwieldy and ramshackle though their empire had become, the Ottomans remained astute into their death-throes. In Egypt they had contrived a sleazy but effective geometry for dividing the rich and exploiting the poor. The Pasha with his Ottoman troops formed one angle; the indigenous religious authorities another; the Bedouin could be used at various points as irregular allies; the base was the divisive mameluke caste. The system had been ruinous for Egypt; it had also prevented any one man from concentrating power in his hands.

Muhammad Ali (whose gifts owed everything to instinct, nothing to learning) recognized that the French invasion had shaken the Ottoman reality as much as the mameluke myth; since the Ottomans were farther from Cairo they were the lesser menace; if Egypt were once united, the power of Constantinople could be defeated or kept at bay. But first the mamelukes had to be destroyed. Muhammad Ali proceeded to do this through maneuvers whose brutality and treachery were worthy of the greatest sultans of the past.

The first maneuver took place in 1805; at this time Muhammad Ali's authority as Pasha of Egypt was everywhere disputed by the dissident beys. The annual cutting of the dam—due this year on August 17—was used as a decoy. Some of the Pasha's agents informed the mamelukes that his presence at the morning ceremony would enable them to seize the unguarded capital. The dam was broken without pomp the previous night while Muhammad Ali secretly posted his soldiers at strategic points. Next morning the mamelukes broke into the city through Bab-al-Futuh and paraded with kettle-drums. In the narrow street "Between the Two Palaces" they came under sudden fire. A good number escaped from the trap; those who did not, took refuge in the great mosque of Barkuk. Their fate was dire. Having surrendered, about fifty were stripped naked and murdered on the spot. The remainder were dragged before the Pasha. One of the leading beys, goaded beyond endurance by Muhammad Ali's taunts, snatched a dagger from a soldier in a mad attempt to kill the Pasha. After this desperate and unavailing act, the remainder were chained up for the night. In the morning they were treated to an alarming spectacle. The heads of those slain the previous day were skinned in their presence and then stuffed with straw. Except for three beys who were released on payment of ransom, the victims of this sadistic show were tortured and killed that night; their heads, also stuffed with straw, were sent to Constantinople as a sign of Muhammad Ali's power over the beys.

It may seem extraordinary that within six years of this *coup de main* the mamelukes would ride into another trap. Events in the interim, including an attempted British invasion, had blurred remembrance; the collective mameluke mind was inured to violence as a way of life; it lacked imagination to foresee that violence might have a constructive as well as lethal aim.

This time—on March 1, 1811—Muhammad Ali used the excitement of an approaching war in Arabia as his decoy. The Wahhabis were a central Arabian sect who objected to the cult of saints (as popular in Egypt as in Turkey) and who disapproved of such practices as the annual procession of the *mahmal*. They had challenged the authority of the Ottoman Sultan in western Arabia by occupying the holy cities of Mecca and Medina as well as the port of Jedda. Muhammad Ali was instructed by the Sultan to organize a punitive expedition; it would be led by his favorite son, Tusun. As an inducement to the mamelukes to cooperate, Muhammad Ali

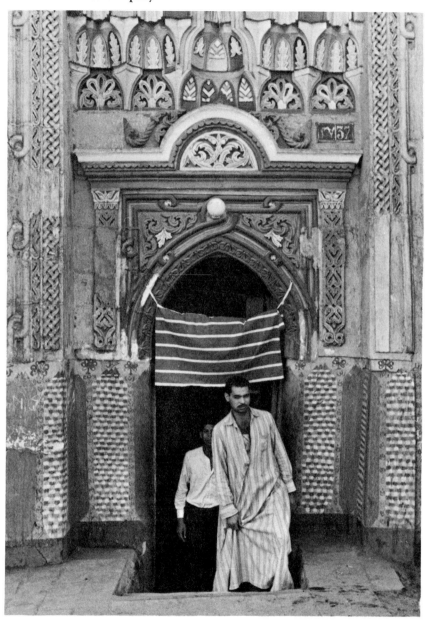

Islam took over the tradition of the Greco-Roman thermae, which the early Christians had opposed. These hammams were more important when water had to be brought on camel or donkey from the Nile. Their role has diminished now that piped water goes to nearly all houses. The entrance to the hammam is shown here. (Sayid Hassan)

had recently restored their fiefs in the Fayum oasis and parts of Upper Egypt.

James Webster, an Englishman who visited Cairo when the events of this March day were fresh in men's minds, has left an account of Muhammad Ali's stratagem.

His plan was effected on the occasion of a public festival. The Grand Seignor had sent his Kislar Aga to Cairo, as bearer of costly presents to the Pasha, and the firman appointing Tusun, the son of Muhammad, to the dignity of a two-tailed Pashalik. The same youth had been by his father nominated general of the army of Arabia. The 1st of March 1811 was the day set apart for the investiture of Tusun: and the ceremony was ordered in the Citadel. The principal portion of the Mameluke body, that indeed most conspicuous for its activity and boldness, under Elfi's successor, Shahin bey, had been enticed some time previously into the city, loaded with honours and attentions, and quartered in an appropriated part of the city. These Mamelukes had been invited to take part in the parades and the festivities of the day; and they consented to do so. In the morning Shahin bey with his staff and officers, apparelled in whatever they possessed of the greatest cost and magnificence, came to the Pasha's hall of audience in the Citadel, to offer their congratulations on so joyous an occasion. Muhammad received them with the greatest affability. They were presented with coffee, and he conversed with them severally, with openness of heart, and serenity of brow. But the serpent lay hidden in its bed of roses!

The procession was ordered to move from the Citadel, along a passage cut in the rock. The Pasha's troops moved first, followed by the Mameluke corps. As soon, however, as they had passed the gate, at that end of the rocky passage which leads to the Citadel, it was shut suddenly against the latter, and Muhammad's forces were ordered to the top of the rocks, where they were perfectly secure from the aim of their victims, and whence they leisurely fired upon the defenceless Mamelukes, and butchered them in cold blood, almost to a man; for escape was difficult, that end of the defile by which they had entered having been also closed, and its breadth, in many parts, being so scanty that two horsemen could with difficulty stand side by side. Of those who were fortunate enough to find shelter in the Pasha's harem, in Tusun's abode, and elsewhere, all were dragged forth, conducted before the Kiaya Bey, and beheaded on the spot. The body of the brave leader Shahin was exposed to every infamy. A rope was passed round the neck, and the bloody carcass dragged through various parts of the city, exposed all the while to the execrations and the contumely of the inflamed populace. The Citadel itself looked like a hideous slaughter-house, newly deluged with the blood of victims, and overstrown with a multitude of reeking carcasses. Dead steeds lay confusedly along the streets with their golden caparisons soiled in the filthy compound of dirt and gore; their knights, some with limbs hacked off, others without their heads, still clenching their scimitars with the last despairing, yet desperate grasp of death, were flung near their war-horses, prostrate in a black puddle of their own life-blood.

The fiction that one mameluke bey jumped his horse over the walls to safety (he was in fact ill, or suspicious, and stayed at home) inspired many of the painters who furnished the drawing rooms of the dynasty.

Four hundred and seventy mamelukes had been killed in the cowardly slaughter. For two days mameluke property was sacked, including an estimated five hundred houses. Throughout the country orders were given to provincial governors to complete the annihilation of the caste. Some beys escaped to Sudan; others survived in Egypt; but their power was finished.

Muhammad Ali's forceful act made Egypt his own exclusive fief. In theory he remained a vassal of the Ottoman sultan; in reality he was the master of a state in which everyone and everything belonged to him. He did not just own most of the land; he owned it all. His power structure was no different from that of the mameluke sultans of the past. He depended entirely on military force. But instead of relying on bought white slaves (the supply of which was to dry up as Russia took over the Caucasus and as the Balkans became independent) he tried the audacious experiment of training brown-skinned Egyptians to serve as soldiers under European or Turkish officers. The purpose for which he used his soldiers was no different from the purpose of Bibars or Barkuk: he wanted to acquire more territory to provide more money for his estate and his enormous family. (His new harem, a workman confided to a visiting Englishman, was intended to accommodate eight hundred women.) Territory supported military power.

What set Muhammad Ali apart from the mameluke sultans was his enthusiastic acceptance not of Western manners but of Western techniques. (All his life he was particularly impressed by the skills of Frenchmen.) Such an acceptance of the West had been as unthinkable as unnecessary for Bibars and Barkuk. In the late Middle Ages Islamic science remained superior to European; the Ottoman

186

army which had destroyed the mameluke sultanate had been the most formidable military force in Europe, not merely the Middle East. But since the late seventeenth century the Ottoman empire had been humiliated again and again by the technical superiority of European, including Russian, armies. The once irresistible janissaries had become society's reactionary rear guard, not its van. (Inspired by Muhammad Ali's actions against the mamelukes, the Ottoman sultan, Mahmud II, was to deal with his janissaries in similar style.) The great empire of Selim and Suliman had been steadily eroded. At first reluctantly, then with increasing ardor, Ottomans argued for the adoption of Western techniques. As the proud inheritors of a complacent Islam, they felt no need for the Western spirit; they required Western drill and Western arms.

Muhammad Ali's acceptance of the West was limited to those aspects of the society which increased a ruler's power. He had no interest in free political institutions, no concern for human liberties. He wanted a powerful army, and since such an army needed officers he established colleges to produce them; he also sent students to Europe. Foreigners of talent were encouraged to come to Egypt to help construct a modern state. One such was Antoine Clot, a Frenchman of poor family who was born in Grenoble in 1793. Having studied medicine while working as a hairdresser in Marseilles, Clot ran into a French merchant who was a friend of the Pasha. The merchant remarked that Muhammad Ali was looking for a doctor to guide the medical services of the Egyptian army. Clot arrived in Egypt in 1825 when Muhammad Ali's considerable, if impermanent, empire was at its height. (At one time or another Egyptian forces, often under the leadership of Muhammad Ali's gifted son, Ibrahim Pasha, controlled Crete, Aden, western Arabia, northern Sudan, Syria, Palestine, and large areas of what is now Turkey.) Clot started a hospital with a medical school at Abuzabel near Cairo. He bravely defied the taboos against dissection (intact since the days of Abdul Latif) and against smallpox introduced vaccination, itself in origin a Turkish practice. His services included combating a cholera epidemic in 1830 and then a bout of plague in 1835. He was created a general in the army, then a bey. Significantly, he was allowed to retain his Christian faith: the regime's encouragement of non-Muslims, including the long-despised Copts, was to be one of its more attractive features. Ironically, the street named in this doctor's honor—a European-style axis providing a link between the railway station and the street leading to the Citadel—became the chief brothel quarter of the city.

Although some of Muhammad Ali's military adventures were against his nominal sovereign, Sultan Mahmud II, both rulers shared similar problems and a similar superficial affection for the West. Both men were to be disappointed. Mahmud II abandoned traditional Turkish costume for braid-edged trousers and fez, introduced Western drill and destroyed the janissaries; Muhammad Ali opened factories, encouraged Western missionaries to bring schools to the Levant, and destroyed the mamelukes. These gestures failed to charm the West. Throughout the century Western influences encouraged the breakup of the Ottoman structure which had started with the revolt of the Greeks; the British used their sea power to strangle Muhammad Ali's burgeoning industrial revolution. This was made possible for them because of Muhammad Ali's position as the nominal subject of the Ottoman sultan. In many ways there is a close parallel between Muhammad Ali's Egypt and the Japan of the Meiji Restoration: the same superficial and rapid westernization, the same local imperialism; Korea, Manchuria, and

Ezbekiah bookstalls in the open air. (Sayid Hassan)

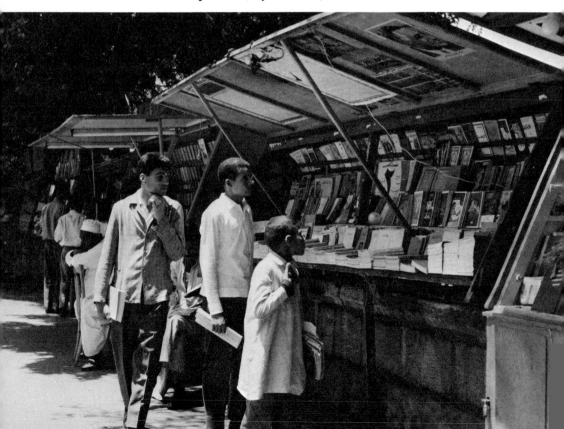

Formosa were to be the Far Eastern equivalents of Arabia, Sudan, and Syria. Both countries, at their different extremes of the Asian continent, realized the need for industrialization, if the West was to be defied as well as imitated. Yet there was to be one important difference. Japan never recognized outside sovereignty; and Japanese industrialization, however much denounced by the Western countries for its "unfairness," was never suppressed. Muhammad Ali's recognition of Ottoman supremacy led directly to the failure of his industrial schemes, under which, if they had succeeded, "Egypt might have emerged into the twentieth century as a small-scale Japan." [1]

In 1838 the Ottoman Sultan had granted to the British the right to trade with any of his dominions, freely, without let or hindrance. On paper, this was an excellent extension of the sacred liberal principle of free trade, luckily applying to Egypt, since Egypt was part of the Sultan's realms. In fact, this freedom for British traders killed dead the Egyptian industrial system, which at that time was one of the few such systems in existence. For so great was England's start in the industrial race, that all competitors, whether the United States, France, or Germany, were forced to erect protective tariff barriers round their economies, to save their new industries from death in infancy. If Muhammad Ali's industries had been allowed to continue past the intermediate stage, to the stage of graduation, Egypt might have built up an economy partly agricultural, partly industrial. Instead, the Ottoman consent to the principle of free trade allowed British traders to undersell the products of Egyptian industry. Egypt was forced back into the role of a primary producing country. One after another the factories were closed while more and more of the country's land was devoted to the new crop, cotton.

Ottoman attempts at westernization were always one step behind Western ingenuity and greed; its provinces, one after another, became Western colonies, Western protectorates, or pro-Western independent states. By the end of the century Egypt was a virtual protectorate of imperial Britain, while its economy was geared to supplying the mills of Lancashire with cheap raw cotton.

Nevertheless Muhammad Ali and his descendants transformed the structure and appearance of Egypt.

Muhammad Ali modified the structure. He made Egypt an autonomous state, whose rulers could decide for themselves at least on internal change. By building the Mahmudiya canal, named in

189

honor of Mahmud II, he restored the link between the capital and Alexandria. By so doing he deserves to be ranked as the second founder of Alexandria, an unimportant fishing village at the start of his reign. The Pasha's effect on Cairo was egotistical. He built a palace at Shubra (the "island of the elephant" had now become a solid if rural part of the eastern bank) and another in the Citadel. He designed a tomb-mosque for himself which was to dominate the eastern skyline: to Pierre Loti, the French traveler, it seemed transported bodily from Stamboul. Otherwise the city remained as unchanged by independence as Muhammad Ali himself, who retained the Ottoman dress and manners which he had brought to Egypt.

"In what corner of Grand Cairo I am to seek for grandeur, I am at a loss to know." The perplexed seeker was an English traveler, R. R. Madden. A man who enjoyed arraying himself in Syrian costume, he traveled widely in the Middle East between 1824 and 1827.

In a city containing three hundred and fifty thousand inhabitants, there is not one tolerable street. Splendid mosques, some of which surpass, in my estimation, those of Constantinople, are built in blind alleys and filthy lanes; the public thoroughfares are hardly twelve feet wide, darkened by mats to impede the rays of the sun, and choked with putrid vegetables and reeking offals, from the various stalls which line the streets. The first thing that astonishes a stranger in Cairo is the squalid wretchedness of the Arabs, and the external splendour of the Turks. The next thing that surprises and confounds him, in every part of Egypt, as well as in Cairo, is the manifest opposition of the modes and customs of Mahometan countries to those of Christendom. Here the head is shaved, the beard unshorn; the men wear petticoats of cloth; the women trousers of silk or cotton. Instead of a hat, a piece of muslin is twisted round the head; instead of a surtout, a blanket is thrown across the shoulders; a carpet serves for a bed; a wooden bowl for a service of plate, a pewter tray for a table-cloth; fingers do for forks, and swords for carving knives. A man salutes without stooping, sits down without a chair, he is silent without reflection and serious without sagacity. If you enquire about the health of his wife, it is at the hazard of your head; if you praise the beauty of his children, he suspects you of the evil eye. The name of the Prophet is in every man's mouth, and the fear of God in few men's hearts.

Madden visited a lunatic asylum and was horrified by the neglect of the tortured inmates. Their daily nourishment seemed to depend

190

entirely on the gifts of the charitable. If on a particular day no one felt charitable, the lunatics starved. Madden lists the Cairo illnesses in order of their frequency: plague, dysentery, ophthalmia, bilious remittent fever, the ague, and inflammatory fever.

His jaundiced view was shared by James Webster, the visitor of the 1820's whose description of the massacre of the mamelukes has been quoted. From the narrow lanes of Bulak (Webster had made the six-day journey from Alexandria by boat) he crossed an area of open fields to Ezbekiah. (Madden, in Ezbekiah on the day of the cutting of the dam, had seen an area of promenade in the morning, a lake afloat with hundreds of craft in the evening.) Adjoining Ezbekiah was "the Frank quarter," where the British consul lived in a secluded lane. Now the Mousky, this area was on the edge of the "native" town.

The scenes which the traveller here meets are powerfully opposed to the expectations of the admirer of eastern poetry. Half the inhabitants of the town are so filthy and ragged, that in England they would be sent to the treadmill for indecent exposure. Their dirt is absolutely indescribable. Few of the streets are wider than 'Change-alley, and they are unpaved and winding. Carriages are never seen. With the thermometer at one hundred and ten, among crowds of Cairenes squeezing and stewing in the avenues, where horses, camels, dromedaries and donkeys, and women muffled and mounted on mules, blocked the place with clouds of small and almost imperceptible dust, which got into our eyes, and the overpowering glare of the sunlight, we had a ceaseless change of temperature at the turn of every street, and the thoughts of the plague, which never leave the imagination of the European. Happy the man who escapes with only bugs and fleas!

Muhammad Ali lost his empire under British pressure in 1841 and his wits in 1848. On his death in 1849 he was succeeded by Abbas, son of his favorite Tusun, who had died aged twenty. Under Abbas there was a brief reaction against the modernizing policies of Muhammad Ali. Abbas, morosely conservative, reduced the army and closed his father's surviving factories and schools. His death at Benha Palace, no far from Cairo, was to be the most interesting thing about his life.

No one was ever punished for his murder, though two variants of what happened exist. A literary pasha wrote that Abbas perished through his policy of favoring certain of his mamelukes more than

191

others. One current favorite, Khalil Derwish Bey, was unbearably arrogant in his treatment of other young mamelukes in the Pasha's employ. These revenged themselves by composing rude nicknames for the favorite. When Khalil reported them to Abbas, they were first flogged, then made to clean up stable ordure in nonmilitary dress. Pardoned, they were brought to Benha to look after the horses. They had neither forgotten nor forgiven their degradation. On the night of July 14, 1854, it was the turn of two youths, Omar Wasfi and Shaker Hussein, to sleep as guards in the Pasha's bedroom. The murderers arrived at midnight and were admitted by the young men. When Abbas tried to escape, Omar Wasfi pushed him back into a room full of knives. The death of the Pasha was hushed up until his corpse had been taken to his Cairo palace by coach. As against this version, a literary Frenchwoman in a book called *Pulling the Curtain on the Secrets of Egypt* argued that the Pasha's maternal aunt, Princess Nazli, arranged the murder. Princess Nazli secured, as bait, two extremely handsome mamelukes and persuaded them to sell themselves in the still flourishing Cairo slave market. As she had foreseen, the Pasha's slave buyer was excited by their beauty and bought them for his master's palace. Again as she had foreseen, her royal nephew appointed them to his bedroom rota. At first the mamelukes feared to attack the Pasha, a burly man of forty-one; but on their second night of duty they summoned up their courage, did the work they had been paid for, collected their fee, and escaped, one to Albania, another to Constantinople.

Yet even Abbas bequeathed an important innovation to Cairo. Reacting from his grandfather's Francophilia—Madden had described Muhammad Ali as being "surrounded by a vile set of Frank advisers, the very scum of Genoa and Marseilles"—Abbas favored the Anglo-Saxons. He encouraged Samuel Shepheard to found a hotel which was to become almost as famous as the pyramids. He gave the British permission to start work on a railway to link Alexandria and Cairo. As a result his corpulent uncle Said, who reigned from 1854 to 1863, could visit his estates in a one-car railway train decorated with arabesques and furnished with dark leather sofas. Said's name was to be connected with another mode of transport. Against British opposition, he gave Ferdinand de Lesseps a concession to drive a canal through the Isthmus of Suez; the northern terminal, Port Said, was to be named in his honor. Thus Abbas and Said, through railway and canal, put Egypt back where it had

Sellers of water and soft drinks, such as this licorice vendor, have always been popular in a city where water was scarce and the Muslim majority was forbidden to drink alcohol. The man on the right is smoking a nargila, *or water pipe. (Sayid Hassan)*

been before the voyage of Vasco da Gama: at the center of world communications.

The man who was to exploit this new strategic importance as well as the new crop, cotton, grown since Muhammad Ali's day, but increasingly important, was the son of Ibrahim Pasha, Ismail. He would transform the appearance of Egypt and make Cairo what it fundamentally is today. In a reign which lasted from 1863 to 1879 Ismail spent lavishly on all the appurtenances of a modern state, from lighthouses to post offices, from schools for girls to hotels for Europeans.

In 1866 S. S. Hill, author of *Travels in Egypt and Syria,* traveled from Alexandria to Cairo. He put up at a Coptic house in the same fringe area where Webster had found the British consul. Visitors

193

were still not a common sight. A crowd of some two hundred people loitered outside, curious to behold a foreigner. But things had begun to change. Hill drove out to Shubra "to inspect the Pasha's palaces and gardens." After leaving the city gate he was much inconvenienced by clouds of dust blowing from the northeast; also by the sun. These inconveniences were of brief duration, "for at hardly one-eighth of a mile from the gate we entered an avenue of acacia and sycamore trees, such as would ornament the vicinity of any capital city in the world. This avenue extends the whole distance from where we entered it to the palace and gardens we were about to visit. The road is a raised way for about half the distance over a fertile plain . . . On our way we met several hundred donkeys loaded with panniers of chopped straw, which is the usual substitute for hay in Egypt, and a long string of camels loaded with many articles of consumption for the town."

The lake by whose borders the beys had built their houses, where Napoleon had lodged and where in the dry season his soldiers had drilled, had been finally drained and turned into a park.

The great square of Ezbekiah, which we now entered, is remarkable for its open and cheerful character, and wants only the moving scene of a similar place in any city in Europe to display many of the appendages to refinement during the hours of relaxation. But what it presented now it presents at all hours. The Pasha and his predecessors have here planted shrubs and laid out walks, and made avenues of the fresh circassia, and thus given form to the ready materials, before the elements that should animate the square are yet conceived. It forms a nearly square space of about a mile and a half, where on all sides are seen to the best advantage some of the finest edifices in Cairo, including a military college, and a long line of ancient houses, evidently the residences of families in easy circumstances. Between the houses and the walks there is a broad road, where may be often seen a stately Arab on horseback, attended by one or two servants on foot, and a *says*, or hostler, who precedes him. Dikes have been raised to form a canal that receives the waters of the Nile, which circulate round the place when the inundations have attained a considerable height; but this again becomes dry when the Nile is lower. The walls on the bank of the canal have been planted with trees, which now flourish in all their freshness and beauty.

The culmination of Ismail's extravagant reign was the inauguration of the Suez Canal in 1869. To mark the linking of two seas

Ismail planned an Opera House which would provide Ezbekiah with the animation so desired by Mr. Hill. To mark the return of Egypt to the center of the world, Giuseppe Verdi was asked to compose an opera with an imperial Egyptian theme; in the event, *Aida* was late, and *Rigoletto* was performed instead. More important to Ismail (under whose reign Europeans had flooded into his country) was the presence of the most glamorous European of all, the Empress Eugénie of France. He housed this lady in a palace which an aesthete would describe as "of doubtful taste but madly sumptuous"[2] but which probably impressed the wife of Napoleon III. The palace was built on the "middle island," known generally as Gezira (or island) and, in its northern sector, Zamalek, after some little shacks which Muhammad Ali had first had built there. For the use of Ismail—now reigning with Ottoman permission as a hereditary viceroy, or khedive—there were main Cairo palaces at Abdin and Ismailiya: "and beyond the limits of the metropolis the names of these gorgeous mansions is legion. At Kasr al-Nil and all along the neighboring banks of the Nile, on the islands of Roda and Gezira, at Giza, Abbasiya, Shubra—everywhere rise the unsightly and ill-built palaces in which viceregal extravagance and ostentation have found an outlet. Not one of all these huge buildings is other than an eyesore. Not one is tastefully furnished. The Khedive's reception room at Abdin Palace used to be a monument of the meretricious style which rejoices in gold and crimson and pierglasses."[3] Ismail's civil list ran to £700,000 or about $3,500,000 a year—twice as much as Queen Victoria's.

Ismail had been able to afford these extravagant whims—and the receptions to mark the opening of the Canal were triumphs of gastronomical overindulgence—thanks to a world shortage of cotton resulting from the American Civil War. Not only was Egypt again at the center of the world; she was also the provider of the "long staple" of civilized dress. The value of her cotton crop soared from five million to twenty-five million pounds sterling. In order to diffuse European ideas, in order to make true his boast that Egypt now belonged to Europe, not Africa, Ismail had apparent allies in the scores of thousands of Greeks, Italians, Marseillais, to say nothing of Lebanese, who flooded to the Eldorado by the Nile. These foreign communities inhabited new quarters that sprawled on the once silt-land between Ezbekiah and the Nile. There were Italianate palazzi for the rich with gardens where solemn green mango and

vivid oranges collected the omnipresent dust; for the poorer migrants there were houses built after the worst pattern of a fifth-rate
artisan's suburb.[4]

This influx of Europeans—no fewer than eighty thousand arrived
in Egypt in 1865 [5]—had a revolutionary effect on the Egyptian
capital. For six centuries Cairo had been divided between the mamelukes and the Egyptians; they had lived, in greater or less comfort,
in one city; palace rubbed shoulders with hovel; in the mosque the
bey and the beggar were temporarily one. Now for the first time a
new phenomenon appears: two Cairos coexisting on one site, an
Egyptian Cairo and a European Cairo, joined by nothing but the
tolerance of the Khedive.

The Egyptian Cairo continued to live as before: not only neglected, it was increasingly destroyed. The modernizing authorities
drove new thoroughfares through ancient beauties (like the dreary
Muhammad Ali Boulevard linking the Citadel to Ezbekiah); if
such European straight lines destroyed irreplaceable mosques and
palaces the authorities were not disturbed. Ismail's Minister of

Mobile refreshment stands for the feast of Sham al-Nesseem. (Eric Nemès)

Public Instruction, Ali Mubarak, asked rhetorically: "Do we need so many monuments? Isn't it enough to preserve a sample?" Since Bab Zuweyla had been a place of execution, he suggested that, like the Bastille, it should be destroyed.

The Egyptian Cairo became a place for tourists and sensation-hunters.

The slave market still existed in the 1860's. It was worse stocked than before.

The most beautiful women were formerly brought from Georgia and Circassia; but this trade ceased with the independence of Greece, and the pashas and beys, with the exception of some of the more wealthy who still obtain Circassians by way of Constantinople, have been since that time obliged to content themselves with the rather tawny Abyssinians, which are brought down the Nile in plenty, and may, when not especially handsome, and before they have been, as the custom is, trained to some occupation, such as sewing, and the housewife's accomplishments, generally be purchased for the moderate sum of about four purses, which is equal to twenty pounds sterling.

Boys were still castrated, their compensation a life of ease and prestige.

The government of Ismail, anxious to impress the West that a modern kingdom now ruled the Nile from Alexandria to Khartoum, hardly bothered with the quarters where most people lived. Hill gives us memorable word pictures to set beside the more tender lithographs of David Roberts. One is from the Mokattam heights.

All is uniform in colour, and of the same shade as the desert, from the roofless dwellings of the artisans to the comparatively grand dwellings of the proudest and most opulent citizens; and even the mosques and the minarets that adorn the town, exhibiting the same feature of common decay, are tinged with deathlike tints of the desert. Some of the minarets do not even stand erect, while others are shattered as if they had been struck by cannon balls . . .

Hill then descends into the streets which he had seen from above. An utter dereliction is their common trait:

Walking through the streets of Cairo, one cannot fail to be struck by the utter want of uniformity or even of completeness in its buildings. If the front is complete, one of the sides or the back has fallen in, or

197

the upper story has not been finished. Hundreds of houses are even seen wanting their whole fronts, while of many, some of the beams have fallen at one end and some at the other, and now rest on the floor of the apartments to which they once formed the roof.

In these areas of Cairo—the word *baladi* (village) came to be used to differentiate them from the *frangi* areas of European influence—the ancient customs of the city continued. Women hid their faces. Gérard de Nerval described nineteenth-century Cairo as the city of the East where women were most hermetically veiled; in a month spent in Cairo Webster had not seen "the face of a single woman of any age in the street, nor any one from the window, save those by whom I was spitten upon." The life of the family was interior, lived in courtyards which could be described poetically:

The inner court is almost as silent and deserted as the guarded windows which overlook the street. We shall see nothing of the domestic life of the inhabitants; for the women's apartments are carefully shut off from the court, into which open only the guest rooms and other masculine and semi-public apartments. After the bustle of the street this quiet and ample space is very refreshing, and one feels that the Egyptian architects have happily realised the requirements of eastern life. They make the streets narrow and overshadow them with projecting meshrebiyas, because the sun beats down too fiercely for the wide streets of European towns to be endurable. But they make the houses themselves spacious and surround them with courts and gardens, because without air the heat of the rooms in summer would be intolerable. The eastern architect's art lies in so constructing your house that you cannot look into your neighbour's windows, nor he into yours; and the obvious way of attaining this end is to build the rooms round a high open court, and to closely veil the windows with lattice blinds, which admit a subdued light and sufficient air, and permit an outlook without allowing the passing stranger to see through. The wooden screens and secluded court are necessary to fulfil the requirement of the Mohammadan system of separating the sexes.[6]

Life was not always as maidenly as this.

Religion, which restricted social life, also gave occasions when it could be indulged. Cairo was famous for its *moulids,* or fiestas connected with the memories of holy men or women. The purpose of a *moulid* was "to glorify God by venerating one of His favorites." The custom of such veneration went back to Fatimid times. Cairo was fortunate in possessing the relics of more of God's favorites than any other Muslim city. The head of Ali's son, Hussein, was buried in a mosque within a stone's throw of al-Azhar; his sister, Sayida Zaynab, was buried in a mosque restored by Abbas Pasha near where the canal had originally branched from the Nile. Three of Hussein's children were buried in the city. Other descendants of the Prophet were joined by a host of holy or outstanding men. Each of these *moulids*—as late as 1938 seventy-eight such fiestas were known to a Scottish connoisseur [7]—was given over to festivities which included transvestite dancing and great deal of noise.

Throughout the nineteenth century the ancient customs connected with the pilgrimage and the cutting of the dam continued unspoiled. Let us hear for the last time (the custom would not outlast that century) an account of the breaching of the Nile:

During the day which precedes the cutting away of the obstructions to the passage of the water, boats gather about the entrance of the Canal, upon the Nile. Towards evening the river between Bulak, the port or quay of Cairo, and the mouth of the Canal, which is about a mile, the water exhibits a scene of gaiety, from the greater part of the boats being very pleasant craft. . . After the departure of the daylight on this evening, some fireworks are exhibited; but the more grand banquets are reserved for the moment of opening the Canal, which, however, is at an hour that renders their effect quite negative. The Pasha, who presided on the important day of this opening, arrived with his suite at about half-past nine o'clock in the morning, and, after passing through a double file of soldiers, dismounted, and took the chief seat in a large tent, reserved for those who were willing to pay for their places of distinction. His Highness took his place with some ceremony, but by what means he communicated his commands to cut the dike I did not perceive. The work was, however, speedily commenced, and coins were thrown into the deep, but yet dry, Canal, and scrambled for by one or two hundred persons, who had descended the banks, until the water rushing down, as it forced, at first its slow, but afterwards its quicker, passage, carried some of the party off their legs, and obliged them to swim to recover the shores, which are accessible on either side. The crowd of spectators on this occasion was very great. Some persons estimated their number at from 10,000 to 15,000; but I saw only one or two of the fair sex among them, and these, to judge from their dress, were quite of the lowest order.[8]

With the speed of the Nile bursting the eroded dam, the Egypt of Ismail was to gallop toward disaster. The two communities which had been living in apparently friendly coexistence—the Europeans and the Egyptians—were to become masters and servants, rulers and ruled.

The Khedive's extravagance could not survive the slump in cotton prices when, after the victory of the North, America began exporting southern cotton once more. Ismail's foreign creditors would not put up with promissory notes. The force of an all-powerful Europe moved in to secure the settlement of Ismail's mountainous debts.

Ismail, desperate for money, now resorted to methods of taxation which reduced the standard of living in his kingdom to that of a concentration camp. Ismail the Magnificent, now known as Ismail the Spendthrift, was bundled off the throne by the real owners of Egypt, the European moneylenders. The son installed to replace him, Towfik, became the enemy of the Egyptians whose material interests had suffered from Ismail's extortions and whose pride now suffered from Towfik's subservience to European advisers.

An army revolt led by Orabi Pasha, a proto-Nasser of the nineteenth century, came near to succeeding. Its basic aims were to introduce some form of parliamentary government to give expression to the wishes of the Egyptian people. It opposed the whole Turco-Circassian pyramid, of which the royal family was the apex.

Just as the British had thwarted Muhammad Ali's attempts to industrialize Egypt, so now for similar reasons they defeated Orabi's attempts to democratize the country. Under the Liberal government of Gladstone, British forces landed in Alexandria and proceeded to restore the Khedive to his full prerogatives. The occupation, the Liberal government insisted, would be strictly "temporary." Next year, the year after, soon, sometime, the soldiers would be withdrawn. Meanwhile, the Egyptian ministry had a British adviser whose word was law. The military occupation was in fact to last more than seventy years and to end only with the dynasty it supported.

Now that Egypt was virtually a British protectorate—sharing the colonial status forced by the "Franks" on all the major Muslim countries with the exception of the rump of the Ottoman empire—the European quarter of Cairo became supreme. The Cairo which has been the subject of this book resembled the old quarter of a city in French North Africa, the native town kept as a picturesque adjunct to the new.

"What is this? Where are we fallen?" asks Pierre Loti in 1907. "Save that it is more vulgar, it might be Nice, or the Riviera, or Interlaken." Loti visits the Muhammad Ali mosque. "Soldiers are on guard there—and how unexpected are such soldiers in this holy place of Egypt. The red uniforms and the white faces of the north: Englishmen billetted in the palace of Muhammad Ali."

The pyramids and the Sphinx have become properties for the tourists of Thomas Cook; the descendants of the Fatimids, tourist

These men go from house to house to remove the cotton from mattresses and fluff it on the wires of their traditional mattress harps. (Eric Nemès)

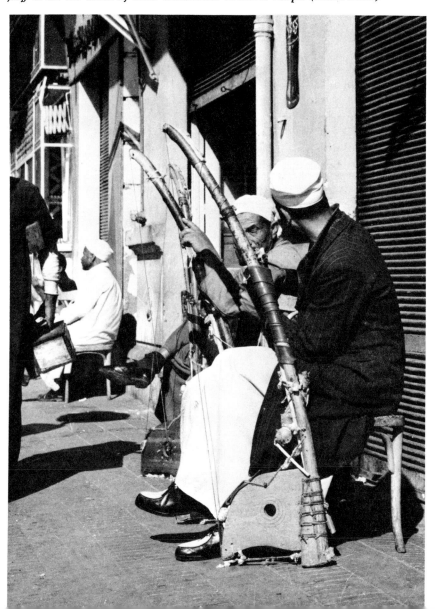

guides. Pierre Loti describes one area near the pyramids at the height of Europe's "belle époque":

> The tourists who have come tonight, and upon whom have pounced the black-cloaked Bedouin guides, wear cap and ulster or furred great-coat: their intrusion here seems almost an offence; but, alas, such visitors become more numerous in each succeeding year. The great town hard by—which sweats gold now that men have started to buy from it its dignity and its soul—is become a place of rendezvous and holiday for the idlers and upstarts of the whole world . . . Little more than a mile away there ends a road travelled by hackney carriages and tramway cars, and noisy with the delectable hootings of smart motor cars; and behind the pyramid of Cheops squats a vast hotel to which swarm men and women of fashion, the latter absurdly feathered like Redskins at a scalp dance; and sick people of a purer air; and consumptive English maidens; and ancient English dames, a little the worse for wear, who bring their rheumatisms for the treatment of the dry winds.

If Europeans could so upset a Breton naval officer, their effect on the native Egyptians was yet more traumatic.

Ahmed Amin, an Egyptian writer, tells how he lived as a child near a British camp; his house adjoined the ground where they played football and cricket. "I was so terrified of their red coats, blue trousers and general bearing that I usually changed my route whenever I saw them coming. My father's view of them was no more rational, but typical of the people's philosophy of surrender. The soldiers were the symbols of God's anger. The Egyptians had oppressed each other for a long time and had forgotten God's laws. The English were God's hand of revenge. They were here to torture and torment them until they saw God's path."

A new generation was to see in Egyptian nationalism the path of God; resistance would take the place of surrender.

CHAPTER 15

Fifty-Fifth Century

Cairo's west-bank precursor, Memphis, had symbolized a human revolution. It was the first great capital of men who had changed from gathering food (whether by picking fruit or knocking down game) to growing cereals in orderly fields and then storing them in vulnerable barns. The constants and variants analyzed in this book or implicit in its story were set in the context of a food-growing society. Cairo's triumphs depended on the delta's cornucopia; its defeats were prompted by the desire of outsiders to control this cornucopia; its people's miseries resulted from a Nile too abundant or too mean.

Its fifty-fifth century would transform this city at the apex of the delta, would banish many of its constants. For this century—the twentieth after the Christian revelation—brought a revolution as fundamental as that which had turned casual hunters into serious farmers.[1]

The industrial and technological revolution created earlier in the West and exported to the East transformed every aspect of Egyptian life.

Lord Cromer, the British proconsul who ruled Egypt during the first quarter century of direct foreign control, claimed in 1901 that "the foundations on which the wellbeing and material prosperity of a civilised community should rest have been laid . . ." In his two-volume apologia, he congratulated "a small body of Englishmen who, in various capacities, and with but little direct support or assistance from their Government or its representatives, have of late years devoted their energies to the work of Egyptian regeneration," on having abolished the whip as an instrument of government, and in having all but abolished slavery and forced labor.

Far more fundamental than the measures of politicians (superficial in many cases and unpopular in others) were the results of work of European engineers.

Until the nineteenth century Egyptian irrigation had consisted of the diversion of the summer flood through canals which flooded the fields for some months and then left them so steeped with moisture as to grow one crop. Nothing was done to store the water for another season. Muhammad Ali had seen the need for a series of weirs at the start of the delta to hold back the water and release it when it was required; otherwise much water flowed wasted into the sea. A scheme for such a delta barrage had been designed by a French engineer, Mougel bey; because of lack of official support, of money, and of technical expertise, this visionary scheme (it proposed to back up the waters of the Rosetta and Damietta branches and release them through three canals) was not put into full effect until 1890. In that year a team of British engineers completed Mougel bey's Nile Barrage in an architectural style recalling the Waverley novels of Sir Walter Scott. Though the barrage gardens became one of the most attractive places for picnics near Cairo, the British had not aimed to amuse the Cairenes; they aimed to increase the yield of cotton in the delta fields. They succeeded.

More important for Cairo was the taming of the Nile to the south of the city. In 1902 two other great weirs were established across the Nile, one at Assiut and the other at Aswan. The latter dam, the work of Sir William Willcocks, was one of the engineering marvels of its day. The effect of the two dams was to diminish the age-old dependence on summer floodwater. As a result the ancient Cairo canal was filled in and turned into an ugly boulevard, the Street of the Misr Canal. In 1957 it became known as Port Said Street (Sharia Port-Said) after the target of the last British attempt to regain control of Egyptian destinies.

204   The taming of the Nile (a process to be developed throughout

The camel corps from the July 23rd military parade, commemorating the revolution of 1952 which forced the abdication of King Farouk. The Hilton Hotel is in the background. (Eric Nemès)

the century and to culminate in the High Dam of the 1960's) abolished the annual ceremonies connected with the flood, the caste of water sellers and the need for sebeels. The water sellers took to selling soft drinks; the sebeels no longer echoed to female gossip; the Nilometer became a museum.

The great religious ceremony of the Cairo year, the start of the pilgrimage, fell victim to a mixture of politics and progress. The destruction of the Ottoman empire atomized the Middle East. In the region of the Holy Places there was no geographical expression of Islamic unity. Different sovereign states (including the new settler-state of Israel) occupied the land route to western Arabia. The holy cities of Mecca and Medina, part of Saudi Arabia since 1926, were ruled by Wahhabis who had long disapproved of such customs as the *mahmal*. In the realm of progress, new methods of transport made possible the "instant pilgrimage," lacking the dangers and the contemplative broodings of the past.

But the greatest change of all was wrought by the Egyptian successors of Antoine Clot. Clot had worked for the Egyptian army, but his disciples worked for the Egyptian people. They accomplished a change more revolutionary than the taming of the Nile. They tamed the diseases which had previously reduced the population. During the nineteenth century the population of Cairo had grown from around 250,000 at the time of Napoleon to perhaps

205

400,000 at the turn of the century. Its pace suddenly quickened. By the late 1960's it had multiplied tenfold. The suburb of Shubra— the island that had grown round the shipwrecked *Elephant,* the country village to which nineteenth-century citizens rode out to escape from city cares—alone housed one million people.

This violent acceleration of population was more destructive of ancient Cairo than the town planning of the previous century. Like logs taken over by wasps, the existing cities, European as much as Egyptian, were colonized by the fellahin who poured into the capital and by their babies who did not die. Palazzi, which in the 1880's had housed the families of European immigrants, cotton brokers and advisers, merchants and entrepreneurs, became divided and subdivided. The cool, eastern mansions so lovingly described by romantic travelers lost their quiet calm as two dozen families shared their space. Under this pressure the segregation into *frangi* and *baladi* collapsed. The roofs of modern apartment blocks sprouted their *baladi* quarters: roof villages of little huts complete with hens and sheep would be established high above the traffic. In the out-lying suburbs, where Italianate villas once dominated leafy avenues, a spate of shoddy building created one of the largest urban areas in the world. The *art nouveau* palace of Habib Sakakini (rumored by its incredulous neighbors to be set on a metal plate that re-volved to catch the appropriate breeze) was beset by tenements. Now that the Nile was tamed, it was possible to build wherever the land was flat. A new northern suburb, Heliopolis, linked to Cairo by a tram, had been designed in the first decade of the twentieth century; it had been the work of a Belgian baron whose own palace was built to resemble a Hindu temple, though the inside was fur-nished in solid Brussels comfort. A southern suburb, Maadi, had been linked to Cairo by a railway. These two suburbs, designed for the well-to-do, were inundated in the same *baladi* flood that over-whelmed Mattariya in the north and Giza in the west; the heights of Mokattam were, for the first time in history, built upon by the wealthy in flight from the poor.

The force of numbers affected the spirit as well as the appear-ance of Cairo. Numbers, as much as western influences, destroyed the harem and its twin symbols of the grille over windows and the veil over faces. The segregation and veiling of women had no more been part of pre-Islamic Arabia than of Pharaonic Egypt. It had never really worked in crowded villages, where women had toiled in the fields alongside men. It had flourished in small spacious towns where there was room for women to be secluded. Crowded Cairo made the veil impossible. Female emancipation advanced in rhythm with the increase of the population. In 1900 the veil had been universal; by the 1960's it was a rarity.

The spectacular growth of Cairo (reflected to a lesser extent in the growth of other towns) had two other important results.

The old upper class, based on country fiefs, now gave ground to political movements representing the public opinion of the towns. The press increasingly expressed the national resistance to foreign or upper-class control; the spread of education gave the press an increasing audience. The nationalist movement of the 1920's, led by Saad Zaghlul, called on a far more coherent and organized support than the movement of Arabia which the British and the Palace had, in collusion, scotched. Though Zaghlul was opposed by the British, his ideas were too generally accepted to be defeated. After his death, his party, the Wafd, suffered from a

Election posters hanging at Bab Zuweyla, the southern gate to the Fatimid city. Criminals were once executed here. (Eric Nemès)

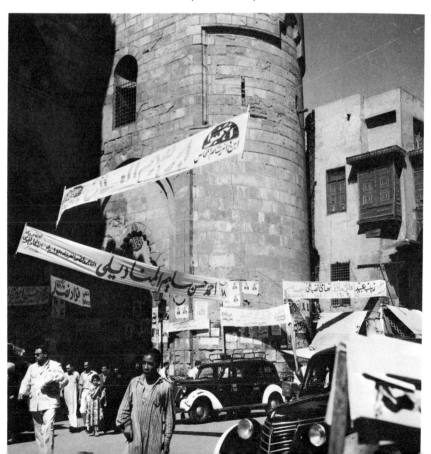

third-generation deterioration in the 1940's. Yet many of his ideals were to triumph in the 1952 revolution. This was in form a *coup d'état,* and the military elements which guaranteed its success were also to be a drag on its progress. But the spirit of Gamal Abdul Nasser transcended that of a narrow military leader. His resistance to the Palace, the old upper class and their foreign supporters, expressed the consensus of Egyptians.

As a second result, the growth of population made industrialization both possible and necessary. This industrialization was a century late. Its growing pains could have been surmounted in the nineteenth century, but foreign control had made this impossible. The new Egyptian republic could ensure that outside interference did not thwart the use of surplus labor in manufacturing goods. It could not so easily defeat inefficiency, shoddiness, and uneconomical waste. All these concomitants of newly developing countries were found in the factories making cement, automobile tires, steel, and refrigerators that turned Helwan, twenty miles south of Cairo, from an Edwardian spa to a proletarian city. Nor could military orders create efficient bureaucrats who would administer the machinery of industry and government politely, as servants of the public.

But the vigor of this young society was as marked as its defects. So was its determination. The new Cairo boasted no remarkable building. (Perhaps the last building of architectural merit was the Museum, built by Abbas II in 1900.) But many slums were pulled down and improved dwellings built for many of the poor. The Revolution and its works aroused sympathy or malice depending on the state of mind of the observer. Critics made the same complaints of inefficiency as they had made against the Russian peasants in the 1920's. Admirers saw in the new leveling of extremes an attempt to create a juster society.

But for good or bad, on June 9, 1967, the people of Cairo did something they had not done before: they played a decisive role in their own history. The same city that had sighed for Tumanbey but cheered Selim, that had prayed against the French but taken no part in the battle of Imbaba, heard their president resign after a calamitous defeat. A city that worshiped success would have repudiated Nasser. But this city had endured foreign rule for centuries and could endure it no more. While people in Tel-Aviv danced at the news of Nasser's fall, people in Cairo crowded the new streets and the old, the *baladi* quarters and the *frangi,* demanding that pre-cisely because the foreigners wanted Nasser to go, Nasser should stay. He was the first native-born Egyptian to rule the east-bank city in its history, the first Egyptian to rule Egypt since the later Pharaohs. The conquest of the myth that Egypt must be ruled by non-Egyptians was as significant as the conquest of the Nile. Only a cataclysm could reverse these victories. Cataclysms were not in-conceivable. If they came no one was more schooled to endure them than Egyptians. If they did not, then Cairo, with new constants and new variants, would continue an urban tradition unequaled elsewhere on the threatened earth.

To Nena

O Noble Lady, no matter how I sought you
I found no truth-substantiated certainty,
My mind-youth tortured by fabrications—
Till you bestowed upon him deep relief
In the forest hut of inexpressibility! . . .

Transcendent Wisdom, Supreme Mother of Buddhas,
Breathing out and in all that lives and stands,
Natural clear light, forever trouble-free, Truth Body Angel—
Let us all enjoy the great good fortune of the Noble Lady!

—From Pabongka Dechen Nyingpo's *Swift Path of Great Bliss*

Contents

THE DALAI LAMA

Foreword

I am very happy to introduce my old friend Bob Thurman's new book, the title of which he derives from the name of one of the buddhas, known in Tibetan as Tsepamey, meaning Infinite Life, which denotes the qualities that buddha principally embodies. He represents the Mahayana view that perfect enlightenment is not merely a peaceful state of cessation, almost like nonexistence. Buddhahood involves a state of complete awareness that finds blissful expression in a compassion that tirelessly embraces all living beings, manifesting whenever necessary to help them reach their own freedom from suffering.

Professor Thurman describes this vision in the context of the vast and extensive practices of bodhisattvas, the transcendent virtues or perfections. He also tackles an important ancillary aspect of this vision, the notion of the past and future lives of all beings. This is based on the Buddha's explanation of the principle of cause and effect, which states that no thing arises without cause, there is no uncaused cause, and no cause loses its effect. Thus, we say that consciousness is always preceded by another consciousness, and always gives rise to further consciousness, much in the manner of the continuity of physical energy. The idea that we live many lives before and many after this present one, the quality of which is affected by our own conduct and motivation, provides the context for appreciating the great rarity and value of life as a free and fortunate human being. Moreover, understanding that all beings have already lived countless lives allows us to accept our interdependence and appreciate that at some time every being has been kind to us in some way.

Most spiritual traditions relate their systems of ethics to some sense of continuity of life after death because the potential consequence of our deeds is what gives meaning to our lives. Understanding actually how this continuity works is considered to be extremely difficult, something accessible only to the mind of a buddha. On the one hand, it is difficult for us to check the existence of past and future lives for ourselves. However, a clear distinction should be made between what is not found and what is found to be nonexistent by science. What science finds to be nonexistent, we should all accept as nonexistent, but what science merely does not find is a completely different matter. On the other hand, the Buddha stated clearly that our awareness of both the impact of our previous lives on this life and the consequences of our present deeds on our future lives is an essential way to motivate a proper sense of ethical maturity and spiritual development.

The question of past and future lives can be difficult for people brought up in the modern world, used to adopting a view that accords with what can be physically proven. But even modern science still does not know with certainty what the facts of consciousness actually are, how it functions, or what its complete nature is. Therefore, I am glad to see that Bob Thurman has addressed some of these issues straightforwardly in this book with his usual vigor and wit.

July 18, 2003

Infinite Life

Introduction:
Invitation to the Infinite Life

was twenty-one years old and a novice monk studying with the Reverend Geshe Wangyal at his tiny Lamaist Buddhist Monastery of America in Freewood Acres, New Jersey. The small settlement consisted of Mongolian, Russian, and Eastern European refugees living in tract houses in the Jersey Pine Barrens. At around 10:15 on a spring morning, I was walking along East Second Street to a corner store up on Route 9, sent to buy a quart of milk for midmorning tea. I was moving briskly west, passing on my left a faded white picket fence that surrounded a small house. As I crossed the driveway, something amazing happened to me.

I experienced a disorienting sensation that I can only describe as the feeling of a push-pressure on my tailbone suddenly dislodging itself. The pressure gone, I immediately saw that I had always been feeling as if I were being pushed along from behind toward my destination, not only to the grocery store on Route 9 but to my destiny in life, to the future in general. The change in sensation gave me a pronounced feeling of relief, a sense of release. I became vividly self-aware of my posture—my brow had been clenched slightly, shoulders hunched up, torso leaning forward, pelvis retracted, and lower back arched. I spontaneously slowed my pace and straightened up my body. A ripple of relaxation moved down my frame, and I felt buoyed by the released momentum.

Looking around me as if for the first time, I noticed the flowers planted beyond the fence I had just walked past, the broader street on my right, and the blue sky filled with fluffy clouds. Then I became aware of a deeper layer of thoughts in my mind, well beneath my thinking about getting to the store, getting the milk, and getting back to Geshe-la and his guests to serve the tea. These deeper thoughts had been circling intently in my head around the Buddhist concept of "beginninglessness." I had first encountered the notion as Geshe-la read to me the Tibetan translation of Nāgārjuna's "Friendly Letter" to the South Indian King Udayi of the Shatavahana Dynasty (circa second century CE). What a funny expression, I'd thought, to talk of "from the beginninglessness . . ." In Western books, "in the beginning" is all we ever hear about. What was this "beginninglessness," I wondered?

All at once, I grasped the concept with full clarity. "Aha!" I thought, "when we say 'in the beginning,' we implicitly assume that there *is* an absolute beginning behind us in time, as if our being and doings were pushing off from a back boundary. I have been driven by that sense of push my whole life, without even realizing it. Amazing! But if life is indeed beginningless, this means that my past has, in fact, been infinite. The future will be too. So there is no big rush to get somewhere. I am mistaken in my compulsion. I can take my time, and take more care, to make sure to go where I want to go. What a thrill! A bit of release, a taste of freedom, no more involuntary pressure—so this is beginninglessness."

I was delighted to begin to understand the Buddhist world I was so drawn to, and amazed to actually *feel* that understanding in my body. I experienced a physical release from a hitherto unrecognized but now obviously bothersome pressure. Returning to the business of the moment, I practically skipped to the store, each step fresh and spontaneous.

A weight was lifted from my body, a veil removed from my heart. I had begun to break free from my inherited life of bondage to enter a new life unbound, an infinite life.

A Blissful Vacation

Is it not everyone's deepest wish to be profoundly and securely happy, joyfully and lovingly able to share that happiness with friends and neighbors as well as all the world's people and animals? To feel an inner bliss that does not depend on this or that circumstance, fortune, or success, but springs from deep within our hearts, from a place of fundamental well-being? To experience a grounding sense of the deep goodness of reality, which fills us with an unconditional joy that energizes our lives? I believe it is. Yet our culture constantly tells us that such joy is not possible, even that it is suspect. It tells us that the world is evil or inadequate and needs fixing. It tells us to think that we need this or that thing or relationship or leader or accomplishment in order to experience even a moment of contentment. They say that deep, unconditional happiness is not just unrealistic, but illegal, immoral, and unhealthy.

Often Buddhist teachings—the Dharma bequeathed to us by so many enlightened ones, which as I grow older more and more has a lifesaving effect on me every day—are misunderstood. They are falsely taught as if the Buddha agreed with all these naysayers, as if he were in fact the ultimate naysayer, the all-time champion of killjoys. "Life is suffering," he seems to have said, "so better to escape from it." How gloomy and sad!

But the truth is, the Buddha definitely did not condemn us to the unhappiness that many conventional societies and cultures, including our own, make us feel is inevitable. On the contrary, he discovered and proclaimed that total freedom from suffering—exquisite, enduring joy—is extremely possible for every sensitive being. It is only the unenlightened, self-centered, and self-constricted being who is temporarily incapable of real happiness. Most of us have a strong yet unwarranted sense of having a fixed, unchanging, limited "self" that is totally separate from all other beings. This combines with our narrow view that our existence is random and terminal; it only starts when we are born and ends abruptly when we die. Fixed and alienated, random and terminal—together these form a vicious combination. In the end, we are left feeling bereft and slightly depressed, living a life seeming to be utterly devoid of meaning. I call this "terminal living."

We can free ourselves from such a terminal existence simply by becoming aware of our misconceptions and their impact on our way of being. Once we have accepted the fact that we ourselves may be the main cause of our own unhappiness, we become determined to understand the problem fully and to solve it as soon as possible. With simple guidance, we easily discover the limiting force to be our own misunderstanding of the reality of the world and of ourselves. The first step toward true contentment lies in confronting the fundamental problem of our rigid self-sense. When we look carefully for our "self," we cannot find it. We discover the error that is the cause of our problem, and we begin to grasp the concepts of selflessness, interconnectedness to others, and infinite life. Now we can set ourselves free to experience the full satisfaction with ourselves, others, and our world that Buddhists call "enlightenment" or "awakening."

The great kindness of the Buddha (and many other enlightened beings who have shared their teachings with us) is that he created a method whereby we can use reason to get ourselves away from the imprisoning "self." That is why we sing Buddha's praises. He has invited us to join a life-long blissful vacation from our domineering selves.

I began studying Buddhism forty years ago and became a monk precisely to go on a blissful vacation. Sometimes I wish I had spent these many years on such a retreat. Maybe after forty years, I would have actually achieved something. Who knows? As it was, I left the monastic community and returned to the U.S. to share the Buddha's message with my American *sangha*, or community. As things go in America, I've been working like a mad dog ever since.

When I came back to New York in 1965, I found there was no support for the blissful vacation I had discovered while studying to become a monk at the Dalai Lama's community in exile in India. I said, "Hey, let's have a blissful vacation." The response was, "Blissful? We've got the Vietnam War. We've got to stop the Pentagon! We've got to stop the corporations! We've got to do important things!" You know, American life. "You want to be bliss-ful?" people asked. "Take Librium. There's no joy in this world. That's unrealistic." Isn't that our society? "Besides, you'll get to experience the bliss of being nothing when you die. Anyway, I've got to get back to work!" I get that same response from people all around the world today—I often even feel that way myself, as things go from bad to worse, when looked at from the materialistic perspective.

But we can change that, you and I. We can join the peaceful, cool, inner revolution. Why don't we have a year-round blissful vacation? We could all form big caravans and wander around, following the sun. It could be sum-mer all the time. Gradually, more disenchanted people would join us. That's what Tibet was like before the Chinese invaded. Since 1409, they were on a blissful vacation, many people wandering on pilgrimage or staying still on retreat. They were on vacation, the whole country—I mean it. A few people had to make *mo-mo* dumplings and a few yaks were sadly sacrificed for food, and sure, some people were not very enlightened at all. It was a bit funky, of course imperfect—but it worked pretty well. With all its grime and low-tech infrastructure, it was the closest any human society so far ever came to ex-periencing the delightful quality of life that the Buddha tells us is our birthright, our destiny. With its inspiration we can create an even more joy-ous society today!

I'm writing this book because I want you to see that your blissful vacation is absolutely possible. There is a life that isn't all pointless, yet full of cell phones and deadlines and total pressure all the time. There is a life that is free, boundless, happy, and full of wisdom and natural purpose. And the great news is that you don't have to go sit by yourself on some mountaintop to gain the insights that I'm going to share with you here. I mean, sure, if you want total enlightenment on a tight schedule, then you will have to go some-day to become a monk or nun or some other kind of professional evolver, an ardent retreatant. But even in the midst of my crazy, pressure-filled New York City life, I am able to experience, joyously contemplate, and discuss with others the immanence of nirvana, the blissful vacation, and relish the aura of total peace and happiness. So you can, too. When more of us do that, we get one step closer to making it real, here and now. And that is precisely what I am going to help you do.

Today—which is the day you read these words, dear reader—I invite you to enter this new realm of existence! Turn back from rushing ahead and face the facts of your life. See it bound by arbitrary limitations. Note how birth and death are imagined as concrete boundaries for no good reason: You can't remember the one and would rather not imagine the other. Take heart. Use your common sense and critical intelligence to awaken. Stop taking for granted your inherited conventional reality. Question even your habitual instincts. Take the plunge into the ocean of boundless freedom. Embrace the mystery. Discover the reality of infinite life!

The Buddha was one of the foremost planetary teachers of the human right, human ability, and human responsibility to achieve the perfect, unconditional happiness that surely is the innermost wish of most people. I follow his inspiring example and write these words for each of you, to help you learn to trust that wish, and to follow the drive of your deepest spirit of intelligent love and courageous goodwill toward a more happy life for yourself and others.

·⊰[Part One]⊱·

·•◄[I]►•·

The Nature of Reality

When I give a talk on whatever topic, at some point I open up the infinite life dimension and invite people to join me in the year-round, lifelong blissful vacation. People often come up to me afterward. They will say, "I love what you said. I hope it's so. But, you know, I still have trouble with that future life stuff." I always say to them, as I say to you now, "The real trouble is with your sense of your present life. You tend to feel boxed in, and you don't know why. As long as you haven't come to feel as common sense, as natural, your life continuity, the reality of your own former and future lives, then you won't be able to be the happy person you really are! So move your mind away from the surface problem and try to look critically at your sense of this life, how it feels, where it comes from, how plausible is it, really?"

If you feel the infinite life perspective is a problem for you, I don't demand that you just drop everything and "believe" in it. Rather, I encourage you to go to work on the issue. I'll keep coming back to it. I more and more have come to feel that if anything positive could result from my teaching, any real benefit for any person, it should be that they get just a hint of the reality of their own former and future lives, that they diminish just the tiniest bit their usual "only this one life" sense of cosmic disconnection, loneliness, alienation, and meaninglessness. I want everyone to be able to see

---

3

more clearly their culturally common belief that, "My life only began when I was born and it ends when I die. So my responsibility to the universe is limited and even my responsibility to myself is limited. Nothing really matters because we'll all be nothing in the end." If nothing else, I want to help you free yourself from that trap, that imprisoning way of thinking. To intensify your spiritual evolution, the first and most important step you must take is to embrace your boundlessness, take responsibility for your infinite continuity, and live your immortality here and now.

Religions make a big deal out of telling people, "You have an immortal soul!" The materialist scientist makes a big deal out of telling them, "You don't have any soul at all! That's only a religious superstition! You die, you're gone, full stop!" The Buddhist "inner scientist" disagrees with the religious claim: "You don't have some fixed inner essence that can be disconnected from your total you and put on a shelf in heaven, staying unchanged immortally while the rest of you rots!" And she also disagrees with the materialist scientist: "There is no full stopping of anything, it's nonsense to say something can become nothing; your consciousness is a something, just like your body! You are body and mind, spirit and soul—the whole 'you' is what is immortal! Always has been and always will be, living and dying, changing and experiencing. The question is not really whether or not you go on, but rather how are you going to enjoy it? How are your friends going to enjoy you, once you're all going to be there together forever?"

When some people hear the word "reincarnation," they automatically think that the person speaking is a nut, a weirdo, or some kind of New Age hippie. It's so ingrained in our heads by our scientific, materialistic culture that the idea is absurd. Carl Sagan thought the belief in future lives was wishful thinking by religious fanatics, an immature clinging to continuing existence by those not brave enough to face extinction. And Carl was a brave man, leaving his tenured position at Cornell to be what many considered a crackpot, running his SETI project to look for intelligent life on other planets.

Why is it so difficult for us to accept the continuation of our personal existence throughout many lives? After all, due to our educated familiarity with the theory of biological evolution, we freely embrace the concept of the evolution of life forms. We accept that we all came out of a primordial stew and that now we're these incredibly complex beings with brains, eyes, and fingers who have created communities, cultures, languages, and highly supportive habitats. We've slowly and miraculously evolved from tiny amoebas into lizards into birds into apes into Shakespeares, Mozarts, Emily Dickinsons, Einsteins, Gandhis, and all kinds of amazing human beings. If we believe that this sort of ongoing physical and mental evolution is possible, then why should it be impersonal and random, a haphazard progression of material forms? Why do we have so much trouble acknowledging a spiritual evolutionary continuum interwoven with the material genetic development? If there are material genes, why can't there be "spiritual genes"?

I'm very sorry to shake up the materialist scientist's sense of history and "progress," but long before Darwin and company, the Buddha and his contemporaries had already "discovered" evolution. He clearly saw that the life-form of the human being was not *sui generis* and was not the creation of a "God," but was evolutionarily connected with all other life-forms, had developed out of them and could also regress back into them. Only he went even further than the materialist scientists. He made evolution a *personal* matter; he acknowledged that it involves the subjective agencies of beings, intentions, and minds. It is not merely an impersonal biological process of atoms and molecules and cells. He saw that living beings do evolve—progress and regress—in a more than strictly physical sense. He taught that we are not merely passive inheritors of genetic codes. We also personally and intentionally evolve ourselves toward higher states of awareness and happiness, or deteriorate ourselves toward lesser awareness and more wretched embodiments. We do so not just in this life, or in a few lives, but over the course of billions of lives, just as it takes billions of lives for a paramecium to become a butterfly.

Why is this so hard to believe? After all, you and I and Darwin and Shakyamuni Buddha were all in the primordial soup together, little slimy creatures with no brains or eyes. And now we are here. Isn't it realistic that our continuity of mental awareness is also here with us, in the same radically transformed and transforming sense that our physical genetic codes are here

---

with us? Why should mind be the one element of reality that is arbitrarily selected to be more nonexistent than matter? Of course, mind cannot be found by means of scientific analysis. But no one has ever found even one atom that can withstand analysis either! There is no thing that anyone has ever found that stands indivisible as a thing in itself. All things, material as well as mental, have only relational, ascribed reality. So it is sheer dogmatism, prejudice, unscientific arbitrariness to insist that matter does exist but mind does not. So an evolutionary biology that excludes the agency and continuity of beings' minds is highly unscientific, philosophically naïve, and pragmatically inaccurate.

I have a theory about why we're so reluctant even to entertain the possibility that our existences might go on: The idea just scares the pants off of us! We find the vista of infinite future lives simply terrifying. Because if we believe we will live on, it inevitably leads to anxiety about the *form* of our continued existence. Will it be good or bad? Pleasant or unpleasant? Will we be human again, angelic or maybe even divine, or insectlike, or something more terrible? When people refuse to believe in their inevitable reincarnation in whatever form their unconscious, instinctual dispositions dictate, they are emotionally trying to avoid the danger of being reborn as a spider, or even worse, in a hell—and the hellfires of the ancestral preachers are crackling away in their unconscious, now and then vividly illustrated in horror movies. That's why we are so desperate to believe that we'll be nothing after death, that the mind is just a buzz of electricity that will one day fizzle out like an old lightbulb. After all, there is a clear relief you can feel, especially when things get tough, in thinking that your life will end someday. We just want to escape.

But don't be fooled by the false promise of security in oblivion. Bars may keep the outside world away but they also imprison you within them. The denial type of defense against an uncertain yet boundless future traps you in a stagnant present. Instead, see your fear itself as the problem and allow your courage to rise as the more natural response. Feel a new kind of strength surge forth from the fullness of your sense of continuing throughout many lives. Forever changing, but forever taking responsibility for seeing that it's forever good!

We often sleep on a difficult problem when we are just too tired to deal with it at night. We all know how it feels to wake up the next morning with that problem still before us. We don't remember it at first—then it hits us. "Ugh," we think, "it's still there." Many of us feel the same way about dying. We try to push the thought away, but every once in a while it creeps into our consciousness with a giant "ugh." We feel queasiness in the pit of our stomachs. How many of us are ready to die right now? How many of us have all our projects accomplished, all the loose ends tied up? How many of us are free of any haunting guilt about negative things we've done? Or on the positive side, how many of us feel that we have already done all we possibly can for ourselves and for those we love?

Thinking along these lines brings to mind the philosopher-mathematician Blaise Pascal's famous wager, in which he establishes that a belief in the existence of God is rational. We can use his principle to support reincarnation, too. From a strictly realistic perspective, should we bet on infinite life and endless consequences to our actions? Pascal would argue that our answer must be a resounding "Yes!" We might as well assume that there will be a future continuity of our personal consciousness, however changed, however disembodied or re-embodied, however connected or disconnected we remain to the "self" we experience in this life. If we make that bet on our own future lives, then we will prepare in whatever way we can to assure that we continue in a good way, in a better embodiment and environment. We will become truly responsible for our thoughts and our acts. Even though we may not remember the previous-life self who made those preparations, we certainly will want to enjoy the results. If our bet is misplaced, and our preparations have no effect because we actually do enter oblivion at death, we will simply not exist to regret having made them. But if we wrongly bet on noncontinuity and therefore do not prepare for the future and have to face it unprepared, then we may suffer seriously in our next existence, and we will very much regret our decision. Even if we don't remember making it, don't know why we are suffering, don't know how to fault ourselves for being so unconscious in our previous life, we will still suffer and regret. Pascal's wager is therefore a very safe bet—it has a clear-cut positive outcome. Whether our personal life is really terminal at death or in fact infinite in continuity, if we bet, like Pascal, on the existence of our life after death, in whatever form, we will be in the best possible position, however things turn out.

Enlightened Theism

The perspective that life is infinite is not by any means unique to Buddhism: All great religions and spiritual traditions of the world teach the illuminating truth and energizing power of embracing the boundless nature of reality. Despite their many differences, the monotheistic religions—Judaism, Christianity, Islam, Shaivism, Shaktism, and Vaishnavism—all posit a belief that an infinite and all-powerful Being creates and maintains the world. They may or may not emphasize a person's boundlessness in the past (as in past lives), but all accept the beginningless nature of God, and all focus on the boundlessness of a person's future with (or without!) God. Each insists that the consequence of true faith and good actions will be endless positive personal continuity (heaven), just as the consequence of bad faith and bad actions will be endless negative personal continuity (hell). While followers of these traditions may be frightened by the negative vistas of infinite and eternal hells, they find the positive vistas of infinite heavenly proximity or unity with the Divine highly illuminating, motivating, and beneficial.

Thus in the grip of their faith, enlightened monotheists expand toward an infinite horizon by emphasizing their sense of connectedness and continuity with God. When they say, "I am reborn through Jesus Christ!" "Stay with me, O God of Israel!" "Allah is great!" "Lord Krishna lives in me!" "Homage to Shiva!" "Save me, O all-powerful Mother!" and so forth, they express the great release of this feeling. Unfortunately, people can get caught up in the egotistical possession of "their God" and often lose track of this sense of boundless well-being.

8

Secular Humanism

On the other side of the spectrum, secular humanists reject the exclusivist and literalist claims of the religious worldviews, finding meaning instead in science and reason. Nevertheless, humanists experience the infinite nature of life, too, in keeping alive their spirit of inquiry and adventure. They touch boundlessness through their curiosity and openness to the wonders of the universe, and feel connected to the vastness of evolution, the limitlessness of the cosmos, the endlessness of the future of their descendants, and the indomitable nature of the human spirit, imagination, and creativity. Think of how infinite you can feel while staring at the ocean, marveling at how those waves have continued tumbling ceaselessly, churning forth life for billions of years. Or consider the profound sense of connection with all life you gain from gazing up at a clear night sky in the wilderness, marveling at the inconceivable profusion of stars in the vast depths of space.

Those who search for the truth, strive for the good, enjoy the beautiful, and live happy and creative lives do so to the extent that their worldview avoids restricting life to a limited and concretized circle of meaninglessness. In their reality, life remains open to the infinite in time and space. Thus secular humanists also already live boundlessly to some degree, although their vision is cramped by the belief that the self's continuum does not proceed into future lives.

Consequences of Infinite Life

The Buddha taught that immense positive potential exists within each and every one of us, just waiting to be unleashed. We are naturally full of love and compassion since we have labored long and virtuously throughout many lives to become human beings. Now, with our highly advanced lifeform relatively free from negative instinctual drives, we are poised and ready to pursue the path to the total bliss that is enlightenment.

The actuality of our past personal continuity is so important because it bears so strongly on our future. Where will we go from here? Our spiritual evolution, like our physical development, is an ongoing process. When you take responsibility for it, you can consciously, and therefore more accurately, aim yourself toward the achievement of a secure state of bliss for yourself and for others. You gain a sense of connectedness with all life that gives you great strength. You become determined to develop positively. You realize how tremendously meaningful is the slightest action, word, or even thought, and so you take ever more care to be virtuous in your acts of body, speech, and mind.

I call this the real "evolutionary insight"—the sense of personal involvement in your own inevitable evolutionary causality. While there is no avoiding the chance that you might experience great negativity at some point in the future, the risk is worthwhile because the evolutionary insight brings with it an infinite horizon of positivity. You benefit from a healthy alertness to the danger of evolutionary self-neglect.

When you realize the boundless nature of your self, you know your immortality and so take responsibility for its good quality. You gradually but perceptibly brighten and energize your world until you break out of your shell, opening your cocoon to spread your colorful wings and fly up into the sunlight. You no longer need fear death, as you know that you will merely pass into another life. You can experience the taste of true freedom for the first time, just as I did when I floated down that street in New Jersey years ago. You can feel confident that you will find fulfillment and empowerment, if not now then at some point in the future. When you frame your present existence in this radically transformed context, you make the shift from terminal life to infinite life, and suddenly everything becomes possible.

The Terminal Life

If the infinite life acknowledged is free and full of endless possibilities, then what is the terminal, constricted, finite life? It is just the opposite—a life limited in possibilities and human potential, a life that does not motivate us to achieve fulfillment for ourselves or for those around us. Where does the bounded life perspective come from? And how can you avoid falling prey to it?

Unfortunately, there are numerous worldviews that bind our lives in concrete finitude, but these can be boiled down to two that are most common and ruinous. One is the terminal life of bondage to nihilistic materialism. The other is the terminal life of bondage to an idolatrous interpretation of spiritualistic theism, whether monotheism or some other absolutism. There are thus both materialistic and spiritualistic forms of bondage.

Nihilistic Materialism

Being a nihilistic materialist does not mean just being materialistic, an avid consumer of material things. Someone who enjoys beautiful things is not necessarily a nihilistic materialist, for example. She may be a spiritual, kind, loving person committed to the best of all possible worlds for all beings, but one who simply wants material comforts while working on those long-term goals. (Perhaps she thinks that she'll be better able to make others happy if she's not too miserable herself along the way.) No, bondage to nihilistic materialism comes from being imprisoned in an unrealistic world-picture. Most of us with a modern education have been conditioned from an early age to accept a philosophically materialistic, so-called "scientific" worldview. This view of reality is not presented to us as a possible theory about the nature of life. Rather, it is presented dogmatically, as if it were a fact, the only thing, the one true reality. We are made to feel as if scientific geniuses had directly and comprehensively encountered this nihilistic world-view and verified it with mathematical precision using machines that produce "hard" data.

According to the nihilistic materialist construct of reality, we have no souls. Spirituality is no more than childish superstition and misplaced sentimentality based on ignorance of the true facts known to scientists. We are created at a certain moment, as yet not fully pinned down by exact measurement, out of the genetically encoded materials of the sperm and ovum of our parents. "We" are, of course, our subjectively conscious selves, whose consciousness and self-consciousness supposedly evolve at a moment when our brain matter and/or socialization reaches a certain, as yet unspecified level of complexity. Once we are conscious, we are granted the status of "persons" and allowed certain rights; our personhood is somewhat respected. However, ultimately we do not actually or substantially exist as we perceive ourselves to exist, and so it seems quite easy for the materialists to deprive us of our life once we break certain rules, fail to conform to the right ideas, or belong to the wrong clan, religion, nation, race, or gender. Killing is lamentable, but we console ourselves with the thought that once the victims are dead they no longer regret having lost their lives, since they simply cease to exist and can no longer remember that they once lived.

At death, the illusion of subjective existence is shattered when the brain ceases to function. We return from complexity and its dreams to the nothingness from whence we arose. During the moments of our lives, we feel conscious (at some usually unacknowledged level) of the fact that death can instantaneously reduce us from self-sensing beings to the insensate nothingness that is our essential reality. We therefore can convince ourselves without too much difficulty, when chronic pain becomes too much for us, that suicide is a viable option, since we picture ourselves slipping quietly into a state of permanent anesthesia.

Assuming that its reality has been proven, we live in bondage to the nihilism of this worldview. We occupy ourselves with materialism rather than spirituality. We feel it is a sign of maturity to resign ourselves to the seeming fact that there is no meaning to our existence—and of course no meaning to anything else either, so we don't have to take it personally. We do have a certain kind of freedom that comes from a devil-may-care attitude about it all, since we feel that a quick exit into nothingness is the worst that can happen to us, no matter what we do or don't do. But we have no rational motivation for sustained effort at personal positive evolution, since whatever we make of ourselves will terminate at death. Nor do we have any *ultimate* motivation to treat others well or contribute to their development, since they also will simply die in the end. We live and work for results in this life only, which we know can end at any time. While we may get enthusiastic about success in some field, enjoying its limited fruits for a while, we do not feel that our efforts will be that powerful or enduring. When times are good, we may be a considerate lover, mate, parent, friend, or colleague, but in tough times we don't have any reason to make sacrifices beyond a certain point of self-interest. Ultimately unmotivated, we lack the power to give something to eternity, so to speak. The concepts of "soul mate," "spiritual friend," and so on are meaningless, although we may find "soul food" tasty.

Some may still find this worldview appealing. It seems to fit the ancient encouragement: "Eat, drink, and be merry, for tomorrow we may die" (and return to quiet nothingness!). How, you might wonder, is this a prison? Here we are with no heavy burdens or big worrisome missions, only free time on our hands. We've got to make some effort to learn how to get along and get ahead. If we're lucky we can live comfortably and then check out whenever we want. Life is no big deal. There are no consequences to our actions; no boring singing in heavenly choirs; no eternal roasting in hell. We live and love and work and play, and then end up in a state that resembles a good night's sleep that never ends. Just exactly what's the problem with this perspective?

I quite agree that things could be worse. I love a good night's sleep myself. I also have been educated to believe in this world-picture. But the question remains: Is it a true picture? Is this the reality of life, death, and the world? What is the evidence for it? How has it been confirmed? Is it a scientific discovery and a rational theory? Or is it a dogmatic fabrication and an irrational delusion? And why does it matter?

I once had a meeting with a neuroscientist about a possible project that would use sensitive machines to measure the brain patterns of experienced yogis. At one point I mentioned something about Tibetan adepts who preserved memories of out-of-body near-death and after-death states, then returned to their previous sensory bodies and brains to tell about it. The scientist, his white coat flapping with his excitement, leapt up and ran around the large hospital conference room, fiercely scolding me, "What are you talking about? Never mention such things in this place. Everyone knows there are no states of consciousness beyond brain death! It is completely confirmed: once the brain is gone, that's it. Anything else is crazy talk. Superstition. Primitive thinking." On and on he went. I was so startled by his emotional vehemence that I felt concerned for his health. I assured him I wouldn't bring it up again, that we would only consider live yogis for the project and that we would stick to meditation states. He calmed down and we completed our meeting.

A day or two later, I was in a cab riding to a different meeting when I startled the driver by bursting out laughing from a total silence. It had taken a few days, but I'd suddenly realized the flaw in my neuroscientist friend's thinking, so radically confused you could easily miss it. By definition, the *only thing* that can *never* be discovered, can never be confirmed rationally, is precisely that which he was so certain about—that is, *"nothing."* "Nothing" is the "one thing" we can be sure ahead of time that no one will ever find. No one can verify that it exists because it does not exist, simply by definition. It is not a thing. It is not a place. Nothing can come from it or enter into it. It has no size or dimension, nor can it have any location. It is not relatable to anything, and so is not really relevant to anything. It is the one word that has no referent: the word "nothing" refers to nothing by not referring to anything! Nothing is not a state of something. So our society's conviction that "nothingness" is the final state of our lives is merely an irrational assumption based on a simple confusion about and, as Wittgenstein would say, a misuse of, language.

All things in nature are *"somethings"* that constantly change into other *"somethings."* No one has ever seen anything become nothing. When wood burns, it does not disappear; rather, heat rises invisibly out of it and ashes are left behind. Ice melts into water, and water evaporates into vapor. Flowers decay into the soil, which in turn feeds the growth of new flowers. "Entropy" means that certain types of energy can become so diffuse that they cease to function in any perceptible way, but that still does not mean that they become nothing. There is, in fact, nothing scientific about our insistence on nothingness.

So where does this feeling of nothingness that seems to lie at the bottom of our lives come from? Since the Renaissance, Western scientists have been fighting to escape from the antirational, dogmatic cosmology of the church, to break the hold of the church over the minds of people. In the past, the church held the populace in thrall by convincing them that it had control over the destiny of their souls: those who refused the authority of the church would meet with eternal damnation and hellfire in the afterlife. Even in this life, the church had the power to destroy any who sought to explore the world using their own senses and reason, launching inquisitions against those who disagreed with their sanctioned worldview. They silenced Galileo and burned Giordano Bruno as well as many other scientists and philosophers. So naturally the scientists revolted. René Descartes constantly proclaimed his allegiance and faith, yet cleverly reduced the soul, consciousness, mind, and even God to a dimensionless point, effectively outside the world that "mattered." Subsequent scientists declared the exclusive existence of "matter," defining the spiritual as beyond rational consideration, reducing the soul to insignificance.

Science has enjoyed great success in the industrial age. Its discoveries, theories, and technologies have enabled us to create great machines that produce spectacular effects. And yet its practitioners have now developed in the universities something like a mother church of "scientism," or scientific materialism, along with their own sort of inquisition to maintain materialist orthodoxy. They have come to enjoy a hold over people's minds by assuring us of their control over the destiny of our souls—ultimately painless entry into guaranteed oblivion. They promise a wild ride on amazing machines while living, and a painless oblivion at the end. They offer security that there will be no hellfire or damnation. Even Hitler and Mao will never burn, though their actions burned so many others. Once dead, they escape consequences, no matter what they did.

It seems that many scientists have succumbed to the temptation of their institutional power. Like the church in days of old, they offer philosophical confusion, metaphysical dogmas, priestly jargon, mathematical magic spells, mechanical miracles, and inquisitorial intimidation to maintain the world-picture by means of which they hold us in thrall. But as we have just seen, they do not have, and by definition cannot possibly acquire, any such certain knowledge that the underlying reality of life and therefore inevitable destiny of our consciousness is nothingness. Therefore we must accept the possibility that we will have some continuum of experience after death that could, after all, be called "a soul."

Nihilists can taste a certain freedom through nothingness. After all, if everything is equally nothing when reduced to its essence, then you can feel a connection to everything in your shared essential nothingness. Nihilists can say to the world, "We share the profound fact that fundamentally we're all equally nothing." However, this kind of connection has the ultimately weak link of nothingness at its center and hence has very little impact.

Ancient Indian philosophers, probably the most sophisticated thinkers the world has yet seen, disagreed on numerous points but agreed on one thing: nihilists are the least fortunate people of all. They have no motivation to join the play of evolution wholeheartedly, no compelling reason to do anything for anyone beyond seeking immediate comfort for themselves and their loved ones in this life. This basic lack of positive drive causes them to waste the precious moments of the self-conscious, critically discerning human lifetime, the lifetime that can lead to the most miraculous achievements and the highest bliss for self and other.

Spiritualistic Absolutism

Spiritualistic absolutism refers to the belief that one's terminal and insignificant life belongs completely to an all-powerful, absolutely Other, Divine Being. While this form of bondage may seem less prevalent today, more like a pre-modern mindset, in fact huge numbers of literate persons in so-called modern societies, such as America, continue to be imprisoned by spiritualistic absolutism. It is not the real teaching of the universal religions, but is a common misinterpretation of all of them (including Buddhism).

All successful religions teach that there is a State or Being or Power which, though it may not be bound to a particular form, manifestation, or concept, is the creative force, fundamental to life, all-powerful and all-knowing, unbreakable by anything else. This Force, fortunately, is full of love, benevolently willing the welfare and happiness of all beings. The founding thrust of these religions is that they encourage humans to orient themselves toward this Ultimate Reality in order to transcend their self-centeredness, their grasping, their pride, and their tendencies to harm others, and to achieve the freedom of infinite life. Therefore, as we have seen, it is entirely possible for enlightened theists to embrace the boundlessness of existence. Religions do open the door to the infinite life perspective. But religions can also be misappropriated precisely when people *lose* their openness to the infinite and become entrenched in spiritualistic absolutism, which has proven to be immensely dangerous throughout history.

Ever since Moses' prohibition of idolatry mentioned "graven images," the Western tendency has been to think of idolatry as the worship of physical representations of gods. We assume that a "graven image" must be a thing, such as the famous golden calf, or even a statue of Jesus on a cross, a Virgin Mary with Christ-child, a buddha or a bodhisattva, a Krishna, Shiva, Vishnu, or Shakti goddess—which physical images people wrongly consider to actually be the Divine Being. But it's not that simple. Is a graven image really only an idol made of metal, stone-carved, printed in a book, or painted on a wall? Is it merely a physical image? Not at all. "Graven" may seem at first to refer only to the physical world, but are there not other ways in which we "engrave" images? Can we not engrave with our speech some verbal image of the divine to which we become attached? Are there not those whose word for "God" becomes the sacred itself, so that they feel moved to kill those who use a different word for the Divine? Can we not hold a graven image in our innermost thoughts? We know the power of the human mind. Therefore, we must count "graven images" as mental and verbal as well as physical representations. And we must define "idolatry" more broadly to mean the replacing of the infinite by a finite entity constructed by our own hands, tongues, and imaginations.

The misuse of the world religions, where their ideas and institutions have caused the most harm to individuals and whole societies, comes from just such *conceptual idolatry,* my term for this most dangerous kind. This occurs when human egotism and selfishness restrict the Divine to merely personal or tribal or national possessions, as exclusive forms, as finite entities; that is, when people conceive of the Divine as idols, whether physical (statues, paintings, mountains, rivers, sky, oceans), verbal (particular languages, sacred sounds, holy books, magic spells), or mental (specific concepts of absolute Beings or Nonbeings).

Such idolatry causes humans to proclaim: "This is *my* God!" "This is *my* divine right!" "This is *my* ultimate reality!" "My beliefs are more important than yours!" "My way is the only way!" Such idolatry lies at the heart of holy wars, crusades, and jihads, and even the secular, ideological movements of capitalist modernization and communist liberation. Such idolatry has empowered mass persecutions, witch-burnings, self-immolations, and many other kinds of religious and ideological fanaticism. Only spiritual absolutists can feel confident enough in the ultimate validity and dominance of their beliefs to kill in the name of their God, or their Reality, believing that they will be absolved and suffer no negative consequences of their actions.

Take, for example, the Muslim extremists who flew airplanes full of people into the World Trade Center towers on September 11, 2001, destroying thousands of innocent lives. Or the Irish Catholic and Protestant terrorists in the U.K., whose constant battles result in bombings that murder citizens who are just going about their daily business. Or the decades of mutual atrocities between Buddhists and Hindus in Sri Lanka. Or the Hindu–Muslim conflicts in India and Pakistan. Or the many mass killings committed by fanatical communists against religious people of various persuasions during the last century. Such religious or ideological absolutists are completely willing to sacrifice their own lives or anybody else's life to a supposedly better, bigger cause—the defense of the absolute dominance of their Gods, their religion, their ideology, or their way of life. Who among us would say that their actions contribute to bringing humanity a step closer to nirvana? Who would argue that they have done anything to help us find happiness and harmony? These are very real examples of the sort of damage that can, and does, result from absolutism still today.

Trapped in a tightly bounded worldview, such conceptually idolatrous spiritual absolutists feel their own lives to be essentially an absolute nothing-ness. They envision all being, reality, destiny, power, and knowledge to belong in the hands of the all-powerful, absolute Deity. They believe that we were nothing before conception or birth, when our inner essence, a mere spark of the great fire of the One, was created from the One. At death, we will return back to the One, where we will again be nothings in ourselves, will no longer have individual continuity or self-awareness apart from the Great One.

People who hold this view lose all sense of freedom because they see themselves as absolutely dependent, the enslaved subjects of the One. They perceive no aim in life other than to obey the orders of those people whom they consider to represent the One, usually sacred texts and high priests but sometimes monarchs, premiers, or presidents. Such people are captured by a paradoxical sense of both utter personal worthlessness as individual selves, and absolute personal power and authority as part of the One. They see themselves as agents and instruments of the will of the One. Since they do not participate in evolution as individuals, they are no longer responsible for the consequences of their thought, speech, or physical actions, nor can they count on good results coming from good deeds. Thus they are disempow-ered in any pursuit of personal development, transformation, or liberation. Like the materialistic nihilists, these spiritual absolutists are in a subliminal sense disconnected from their own lives. They consider any tangible evi-dence of themselves to be, ultimately, nothing, feeling the fundamental core of things to be an obliterating light, just as the nihilists look forward to an obliterating darkness.

Spiritualistic absolutism does have a good side to it, of course, a liberating interpretation, just as does materialistic nihilism. After all, absolutists believe that something greater than they is what is truly real. Depending on their religious background, they may believe in their own endless future continuity, either in heaven or in hell. They may be motivated to act in a way that ensures they enjoy the benefits of the former and avoid the horrors of the latter, and hence behave in a manner that is generous, kind, and gentle to other beings.

Furthermore, it is possible that spiritual absolutists can experience some sense of the infinite life. They tend to think of themselves as having been created by the One, which allows them to feel they are part of the Divine. The more they emphasize this tie, the more they are able to enter the boundless life, connecting with the infinite through the One's connection to everything.

A very important point I'd like to emphasize again here is that this critique of idolatrous spiritual absolutism is not a critique of theistic world religions in general, but rather a critique of the misunderstanding and misuse of these religions. All the world religions share in common ethical precepts about love and mercy, wisdom, compassion, generosity, altruism, and so forth. What matters most is that spiritual persons can believe in whomever they want with all their hearts, and yet at the same time take the prohibition against idolatry seriously enough to avoid viewing their conception of the Ultimate Reality as exclusive of what others believe it to be. The statements in many of the world religions' scriptures about how "this way is the only way" to salvation or liberation can be understood as hyperbolic affirmations expressing strong emotional commitment in a specific context, rather than as dogmatic statements valid for all time and for everyone on the planet. The transcendent, infinite Being or Power simply must not be imprisoned within any particular absolutized belief system.

No living person holds exactly any of the worldview types described above. We all have a bit of the spiritualistic absolutist, a bit of the nihilistic materialist, a bit of the open-minded theist, and a bit of the secular humanist within us. And yet when we understand the two primary types of extremism that can enslave us in the terminal life, we are able to free ourselves from the materialistic or spiritualistic bonds that can lock us in the prison of stagnation, insignificance, and evolutionary aimlessness, devoid of boundless horizons. We can break out of delusional confinement by tribal conventions into the infinite life of opportunity and creativity that awaits us.

A New Reality

In encouraging you to accept your life as infinite, I am asking you to transform your concept of reality. I am calling on you to deepen your natural insight. I am empowering your plain common sense. I am encouraging you to open your heart to a new understanding of yourself and your world.

It is always best to live in tune with reality. It is strenuous to live in denial. When we strain to preserve wishful thinking, we must hold off the pressure of the real by investing more and more energy in the unreal. We all know how trying to maintain even a white lie can be confusing and exhausting. Realism is simply practical: it is the essential adaptive quality of human beings and all successful animals, and so it can be cultivated limitlessly without fear of going too far. Why try to deny it? Why not embrace the reality of infinite life?

In inviting you to shift your perspective, I am similar to the rebel leader Morpheus in the popular movie *The Matrix,* when he offers Neo, his latest recruit in the battle to free humanity, a new perspective on life. Neo must choose between a red pill, which will allow him to discover the truth, or a blue pill, which will return him to his ignorant, imprisoning, yet familiar reality. Like Morpheus, I am offering you a new way of looking at the world. Will you take the red pill or the blue pill? Will you choose to expand your concept of reality? Or will you choose to be "safe," to continue to live with your preconceived notions despite the fact that they may be false and thus will radically constrict your ability to improve your situation and that of those around you?

Let me be crystal clear from the very beginning that this movement from terminal existence to infinite living, from bound to free personhood, does not require a "conversion" to some sort of religion, either Buddhism or any other. You can accept this new reality within the context of your existing worldview or religion. I am sort of a lax Buddhist myself, that happens to be my way. It doesn't have to be yours. Most Buddhists do not seek followers. They do not try to convert the world to one particular religion, as much as they may love the Buddha's Dharma themselves. They are more like psychologists, scientists, or educators—they want people of all religions or no religion to become more aware, to think critically, to understand reality better, and so allow themselves to be more happy and helpful to others.

In my case, I enthusiastically chime in with the Dalai Lama's call for the leaders of all world religions to abandon once and for all their campaigns to convert everybody. The time is past for religious institution-building, religious competition for market share, and religious imperialism. It has caused great violence and harm in the past, and, if continued with the modern machinery of mass communication and coercion, could cause untold misery in the future. None of the founders of the great religions wanted to cause any injury to anyone. Their belief systems are radically misunderstood and cruelly misused when harm is done in their names.

No, you are free to keep your current belief system, whether it happens to be religious or secular humanist. Within whatever chosen tradition, there is a broad range of interpretations, some more realistic than others. Your imperative is simply to choose the most realistic view.

All spiritual traditions, as well as secular humanism, are based on a specific picture of reality. Yet they all make room for mutual inquiry, constructive criticism, creative reevaluation, and liberal reinterpretation in light of scientific discovery. For example, most great historical spiritual founders, including the Buddha, Isaiah, Mahavira, Zoroaster, Lao-tzu, Confucius, Plato, Jesus, and Muhammad, in order to communicate with the people of their times, seemed to accept the conventional ancient view that the world is flat. Today, most of their followers are still capable of great faith and devotion but feel no need to deny that the world is, in fact, round. They have changed their view of reality in this respect, departing from that of their prophet or teacher. Yet they remain faithful members of their traditions. They still value the relevant information those teachers imparted— insights about the human heart, mind, and soul, which seem true and useful even now.

So please, remain a faithful and observant Jew, Christian, Muslim, Vaishnava, Shaiva, or Shakta, simply expanding your joy and tolerance by focusing on the infinite dimensions of your deity. Or remain a liberated secular humanist, recognizing that your sense of the boundless mystery of the universe is what makes you feel free and enables you to find meaning in your life, while increasing your tolerance of your own spiritual urges and those of overtly religious people. There is no need for anyone to become a Buddhist. Whatever your belief system, this book is for you.

I invite you to embrace a new reality. It is not a matter of religion—it is a matter of fact, a matter of science, a matter of experiment, and a matter of awareness. I invite you to awaken to the infinite life you already have, no matter what your worldview. I invite you to take up responsibility for your own evolutionary destiny. I invite you to take advantage of your priceless human opportunity to make a definitive turn toward ultimate security, complete freedom, and unbounded happiness.

Conceiving the Spirit of Enlightenment

The invitation to the infinite life is not controversial in the sense that it is universally beneficial and therefore can be neither extended too casually nor accepted too prematurely. Embracing the reality of infinite life does not mean making a leap off a cliff or involving yourself in a dangerous experiment. On the contrary, it is the most obvious, practical, commonsensical, realistic decision you can make.

However, the invitation does have a further implication that might seem daunting at first. So I am going to present it as optional for the time being. I'd rather have you shy away from this aspect of infinite living until you feel more comfortable with your new perspective than deny yourself the benefits altogether. Worse yet, you may enthusiastically embrace this principle, but then, due to lack of appropriate preparation, fall back in discouragement and become cynical, rejecting the entire premise of continuous existence. Be forewarned.

The further implication is as follows: *Embracing infinite life means embracing infinite interconnection with all other beings.* If life is beginningless and endless, and death nothing but a swift transition from one existence to the next, then you and everyone else have already been living together forever. Therefore, you have had endless different relationships with them—as they have had with you. We have all been each other's mothers, fathers, lovers, best friends, and worst enemies, and we will continue to be everything to each other throughout time. So in order for our lives to become completely actualized in enlightened happiness, all other beings must also experience their lives as full of happiness. We can leave out no single being. Like the Three Musketeers, we are "all for one and one for all." We cannot liberate just ourselves from suffering, because it is impossible to achieve fully perfect bliss if anyone is excluded from it. Infinite interconnection logically mandates infinite responsibility.

I offer the following analogy when I speak to audiences about the concept of interconnection, though it is perhaps most meaningful to New Yorkers. Imagine that you are seated in a subway car. Other people are riding in the car, too. You try to notice them as little as possible as they come and go. You read your newspaper or book; you stare down at your feet and hands—anything to avoid eye contact. You know that if you look too closely at someone, he might take offense, or worse, develop a predatory interest in you. If someone looks closely at you, you shrink back and feel afraid. Your whole relationship with fellow passengers is based on the concept that you and they will soon get off the train and go your separate ways, never to meet again. In the meantime, you just want to bother each other as little as possible.

Suddenly, you hear a metallic screeching of brakes as your car veers off into a hidden tunnel. Iron grilles clang down over the windows and doors, trapping you inside. Then a deep voice with an Austrian accent like the proverbial mad scientist or realpolitik Strangelove comes over the speaker system. "You are being kidnapped!" the voice announces. "Zis is an experiment. It is a qvestion of national security. Zere vill be no recourse, no matter who you are! You vill spend the next year in zis subway car. Food vill be brought to you. You can use ze bathrooms vich are in ze control booths. Your families vill be informed zat you are avay on a purpose of national security and zey vill see you eventually, but zey vill not find you until then. You vill have good food, reading materials, blankets, medicine for illness, and everything else zat you need. But you vill see no one besides ze people who are on zis train viz you right now!"

At first you and the others freak out, shout at the speakers, have panic attacks, yell at each other, weep, and so on. But then eventually it sinks in. You may be stuck in the car for a year, or however long! You are in the hands of a mad scientist! Now how do you look at the people in the subway car with you? They will be your companions for the foreseeable future. You won't be able to avoid them any longer. You suddenly find yourself committed to them in an entirely new way. You need to develop relationships with them. They may become your friends or foes, but either way they are like family because they are all you have for a year. You recognize that in this difficult situation your happiness depends on theirs.

When you normally ride on the train, getting on and off at will, it would be rational to be fairly unconcerned with your fellow passengers, unless you happened to recognize someone you know. You'll probably never see them again. Someone you would address might turn out to be a troublemaker. Why bother? You are not connected to them. Best to live and let live. So you bury your face in your reading matter. Or if you've forgotten to bring anything, you read the ads up on the wall. You avoid all contact. A reasonable way to spend your subway ride.

The terminal lifestyle is similar. It is foisted on you by the dominant worldview of our scientific materialist culture. You and others began from nowhere, coming out of nothing, though you have inherited bodies related to your parents, et cetera. You and they will die and go back into nothingness. So why get that involved with any of them? You have connection to relatives and parents. You might feel passion for someone at some time and start a new family. You might feel a continuity through your offspring. You might want fame and want to be remembered by strangers for some outstanding accomplishment or creation. But you are unconsciously aware that you won't be aware after death of however famous you might be, what your descendants are doing, and so forth, so the amount of effort you can draw from such a limited result—*for you personally*—is so limited it would not be normal for you to make a huge effort to do anything. Better to stay comfortable for the time being, which is all the time you have. If someone talks of *saving the whole world, doing something for eternity,* you dismiss them as having a messiah complex, as being a megalomaniac.

When the extraordinary situation of our analogy occurs, you are jolted by the realization that you have to be involved more deeply with the other passengers on the car. Whether your relations with them are good or bad will now have long-term impact. You now feel compelled to take them seriously, to relate to them passionately. Your happiness depends on them. It becomes instantly clear that the ideal mode of coexistence for all confined together in the car is for each one to feel content and peaceful. No one can be ignored if they freak out. The whole car must take them seriously. So everyone becomes strongly concerned with your state of being, and you become vitally concerned with their state of being. Because you all cannot avoid being interconnected for the foreseeable future.

So now the infinite life perspective makes you see that you have always been sort of stuck in a subway car with every single other person on the face of the Earth. You and they have been born and reborn infinite times in the past, hence have shared relationships in infinite variety with infinite others. Hence, there is no being in the universe who has *not* been your father, your mother, your lover, your brother, your son, your daughter, your friend, your enemy, your protector, your destroyer—and you have been all of those things to them. Now you only know a few of them, because you can't remember the experiences of those infinite past lives. Furthermore, you are contained with them in an infinite future continuity wherein you will once again be all things to them and they will be all things to you. Since every effect has a cause and every cause gives effect, whether you will be good to them and they will be good to you depends on, among other conditions, how you treat each other today. Every thought, word, or deed, every slight interaction— a glance, a facial expression, a casual word, a gesture, however trivial seeming—becomes immense, since it will have *infinite consequence.*

The only commonsense decision you can make in this situation is to take each moment with the utmost concern, become passionately engaged with every being at every moment. Every tiniest thing must be *optimized*, to have *optimal positive effect*, in the moment and in the infinite continuity of consequences of that moment. You have entered the realm of Nietzsche's "eternal recurrence," where you never do anything unless you affirm your willingness to repeat that act again and again, eternally, and enjoy its consequent experience again and again eternally. So just as the only thing you could wish for from all other beings is their total love and compassion, their wish for you never to suffer and always to be happy, so you yourself feel it is altogether natural and fully commonsensical to feel only love and compassion for them, every single one of them, willing them never to suffer and always to be happy.

Thus, once you have adopted such an attitude of infinite interconnectedness, you naturally want to liberate not just yourself but all beings from suffering. The Buddha calls this "the conception of the spirit of enlightenment." It is the soul of the bodhisattva, the person who dedicates him- or herself to helping all beings achieve total happiness. When you open to the inevitability of your infinite interconnection with other sensitive beings, you develop compassion. You learn to feel empathy for them, to love them, to want their happiness. You want to keep them from suffering, and you do so just as if they were a part of you. You don't think your behavior makes you special. You don't congratulate yourself for helping others, just as you wouldn't congratulate yourself for healing your own leg when you hurt it. It is natural for you to love your leg because it is one with you, and so it is natural for you to love others. You would certainly never harm another being. As the great Buddhist adept Shantideva (eighth-century Indian sage) wrote, "How wonderful will it be when all beings experience each other as limbs on the one body of life!"

In a way, this notion of universal responsibility is just as commonsensical as the acceptance of infinite life. We are merely adding the lives of others to our own, recognizing our inevitable interconnection.

But it might not be prudent for all of you to pursue this further implication of the infinite lifestyle right away. It is so important to conceive this spirit of enlightenment, as it results in such a quantum transfiguration of the soul, that you should never dive into it unprepared. You might feel momentarily inspired, but then get discouraged and lose your determination, and the negative evolutionary momentum from such a reversal would be too severe. For example, you might start out wanting to save all beings from suffering but quickly get annoyed with someone just beyond hope. You'd end up feeling alienated and not giving a damn about anyone, abandoning altogether your belief in infinite life and all the positive work you'd accomplished.

Surely many of you have already developed a compassionate spirit, either in previous lives or from following altruistic teachings in this life. So for you it is not such a shock to open to infinite intertwinement with all beings, what the delightful Vietnamese Zen master Thich Nhat Hanh calls your "interbeing" with them. For you, I mention it here at the outset, and for the more cautious, I encourage you just to think of it as an experimental idea for now.

Opening to the Infinite Lifestyle

This book is about the great variety of methods you can use to live a happy, fulfilling, and infinite life of what I like to call "evolutionary sport." You can become a true sportswoman or sportsman in the game of life. You can choose to take up the challenge of competition with yourself, transcending your inherited self-limiting instincts, your conditioned ingrained habits, your carelessly self-destructive addictions to the terminal lifestyle. You can release yourself from the prison of the meaninglessness of consumer culture and from the constraints of absolutist beliefs.

But it is not worth reading another word of this text, for it is not possible to make good use of a single method or art presented here, if you do not dare to experiment with opening up your life to the infinite perspective. If you are looking for a cell in which to lock yourself away from danger, a hole in which to hide, a mechanism in which to entrust your precious self-image, then you should give this book back or throw it away. It will only waste your time.

So I urge you now, once more, to accept the possibility of infinite life, even just as a temporary experiment. Try it on, for size and effect. We all have the potential to travel the path offered to us by the Buddha and presented in this book, as well as in other world religious, humanist, and scientific teachings that flow from the same experience. We all have the ability to walk out of the gloomy prison of self-limiting, uncritical existence into the bright daylight of a boundless, deeply meaningful, and tremendously satisfying existence, with its attendant playful, exuberant, joyous wisdom.

The infinite life is life unbound by time or space. Deaths are only doorways, transitions from one life-form to the next, just as sleep is only a passage from evening to a new day. Your every movement of body, speech, and mind arises from a beginningless past and resonates into an endless future. You are free and boundless in dimension, and also very real and unique. You are lost in oneness with the awesome infinite, yet you have infinite importance due to your total interconnectedness with all other beings. When self-centered and unhappy, you are a big problem for them, often engaged in life-and-death struggles. When enlightened, self-transcendent, boundlessly open, and truly happy, you can be the living solution to all their problems.

Open your eyes and look at yourself carefully. Expand the concept of reality that you live by—your awareness of, and responsibility for, your own personal continuity. Everything you do now, your very breathing, flows from your sense of yourself as a living continuum and your drive to improve your state of being. You are a dynamic evolutionary process. There is no limit to how far you can develop positively into higher states of spirituality, understanding, love, happiness, and creativity.

⋯⋙ 2 ⋘⋯

Buddhism:
A Joyous Science of the Heart

Speech is a powerful thing. When I speak and you listen, we share our minds with each other. We become one mind, which is bigger than both of our usual minds. I put more thought into what I'm saying because I feel the traction of my words in the terrain of your mind. You let my words flow through you while your own reflections eddy and swirl around my current of thought.

As I engage you in this book, I feel deeply conscious of the responsibility I have when I enter your mind. My words are drawn forth by your interest. I believe there is value in what I say, since the words came to me in turn from other, more enlightened minds. Many of these teachings and methods were first spoken by great philosophers back through time, in this case back all the way to the Buddha. They were a great help to me, so I hope they will help you, too.

I do not try to calculate some sort of effect upon you with my words. Rather, I speak to you from my heart. But my heart is not dumb—it senses your heart. I am moved to speak out about the surges of the heart that can bring relief, movements of the mind that have immediate and noticeable effects, movements of the spirit that call forth feelings of freedom, peace, grace, and love.

I myself do not pretend to be enlightened. But thanks to my practice, I have felt some blessed releasing surges of the heart. I have moved my mind, occasionally, in a positive direction. This has given me the hint that others before me were enlightened. I have been able to verify for myself that these lessons work: they open the heart, they sharpen the intelligence, and they liberate the mind. And so I feel the desire to tell you about them, in the hope that they will help you achieve some degree of happiness and freedom in your own life.

Buddhist Psychology

You can use enlightening Buddhist practices to transform your life. Unfortunately, many people do not know it, but the Buddhist Dharma, or teaching, is actually a scientific system of psychology, developed in India and further refined in Tibet. It is a psychology that works. I call it a "joyous science of the heart" because it is based on the idea that while unenlightened life is full of suffering, you are completely capable of escaping from that suffering. You can get well. In fact, you already *are* well; you just need to awaken to that fact.

And how do you do this? By analyzing your thought patterns. When you do, you realize that you are full of "misknowledge"—misunderstandings of yourself and the world that lead to anger, discontent, and fear. The target of Buddhist practice and the constant theme of this book is the primal misconception that you are the center of the universe, that your "self" is a fixed, constant, and bounded entity. When you meditate on enlightened insights into the true nature of reality and the boundlessness of the self, you develop new habits of thinking. You free yourself from the constraints of your habitual mind. In other words, you teach yourself to think differently. This in turn leads you to act differently. And *voilà!* You are on the path to happiness, fulfillment, and even enlightenment.

The battle for happiness is fought and won or lost primarily within the mind. The mind is the absolute key, both to enlightenment and to life. When your mind is peaceful, aware, and under your command, you will be securely happy. When your mind is unaware of its true nature, constantly in turmoil, and in command of you, you will suffer endlessly. This is the whole secret of the Dharma. If you recognize delusion, greed, anger, envy, and pride as the main enemies of your well-being and learn to focus your mind on overcoming them, you can install wisdom, generosity, tolerance, love, and altruism in their place. This is where enlightened psychology can be most useful.

Psychology and philosophy are really one entity in Buddhism. They are called the *inner science,* the science of the human interior. In the flow of Indian history, it is fair to say that the Buddha was a great explorer of the human interior rather than some sort of religious prophet. He came into the world at a time when people were just beginning to experiment with self-exploration, but mostly in an escapist way, using their focus on the inner world to run away from the sufferings of life by entering a supposed realm of absolute quiet far removed from everyday existence. The Buddha started out exploring that way too, but then realized the futility of escapism and discovered instead a way of being happier here and now. He made interior freedom available to everyone by teaching people to gain insight into reality and then deepen their experience through meditation. Further, he created a *sangha,* a lay and monastic community where people could go to receive teaching and support for their interior explorations.

Before Buddha's time, societies never had much interest in psychology or philosophy. They had religions and rituals, but they just wanted their citizens to work and obey, not to question their existence or the meaning of life. They wanted the warriors to fight battles, the farmers to plant, the merchants to exchange goods, and the priests to neatly explain why things had to be the way they were. That's all the rulers of India wanted then, and the same holds true in almost every other society throughout the history of the world.

In order to create the inner science of psychology, the Buddha had to take extreme steps. He had to leave his beloved, adoring wife and lovely infant son. He had to renounce his position as prince and future ruler. He had to abandon his father, the king, in deep disappointment. After all, his father was about to retire and have his son take over the royal duties. But the would-be Buddha, Prince Siddhartha, said, "I'm going to retire myself. I'm off to the jungle to meditate. Why? Because I don't want to be just a prince, don't want to be a general and fight battles to defend the country. I want to help my people with their deepest problems. I have an interior that I need to explore. I want to find out the meaning of life. I want to discover the nature of my thoughts and my emotions. And I think that's what everyone needs to do. We have enough food around here. We have enough battles. We have enough goods. We have enough childbearing. We have enough everything. What we need to do is find out *why* we are doing all of this. What is the reason for it? Is there a better way?"

So the Buddha took off, leaving his old life behind, and went into the jungle to be by himself so that he could quietly investigate the inner world through meditation. After many years, he gained tremendous insight into the functioning of the human mind and the problems we create for ourselves. He came to understand how negative states develop, how those negative states can be replaced by positive states, and how those positive states can be cultivated without limit. The Buddha realized that the human life-form is the ideal life-form in which to do that cultivation, each person ultimately by themselves but with the help of therapists and teachers and philosophers. And that was the birth of psychology, really: the beginning of the systematic scientific exploration of the way the mind works.

Buddhist psychology is a do-it-yourself science. As the philosopher Vasubandhu put it, only by discovering for yourself the facts of your own reality, your psyche, your life, your society, the way your mind thinks, the way your body senses, and the way the world works will your neurotic addictions be cured. And without curing your addictions, you are hurled again and again into the ocean of unsatisfactory existences.

But what about Western psychology, you might ask? When I think about that kind of psychology, it reminds me of what Gandhi once said about American civilization. When asked what he thought of it, he replied, "American civilization? Now that would be a good idea!" So I say, "Western psychology? Now, that would be a good idea!" It would. But it's really still in its infancy. That's because the West as a society has been plagued for thousands of years by poverty, authoritarian social structures and rulers, and militarism. The West has not been, until recently, a rich place. Western societies have not really had time or resources to devote to people's psychological development and well-being. Those people who had problems with their inner lives, with fitting into the machine of the greater social purpose, were mainly cast off into a corner and forgotten. Maybe they played the village idiot role, or, if they were lucky, they wandered off and found a Christian monastery. But no one paid much attention to them. People who were insistent and vocal and therefore attracted many others to developing the interior life tended to get crucified or burned at the stake or locked up, because Western societies viewed them as troublemakers.

Western psychology developed during the era of industrialization. Freud and Jung lived in the wealthier societies of central Europe. Members of the middle class finally had a little time and money to explore their general state of being. When their interiors were maladjusted or abused or neglected, they could find someone to work with them. So these early psychologists began to ask themselves: How does the mind work? What are the problems with the mind? How can these problems be fixed? But their main purpose was only to re-adapt these misfits back into the machinery of industrial society so that their patients could work, function, and "be normal" again. As Freud himself said, his therapy was designed to help people get rid of neurotic suffering so that they could get back to ordinary suffering. There was never any mention of complete freedom from suffering as the definition of health, or even a livable option.

Today in the West, we are trying to further develop this nascent science of psychology. Unfortunately, we don't have a strong base to begin from and we have a big handicap—we are caught up in nihilistic materialism. We are taught to believe that only matter, and not spirit, is real, that the mind is only the brain. So now psychology is pursuing an imprisoning and dangerous path, namely neuroscience, in which the mind is believed to be reducible to chemical and electrical signals in the brain that can be entirely manipulated by drugs. And the primary goal is still to "cure" people, to control their wayward thoughts so that they can fit right back into everyday, eat-work-sleep life, unquestioning and unconcerned about the meaning of it all.

Take the plight of today's schoolchildren in America. Their metabolism is flooded with sugar from infancy. Their minds are deluged with cartoon television, filled with violence and hyperactive drama. Commercials flood them with desires for more sugar, for more hyperactive equipment. When they get to school, they naturally have "attention deficit disorder" (ADD), a supposedly medically diagnosable disease cooked up by our industrial psychology, unwittingly in service to consumer pharmaceuticals. They then are prescribed Ritalin or other amphetamine-type drugs, which supposedly rebalances their "brain chemistry," but actually is addictive and leads to deep internal hyperactivity, ending up with manic depressive states, that are again to be rebalanced by a battery of antidepressants. Buddhist psychology helped us somewhat as parents to avoid the worst of this cycle with our children, and we somewhat moderated the debilitating elements of their growing up in consumerist society. I say "somewhat" because it is very difficult to be totally pure in this world, and perfection is elusive.

What is the solution to this destructive treatment of our children? Do we really need Buddhist psychology to reinforce our common sense? Clearly, we should limit sugar intake drastically, remembering that cereals, breads, and many other supposedly healthy products are laced with sugar by our commercial food industry. Limit the television exposure (eliminating it altogether may end up remanding our children to neighbors' houses) to public broadcasting, nature shows, science shows, perhaps the worlds of Sesame Street–type education shows. Allow absolutely no commercials. Read to your children, teaching them by example to focus their attention quietly on one thing for sustained periods of time. Perhaps include them in periods of quiet meditation, in nature, by streamsides, on mountain slopes watching clouds. In this way, you help them avoid becoming enslaved to consumer culture.

According to the Dharma teaching, psychology is about understanding what human beings are made of, how our world works, how reality is put together, and how our minds function. The purpose of doing this, ultimately, is not to adjust people to go back and live according to how society tells them they should live, so that they can fit into some meaningless, supposedly wealth-producing, militaristic scheme. That's a total waste of human life. If somebody has the good sense to be depressed, malfunctioning, hallucinating, dropping out of society because their mind-body complex is saying "no" to the whole nonsense and looking for some better way of being, a liberating psychology should not try to stuff them back into the box. They should not be just rushed straight ahead, encouraged to wash the dishes, do their jobs, and pounce on the enemy, just because that's what everybody else is doing. People who have the sensitivity and insight to see through the meaninglessness should be able to find someone to help them discover freedom, which is what they are looking for. They should be supported in their endeavors.

That is the big difference between Buddhist and Western psychologies. The original liberating psychology *is,* in fact, the Dharma, and the Dharma is a wonderful thing. These days, some veteran enlightenment practitioners are becoming therapists because they realize it's an effective way in which they can deploy this amazingly practical psychology in the West without stirring up all sorts of religious issues by calling it "Buddhist."

Most Westerners really do need therapy. I certainly do! Fortunately, I'm lucky enough to have a wife who gives me constant instruction and support, as well as wise teachers, including the Dalai Lama, to guide me. In general, we are overstressed, overworked beings who don't even believe in a soul and think that pills should cure all our problems. Many of us have inherited individual traditions of family abuse, suppression, and neglect, as well as societal traditions of racism, prejudice, and religious fanaticism. It's no wonder that modern society is so grisly and gloomy. It's no wonder that when people first encounter the wonderful Buddha Dharma, the joyous science of the heart, they recoil. When someone proclaims, "Come and join us. You can heal your mind and body through enlightening practices. You can be free!" Westerners initially react by saying, "Oh no! The Buddhists are taking over! They want us all to be Buddhists. It's a religious cult. It's weird. Let's run away as fast as we can!"

But most teachers of enlightenment are just out there offering their healing and liberating therapies. It's their profession, as it was the Buddha's. He was the first great therapist. He was the original Freud, the ultimate Jung. Like the Buddha, enlightenment-oriented teachers just want to share their insights with you, as any caring scientist or doctor would. It's just up to you to take the first step by deciding to engage in inner exploration. You can draw your own conclusions and implement your own healing methods. You can keep your own religion, too, though you may soon feel like making changes within it, embracing the more open interpretations available within its doctrines.

Buddhist psychology is a joyous science of the heart. It operates on the assumption that we can use our own sophisticated minds to realize our selfless and thus transformable nature. It teaches us how to take apart our absolutized self-sense in a useful way so that we are no longer in conflict with reality as we normally are, kicking and screaming and miserable but pretending that we've got it all together. It teaches us to free ourselves from our demons by understanding our true place in reality: ultimately selfless while relatively present, aware, and interconnected with all other beings. It teaches us to embrace infinite life. And it teaches us compassion, caring for others rather than obsessing over ourselves.

Transforming Your Life

There are six, or seven, or ten transformations that release the terminal self into infinite life, set forth by the Buddha as the transcendent virtues (*pārāmita* in Sanskrit). During the last two thousand years, by putting these transcending patterns into practice, many millions of individuals in many civilizations have transformed their lives from quiet desperation into happiness.

In each chapter, we'll examine one of the basic Western thought-traps: self-preoccupation, dissatisfaction, depression, pride, envy, and hatred. These habit-patterns ensnare you and prevent you from achieving true happiness. Focusing on the unbounded nature of your existence can change your perspective on your problems and issues, transforming neediness into contentment, resentment into forgiveness, and selfishness into compassion. You can try out a whole new approach to life. Then we'll explore how you can put your new ideas into practice in the world, turning your thoughts into action. We'll examine the repercussions of your personal changes on society and on the fragile, opalescent planet. We'll see how personal transformation *is* social transformation.

Each transformation chapter includes a section called "Practice." These set forth meditation sequences that aim to enable you to understand, experience, and enact the transformations rather than simply reading about them. These sections are the key to your success. Why? Because meditation is the time-tested technique for analyzing old thought-habits and developing new thought-habits and new behaviors. It permits us to gain better control of ourselves. Our bodies and minds are our prime tools for dealing with life. We must develop greater and greater mastery of these tools, as well as improve their quality and capability. Just as we use yoga of the body to enhance its resiliency, strength, and prowess, so we use yoga of the mind for the same reasons.

Meditations are not just one type of practice; there are calming, creative, and critical insight meditations. You should always begin meditation sessions by calming your thoughts and quieting your body. You can easily learn to meditate on letting go of thoughts in order to lessen stress, find pleasure just in being, enjoy calm, peace and quiet, and gain greater detachment from environmental stimuli. Once this is readily achieved, we can focus on creative and critical meditations—meditations on specific topics that will help you to achieve your goals. These are called "practices" because they are not just pursued for their own sake, they are advance rehearsals for your performance of the accomplished abilities, insights, and virtues in your daily life. These meditations will enable you to sustain and intensify your thinking in order to reach insights and conclusions that are transformative. They will serve to make intellectual insights visceral and aspirations practical.

It is not necessary that you accomplish each practice in one sitting or that you finish them all while reading the book for the first time. In one sense, this is a regular book with a message, just waiting to be picked up and read. But in another sense, it is a workbook, in that the practices are there for you to use again and again. As you become more advanced in your practice, you

———

may choose to spend many meditation sessions or a whole retreat on the themes set forth in just a few paragraphs in one chapter.

Physical Preparation

It is considered very important in contemplative traditions that you pay careful attention to the context in which you meditate. The setting and context play an important role in determining the result of the session. So I want to describe the optimal setting for you here.

First, you should try to create a special spot in your house or apartment where you regularly sit down to contemplate. Just as you have a special room to exercise in, and don't usually do push-ups or ride your exercycle in the living room, you need a special space to meditate. My meditation room is a largish closet that I've fixed up. It should be quiet and pleasant, a space where you enjoy being. You might put up a picture of an inspiring person or place on the wall you face. On a small altar or shrine in front of it, place some pleasant offering—a candle to symbolize light or an object of sight, a flower for beauty, a bowl of fresh offerings to please the taste, a beautiful cloth for texture, perhaps an incense burner for pleasant scent, some little cups of water symbolizing sweet sounds and all good things. You'll also need a meditation seat that's comfortable for you. The most comfortable, I find, is the Zen-type rectangular cushion mat with a round sitting pillow in the center. If you have trouble sitting cross-legged, place a comfortable chair there, though then you should start to work on gentle and gradual yoga stretching so you can eventually sit cross-legged after a few weeks or months. Now your room is set up properly.

Once you take your seat, adopt a comfortable cross-legged or sitting posture. Lay your hands flat in a relaxed posture in your lap, with the back of the right one lying flat upon the palm and straightened fingers of the left. Straighten your spine, and drop and relax your shoulders. Now tuck your chin down a bit so that your nose-tip feels in line above your navel. Put your tongue up to touch your palate just behind your teeth, but do not strain. Keep your eyes half-open with a loose focus of your vision a few inches in front of the tip of your nose. Breathe in normally, counting each in-breath up to ten or twenty and then starting again at one. When distracting thoughts start to run away from the counting, let them go on their own, pull your attention back from them, and resume counting or start over again at one. When you master counting, you can develop mindfulness about your breathing process, noticing everything about the act of breathing in and breathing out, without forcing it to be slower or deeper, just observing the inflow and outflow. Spend a little while settling down in this way, sitting peacefully in your pleasant spot, calming and resting, and your energy will build up for your meditation practice.

Mental Preparation

The physical arrangements of the room and your body are important and helpful, but not as important as creating a special space in your mind, an ideal place for transformation and liberation. Before you begin meditating on your chosen theme of the session, it is crucial that you open your mind up to your own vast potential. If you enter the practice leaving your habitual self-image and reality constructs intact and unopened, you are programming yourself to emerge the same as when you begin. "Show me your beginning and I'll show you your end!" is a wise adage. In order to open yourself for new experiences and understandings, you need to imagine yourself in a space where you feel most able to realize your true nature. The preparatory practice below comes from an ancient tradition known for optimizing your opportunity for success in the subsequent practices. I highly recommend that you try it before starting the practices described in each chapter. It is open to modification according to your personal taste and experience, of course.

First, use your inquiring, scientific mind to inventory your reality construct, your sense of your situation in the universe, questioning whatever you take for granted and taking special note of the uncertainties prevailing around you. What do you know really? How do you know it? Where are you really—on a planet spinning a thousand miles per hour, held by gravity above oceans of fire, water, and earth, within an ocean of air, circling a sun ninety-two million miles away, itself orbiting at an even greater speed on the galactic arm? What are you really, how many billions and trillions of sub-atomic energies or atoms, cells, how many countless neurons? What about your subconscious? Is it a personal store of inchoate memories, or a bundle of instinctual drives imprinted on physical molecules? Continue posing questions to yourself in this manner, melting away your habitual sense of certainty about your nature, structure, location, and presence within an assumed world-picture. Dissolve into "unfindability" and feel yourself rest in the unknown openness.

Now picture the following, or something analogous that you prefer: You arise in a luminous, buoyant body on a grassy bluff at high altitude over-looking a vast, crystalline glacial lake. The sun glints for miles and miles off its aquamarine waters, and majestic Himalayan mountain peaks rise up around it on all sides. Fluffy clouds float in the sunny, deep blue sky. Behind you to the north, the majestic snow-covered dome of Mount Kailash radi-ates magnificently like a prism, refracting the white sunlight into rainbows of blessing. In front of you, in the lake, is a small island on which minor deities and guardian spirits roam. Dragons sun themselves along the shore. In the center of this island grows a giant tree, reaching almost up into the heavens like the beanstalk Jack climbs in the story. Jewelline flowers and fruits cover its massive branches, making it seem like a huge Christmas tree with glittering ornaments.

At the crown of the tree rests a giant lotus flower, on which stands a lion throne made of many precious gems, on which sits the person who you think is the most enlightened, most all-knowing, most loving and compassionate person in the universe, whether human or divine, the person whom you would choose above all others to be your spiritual, intellectual, and moral mentor. Visualize this person to be large in size, brilliantly radiant, with a body made of light like Obi-Wan Kenobi's after he has died in the later *Star Wars* film. Around her in the tree sit a host of other mentors and benevolent beings. She or he is looking down upon you with a dazzling smile, and a tube of golden light descends from her heart to reach the crown of your head.

Blessings in the form of liquid, jewel, rainbow lights coilingly flow down the golden tube and flood into your body and mind. Their blessings bring your body and mind inexpressible bliss and happiness, driving out the shadows of your confusions, anxieties, doubts, fears, and worries, and bringing you instead confident energy, clarity, joyous enthusiasm for understanding and good feeling.

As you slowly fill up with light and energy, you ready yourself for your meditation practice as a beneficent being with no limit to your potential. You have rid yourself of any preconceived notions about your own inabilities. Now you notice that around you on the grassy bluff, a vast crowd of ordinary sensitive beings has gathered. People and animals (in semihuman form) whom you know personally—those you love, those you hate, those you feel neutrally toward—all stand in the front row. They do not see the island, or the tree filled with mentor persons. But they look toward you and they are aware of how you are filling with light. The blessings begin to overflow from you to them, so that your light washes away their negative thoughts and feelings. Naturally, your loved ones are delighted and your neutral acquaintances are pleased and intrigued. And even your enemies are fascinated and blessed by the light that reflects from you.

Now turn your attention toward the mentor beings that have gathered on your behalf. Celebrate their presence by sending them waves of gratitude for their blessings. If you like, visualize yourself making fantastic offerings to them: commissioning symphonies, creating beautiful works of art and literature, sending clouds of exquisite scents, delicious foods, soft and precious cloths, beautiful lands, jewels, whatever you can imagine. Apologize for your past negative attitudes and deeds, resolve never to engage in them again, and ask your mentors' gracious assistance in helping you maintain your new resolve. Now be sure to rejoice in all the good deeds you and other beings have done, even those of your enemies. Request that the mentor beings turn the wheel of teaching, sending down the rain of Dharma truth and liberating insight. Ask them not to leave you lost in the world of suffering, but to stay with you and all sensitive beings until you are awakened and secure in reliable happiness. Finally, resolve to earnestly pursue the quest for full enlightenment, wisdom, and compassion for the sake of yourself and all other beings.

You are now ready to turn your attention to the meditation practice itself, forgetting about this entire picture, just sensing it's there. Follow the instructions for the practice as described in each chapter. When you conclude your meditation, come back to the image described above. Let your mentors and their magical environment merge completely into your heart and soul. Then melt yourself into pure light and flow into the hearts of those people who stand around you. Dedicate whatever merit or virtue you may have developed during your practice to them, expecting no selfish reward or recognition for your achievements. Once you've emerged from this state of melted oneness into your ordinary existence, you will go about your daily routine with these new insights very much a part of the renewed you.

Don't worry if, especially at first, you find it difficult to imagine all the details of your mentor, the other beings around you, the lake, island, tree, mountains, and clouds. At a minimum, think of yourself in a space filled with light and blessings, and with beings you care for spiritually present to assist you. What's most important is that you visualize yourself on top of the world, empowered, and then just know that you are there. It's like when you enter a room for the first time, how you look around at the floor, walls, and ceiling. You might note some details of the moldings, window frames, drapes, furniture, carpet, and so forth, and then you forget about them and engage in whatever thoughts are occupying you at the time. But the picture of the room remains in your background awareness, as proven by the fact that you might jump up to go out the door without thinking. And the room itself certainly affects your mood, whether it is uplifting in its beauty and elegance or depressing in its ugly mess. The image you create for yourself with the practice described above functions in much the same way as the room.

You should feel free to employ this preparatory practice to whatever degree of elaboration you desire and enjoy each time you work with the meditations presented in the book. However, don't try to visualize too much at one time, which will only leave you feeling frustrated. Remember to open and close with the image of your ideal place and mentor person, but then let that vision go as you engage in your specific practice. The goal of this exercise is to make you feel fully energized and indomitably capable of realizing your aims, as well as to remind you to dedicate your accomplishments to supreme fulfillment for all. Creating for yourself even a minimally appropriate physical and mental setting within which to practice will greatly empower you and accelerate your progress.

If you have trouble meditating, if you are bothered even by the concept of meditation, if it just feels too artificial for you, then simply read the book, returning again and again to passages you find inspiring and illuminating. After all, reading is a form of meditation, as is going to the theater or a movie, or watching television—above all, watching commercials is meditation, though it is intended to be disempowering in that it aims to make you feel you can't do without the product advertised. Even sitting on a bus with random thoughts flickering through your mind, memories of past events, anxious or eager anticipations of future events, tunes, images—even this is meditation. Your sense of self and your sense of your environment and world is not just a fixed thing that sits in you and around you like a skeleton and a tent; it is a constructed picture within and without. Your mind constantly refreshes the picture by scanning over it and ruminating about it, just as the photon gun at the back of a TV set fires light and color so many times a second within a pattern to refresh the picture on the screen. So it is not a question as to whether you should meditate or not. You are meditating all the time. And so the big question is, Are you choosing what you meditate upon, is it what you want to become your ability and reality? Or is it all too often what the powers and principalities around you want you to hold as you and your reality? Your culture, your religion, your society, your government, the commercial industries that need you as participant, believer, member, subject, and consumer?

The bottom line is that you can take responsibility for how you occupy your mind. You can convert negativity into positivity in your life by opening yourself up to the ancient and well-proven philosophies available from the teachers of liberation who have flourished in history. You can study their teachings, not only as a spiritual seeker but also as a scientific investigator, and you can find what makes sense and see if it is verifiable in experience in the world. In so doing, you will transform not just your own individual existence, but also the lives of those around you. Each of us is like a bubble of awareness. When we transform ourselves, free ourselves from inner knots and blemishes and blossom out our inner beauties, our new openness and blissful pleasure resonates instantaneously and reinforces liberation and satisfaction in the other bubbles. Changing ourselves for the better changes the world for the better. Rehearsing positive changes through intelligent meditation practice makes us more capable of performing the more positive world, creating it in our infinite living and sharing it with others.

·≈❙ Part Two ❙≈·

·⊰ 3 ⊱·

Wisdom

Preamble: Selflessness

At one point in the early 1970s, after I'd gotten my Ph.D. and started teaching Buddhism, I went back to visit my old teacher, the Mongolian lama Geshe Wangyal. We were working on a project to translate a Buddhist scientific text from the Tibetan. We were six or seven people gathered around a kitchen table, and Geshe-la began to talk about the inner science of Buddhist psychology, the Abhidharma. He was reading us a few verses about the insight of selflessness, the deep release of becoming unbound, when I began to feel a little dizzy, even nauseous. It was a funny feeling. It felt slightly like a vibration spinning in my head. The vibration came not from Geshe-la, but from this ancient tradition. It was as though my habitual mind couldn't quite find traction. I realized that if I fought it, the sensation would only get more nerve-wracking and I would only feel more nauseous. So I didn't fight it. Instead, I let go and relaxed, and soon I was able to orient myself in another way, away from my "self." I felt like I was slowly but surely loosening my self-centered perspective on life and the world. In a useful way, a strengthening way, I was beginning to experience the great Buddhist mystery that is the selflessness of subjects and objects.

The Buddha based his psychology on his discovery of actual and ultimate reality. This he called "selflessness" and "voidness," or "emptiness." Some people love these words from the moment they hear them, but others are frightened by them. People often ask me, "Why did Buddha have to be such a downer? Obviously nirvana is a happy, cheerful state. So why didn't he just call it 'bliss' or something? Why did he have to label the reality he discovered with negative words such as 'voidness,' 'emptiness,' and 'selflessness'?" When people respond negatively to these terms, it's often because they're worried that the words imply they are going to die, disappear, or go crazy in their attempts to seek enlightenment. And that's exactly why the Buddha called reality by those names. He did it on purpose, to liberate you! Why? Because the only thing that's frightened by the word "selflessness" is the artificially constructed, unreal, and unrealistic self. That self is only a pretend self, it lacks reality, it doesn't really exist. That pseudo-self seems to quiver and quake because the habit that makes it seem real wants to keep its hold on you. So if you're seeking happiness and freedom, then you should want to scare the heck out of your "self"—you want to scare it right out of your head!

Actually, *it* is constantly scaring the heck out of *you*. Your "self" is always busy terrorizing you. You have a terrorist in your own brain, coming out of your own instincts and culture, who is pestering you all the time. "Don't relax too much," it is saying, "you'll get stepped on. A bug will bite you. Someone will be nasty to you. You'll get passed by, abused, sick. Don't be honest. Pretend. Because if you're honest, they'll hurt you." And it's ordering you, "Be my slave. Do what I tell you to do. Keep me installed up here at this very superficial level of the brain where I sit in my weird Woody Allen–type cockpit. Because I'm in control." Your falsely perceived, fixated, domineering self is precisely what's getting between you and a fulfilling life.

Early on, some of the Western psychologists who were beginning to learn from the Buddhist tradition—members of the transpersonal and other movements—came up with the idea that the relationship between Buddhist and Western psychology is this: "Western psychology helps somebody who feels they are nobody become somebody, and Buddhist psychology helps somebody who feels they are somebody become nobody." When I first heard this, I was at an Inner Science conference with the Dalai Lama. Everybody laughed, applauded, and thought it was a great insight. The Dalai Lama just looked at me and kind of winked and was too polite to say anything. I started to jump up to make a comment, but he stopped me. He told me to be quiet and let all of them ponder it for a few years until they realized the flaw in their thinking. Because of course that idea is not even remotely correct.

The purpose of realizing your own selflessness is not to feel like you are nobody. After he became enlightened, the Buddha did not sit under a tree drooling, and saying "Oh, wow! I'm nobody!" Think about it: If he just "became nobody," if he escaped from the world through self-obliteration, then he wouldn't have been able to share so many teachings here on earth, to work for the good of all beings for years and years, long after he achieved nirvana. He would've just stayed in his "nobody" state and forgotten about all of us poor humans busy suffering through our miserable lives.

The reason why we sometimes think that the goal of Buddhism is just "to become nobody" is that we don't understand the concept of selflessness. "Selflessness" does not mean that we are nobody. It does not mean that we cease to exist. Not at all. There is no way you can ever "not exist," just as you cannot become "nothing." Even if you go through deep meditation into what is called "the realm of absolute nothingness," you will still exist. Even if you are so freaked out by a tragedy, such as losing your only child, that you try to end your existence completely, you will still exist. I have a healthy respect for tragedy. We do have terrible tragedies. Personally, I don't bear misfortune well; it knocks me out. But there is no way to become nobody. Even if you were to succeed in killing yourself, you will be shocked when you awaken to disembodied awareness, out-of-body but still a somebody, a ghostly wraith who wishes he hadn't just done that. And a terribly unfortunate living person who has been so brutalized that he blanks out who he was in a seemingly impenetrable psychosis is still somebody, as everybody else around him knows.

Our mind is so powerful that it can create a state of absolute nothingness that seems totally concrete. Thousands of yogis in the history of India and a few mystics in the West have entered such a state of nothingness. But no one can stay there forever, and it is not where you want to be.

Have you ever had a minor experience of nothingness? I've had it in the dentist's chair with sodium pentothal, because I used to eat a lot of sweets and not brush my teeth as a youngster so I had to have teeth pulled. They give you this knockout anesthetic, and if you are a hard-working intellectual, you are tired of your mind, so you think, "Oh great, I'm going to be obliterated for a little while." You're really pleased, and you feel this little buzz, and you're just about to get there. You're going to experience nothingness, a little foretaste of the nihilistic notion of nirvana! But suddenly the nurse is shaking you awake saying, "You've been slobbering in that chair long enough. Get out of here." It's over. You started to pass out, wanting to be gone, but now you're suddenly back with no sense of having been gone at all! And that's what it is like in the state of absolute nothingness. It's like being passed out in the dentist's chair. There's no sense of duration of time. But eventually you wake up, totally disoriented with a nasty headache, and you never even got to enjoy the oblivion.

So we can never become nothing, as appealing as that may sound to those who are addicted to the idea of nothingness after death. We are always somebody, even though we are selfless in reality. We are just different sorts of "somebodies" than we used to be. "Realizing your selflessness" does not mean that you become a nobody, it means that you become the type of somebody who is a viable, useful somebody, not a rigid, fixated, I'm-the-center-of-the-universe, isolated-from-others somebody. You become the type of somebody who is over the idea of a conceptually fixated and self-created "self," a pseudo-self that would actually be absolutely weak, because of being unrelated to the reality of your constantly changing nature. You become the type of somebody who is content never to be quite that sure of who you are—always free to be someone new, somebody more.

That's the whole point of selflessness. If you don't know exactly who you are all the time, you're not sick, you're actually in luck, because you're more realistic, more free, and more awake! You're being too intelligent to be stuck inside one frozen mask of personality! You've opened up your wisdom, and